Riding the Tiger

Riding the Tiger

The Middle East Challenge After the Cold War

EDITED BY

Phebe Marr

National Defense University

AND

William Lewis

George Washington University

Westview Press

BOULDER • SAN FRANCISCO • OXFORD

Copyright © 1993 by Westview Press, Inc.

Published in 1993 in the United States of America by Westview Press, Inc., 5500 Central Avenue, Boulder, Colorado 80301-2877, and in the United Kingdom by Westview Press, 36 Lonsdale Road, Summertown, Oxford OX2 7EW

Library of Congress Cataloging-in-Publication Data
Riding the tiger : the Middle East challenge after the Cold War /
    edited by Phebe Marr and William Lewis.
        p.   cm.
    Includes index.
    ISBN 0-8133-8479-6. — ISBN 0-8133-8663-2 (pbk.)
        1. Middle East—Politics and government—1979–   I. Marr, Phebe.
II. Lewis, William Hubert, 1928–   .
DS63.1.R53   1993
956.05'3—dc20   92-46572
                                                                           CIP

Printed and bound in the United States of America

The paper used in this publication meets the requirements of the American National Standard for Permanence of Paper for Printed Library Materials Z39.48-1984.

10   9   8   7   6   5   4   3   2   1

Contents

Preface

This book is the outgrowth of a collaborative effort by a small group of national security analysts associated with the Institute for National Strategic Studies of the National Defense University, government officials responsible for pondering defense and foreign policy issues, and academics with long experience in Middle Eastern affairs. In the past several years these scholars, policy analysts, and military planners have been focusing on the impact on U.S. goals and interests in the Middle East of three seminal events—the ending of the cold war, the collapse of the Soviet Union, and the invasion of Kuwait by Saddam Husayn and the subsequent Gulf War. The authors' individual studies have been nourished by frequent intellectual exchanges with one another and by their participation in numerous academic meetings designed to explore the future of U.S. relations with the Middle East.

It is their conclusion that these dramatic events have masked basic forces that have been operating in the Middle East and in Southwest Asia over the past several decades. The group of analysts and academic specialists involved in the preparation of this book believe that U.S. policymakers should concentrate on these forces in their formulation of regional policy for the decade ahead. Several events of the post–Gulf War period, notably the collapse of the Soviet Union, the initiation of a serious Arab-Israeli peace process, and the emergence of new Muslim nations in Central Asia and the Caucasus, have opened opportunities for new U.S. policy initiatives in the region that extends from North Africa through the Middle East to Southwest Asia. Both the emerging challenges and the opportunities should prompt a reexamination of traditional U.S. interests in the light of a more disorderly and complex international environment. This volume will define the forces that are likely to shape the region in the coming decade and will suggest a U.S. policy agenda for the 1990s.

The editors themselves have contributed to this study, but the successful completion of this book is the fruit of the intellectual input of the several contributors who have brought to it their knowledge of a variety of academic disciplines and their experience in various subregions of the diverse Middle East area. We would like to acknowledge their patience and their willingness to undertake the revisions made necessary by rapidly changing events. In addition, the appearance of this volume would not have been possible without the strong support of the Director of the Institute for National Strategic Studies (INSS), Dr. Alvin Bernstein, and the Institute's Deputy Director, Dr. Stuart E. Johnson, whose enthusiasm and encouragement were essential. We are also grateful to the support staff of INSS, and in particular to Linda Chambers, for their patience and help in preparing the many "final" versions of the manuscript.

As is traditional and fully warranted, the undersigned assume full responsibility for the overall organization, cohesion, and quality of the study. The ideas and information in this volume are those of the authors and editors and do not reflect the views of the National Defense University, the Department of Defense, or the U.S. government.

Phebe Marr
William Lewis

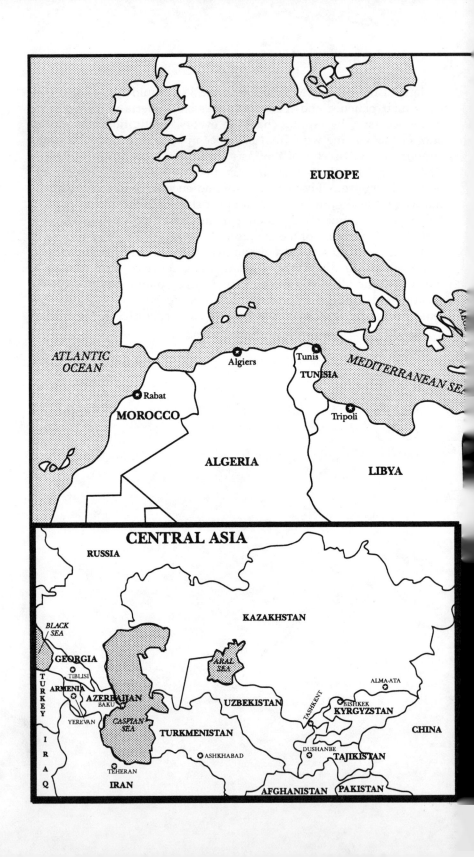

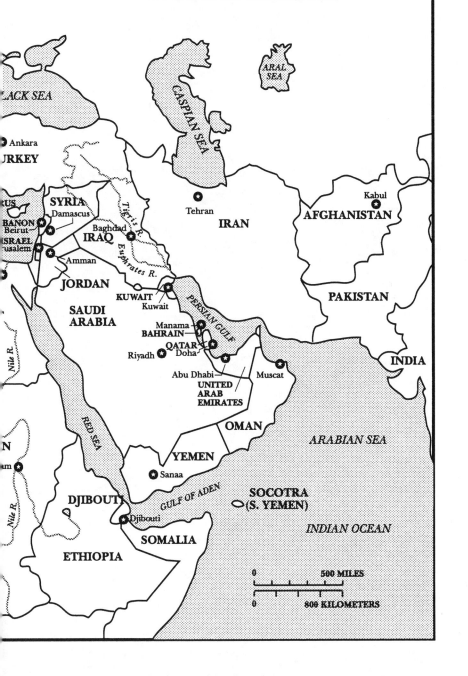

THE MIDDLE EAST
&
NORTH AFRICA

BLACK SEA

Ankara
TURKEY

ARAL
SEA

CASPIAN SEA

RUS
SYRIA
Damascus
BANON
Beirut
ISRAEL
usalem

Tigris R.
Baghdad
IRAQ

Euphrates R.
Amman

Tehran

IRAN

Kabul

AFGHANISTAN

JORDAN

KUWAIT
Kuwait

SAUDI
ARABIA

Manama
BAHRAIN
QATAR
Riyadh   Doha

PERSIAN GULF

PAKISTAN

INDIA

Nile R.

Abu Dhabi
UNITED
ARAB
EMIRATES

Muscat

RED SEA

OMAN

ARABIAN SEA

N

YEMEN

Sanaa

am

Nile R.

DJIBOUTI

GULF OF ADEN

Djibouti

SOMALIA

ETHIOPIA

SOCOTRA
(S. YEMEN)

INDIAN OCEAN

0   500 MILES

0   800 KILOMETERS

Introduction

The Historical Record

Throughout the nineteenth and twentieth centuries, U.S. involvement in the Middle East was dominated by religious, philanthropic, and academic organizations. Presbyterians first arrived in Lebanon (then part of Syria) in the 1820s, subsequently founding the American University of Beirut. In the late nineteenth century, missionaries from the Reformed Church established a string of missions in the Persian Gulf from Iraq to Oman.

Prior to World War II, official interest in the Middle East was mainly limited to the defense of commercial interests, principally oil. There was a brief period of strategic interest in the Middle East during World War I when the Allies were cut off from Middle East oil and the United States, then the leading producer, became the principal supplier for the Allied war effort. Strategic interest reappeared during World War II for much the same reasons. But in the interim, there was little official concern beyond that of assuring the U.S. oil companies that they were granted the same competitive advantages as were European oil companies.

Official appreciation of the geostrategic importance of the region changed dramatically during World War II. The Middle East was increasingly viewed by the U.S. and British military planners as a significant theater of operations, one which would serve as a launching pad for the insertion of Allied forces into southern Europe as well as a transit zone for movement of desperately needed military supplies to support the armed forces of the Soviet Union. To meet both objectives, some accommodation with nationalist leaders in North Africa, the Near East, and Iran, still under European tutelage or influence, was required, and under the direction of President Franklin D. Roosevelt, U.S. assurances on post-war political freedoms were extended in an early attempt to balance strategic interests and democratic values.

The Middle East assumed even greater strategic significance during the period that one U.S. scholar has characterized as "the long peace."[1] The cold war generated requirements for access to military facilities in the region, alliance formation on the part of the United States, and transfers by Washington of military supplies to favored friends and allies. By the end of the 1950s, the United States had a substantial military presence in the region. The political and military hinges of strategy had a northern and southern component. The northern tier embraced Greece, Turkey, and Iran—with Tehran as the quintessential pivot, and the southern tier embraced the monarchies of Saudi Arabia and Ethiopia.

Meanwhile, strong U.S. support for the creation of the state of Israel and its recognition by the United Nations (UN) in 1948 forged a relationship with this eastern Mediterranean nation that has been a pillar of U.S. policy ever since. These ties were buttressed by support for Israel, based on cultural affinity and shared democratic values, and by increased strategic cooperation after the 1967 war. U.S. support for Israel, however, created continual frictions with Arab states opposed to its recognition and complicated attempts by the United States to strengthen its strategic relations in the Arab world.

U.S. Interests During the Cold War

It was in this cold war era that the now "traditional" definition of U.S. interests in the region crystallized. These were:

- Containment of expanding Soviet influence in the region
- Support for Israel's sovereignty and security
- Access to oil at reasonable prices, predicated on growing Western and Japanese dependence on Persian Gulf and North African oil resources
- Stability for Arab and other regional friends, whose military facilities and political backing were essential for containing the Union of Soviet Socialist Republics (USSR)
- Access to the region for peaceful commerce

Events of the 1970s reinforced these interests as guideposts of U.S. policy. When Britain abrogated all its defense responsibilities in the Gulf and the foreign oil companies gradually lost their oil concessions, U.S. interest in oil became strategic as well as economic. With American involvement in Vietnam, President Richard M. Nixon embarked on a strategy of transferring weapons to regional allies prepared to bolster their self-defense capabilities. In the Persian Gulf, when the Shah of Iran signaled his willingness to become the Persian Gulf "policeman," Washington accepted. A 1972 presidential decision initiated a major arms sales program for Iran but sought to balance it on the Arab side of the Gulf with arms sales to Saudi Arabia in what became known as the "two-pillar" policy. Iraq, in this period, was relatively hostile to Western interests.

However, by the end of the 1970s the assumptions underlying this policy had begun to crumble. The "two-pillar" policy failed to prevent the Soviet invasion of Afghanistan in 1979, or the 1979–1980 revolution in Iran that carried the Ayatollah Khomeini to power, causing the collapse of one of the two key pillars. The following year, the eruption of armed conflict between Iran and Iraq brought the Persian Gulf to the brink of instability, threatening Western access to vital oil supplies. Toward the end of the 1980s, a Palestinian uprising in the West Bank and Gaza shattered complacency about Israel's occupation of these territories and initiated a process of rethinking on the Arab-Israeli conflict. "New thinking" about the region gained momentum with Mikhail Gorbachev's rise to power, his search for accommodation with the West, and the subsequent realignment of U.S. strategy toward the Soviet Union. By the end of the decade, the cold war had ended and by 1991 the Soviet Union had collapsed. With these cataclysmal events, containment of Soviet influence ceased to be a political-military objective.

The Post–Cold War Environment

A by-product of the implosion of the Soviet Union and the collapse of the Warsaw Treaty Organization was the emergence of a new international security environment. More than four decades of stability in a bipolar Europe gave way to ethnic rivalries and widening crises in East and Central Europe—epitomized by the barbarism of civil wars in the former Yugoslav federation. The Western European constellations of NATO (the Atlantic Alliance), the EC (European Community), WEU (Western European Union), and CSCE (Conference on Security and Cooperation in Europe) struggled with these problems with outcomes that were problematic at best. Clearly, Europe was becoming an area of widening instability, reflecting a diminished capacity to assume major burdens in peripheral geographic areas such as the Middle East and Southwest Asia. Even the trend toward Western European unity in 1992 was slowed by marginal votes in Denmark and France on the Maastricht Treaty, the instrument designed to bring closer financial and political union by the end of the decade.

Western European governments, reflecting diverse interests and policy goals, often differed with the United States in their perceptions of the basic challenges to Western interests emanating from the Middle East. While a military coalition was assembled under United

States leadership to deal with the Iraqi invasion of Kuwait in 1990, economic difficulties in Europe and the United States suggested that a comparable response would be difficult to produce if future circumstances should require it. As governments seek solutions to economic and national security concerns, historical rivalries are likely to resurface that will reflect divergent approaches to regional security priorities. In the Balkans region, for example, Russia and Ukraine tend toward policies favoring the Serbs, while Germany aligns itself with Slovenia and Croatia. Similar realignments are beginning to unfold in the Middle East as the bipolar period comes to an end and the dissolution of the Soviet Union becomes complete. Syria, a former dependent of Moscow, seeks new ties for arms and economic assistance; Turkey and Iran seek to extend their influence into the Soviet Central Asian republics; and Iraq and Libya, reduced to pariah status in the community of nations, seek economic and political ties wherever they can find them.

The new, more multipolar, world raises significant issues of diplomacy for the United States, as the only putative "superpower" remaining. Will Europeans, intensely involved in their own continent, be willing to share some of the burden of maintaining stability outside of the NATO area? Will coalition diplomacy be an effective agent in dealing with rapidly emerging crises? Will the United Nations continue to function under the leadership of the industrial powers, as it did in the 1991 Gulf War, or will it be reshaped along lines more amenable to the concerns of developing countries?

New Regional Imperatives

The removal of Soviet power and influence from the Middle East and Southwest Asia is producing other consequences. The withering of postwar security alliances and guarantees is creating fresh incentives for some states to strengthen their military arsenals by acquiring weapons of mass destruction. Most experts agree that the accumulation of advanced weaponry—conventional and unconventional—will add to the sense of instability in the region, and make crisis management more difficult. At the same time, long dormant ethnic, nationalist, and sectarian sentiments have now risen to the surface. National borders are no longer sacrosanct and are increasingly seen by dissident groups as obstacles to realizing the full benefit of deeply held ethnonationalist sentiments among many groups including the Kurds in Iraq and Turkey, the Sahrawis in the Western Sahara, the Palestinians in the Arab world "diaspora," and numerous ethnic groups in Central Asia and the Caucasus.

Emerging demographic patterns in North Africa and adjacent areas will be a further challenge to stability and order. The management of population growth, including strategies of resource allocation, education, and welfare services, is taxing the capacity of many governments. This has led in some instances to mounting pressure for reallocation of traditional distributions of political power; elsewhere, secular ideologies of Western origin are being replaced by traditional Islamic values. For those unable to find accommodation in their own societies another outlet has emerged. Emigration from poorer states—Morocco, Algeria, Egypt, and Turkey—to more affluent European countries along the northern Mediterranean littoral is growing and, at its present rate, could constitute a source of cultural, economic, and political difficulty for host governments in the decade to come. Emigration trends have already served as a catalyst for the creation of alliances among rightist political parties in France, Italy, and Germany.

Disaffection by increasingly large segments of less affluent societies of the Middle East and North Africa over the failure of governments to deal effectively with pressing domestic problems has kindled the drive for political reform and, in some instances, radical change among Middle Eastern constituencies. This is often reflected in the emergence of Islamic revivalist movements. In its most extreme manifestation, militant Islam seeks to topple government authority through violent tactics. Often erroneously characterized as Islamic fundamentalism, this rejectionist phenomenon assumes many forms. In some societies, revivalism finds expression primarily in the social realm. In some, change is sought through participation in electoral processes, notably in Egypt and Jordan; elsewhere, as in Algeria and Tunisia, military regimes refuse to permit democratic processes to unfold without policies that exclude religious parties. The point must be stressed that militant Islamic groups do not constitute a monolithic movement; nor are all the growing number of adherents of Islamicist doctrines militant. There is at least one conspicuous example of a "fundamentalist" Islamic regime cooperating with the West—Saudi Arabia.

The majority of populations in the Middle East share an inherent suspicion of outside powers and influences, which is historically well grounded. The lengthy period of Western colonialism, followed by cold war rivalries and foreign interventionism, and the current economic and political difficulties create a sense of doubt about the purposes and intentions of foreign intrusions. Particularly irksome is the sense of dependency felt by some Middle Eastern countries, the inequitable distribution of resources in the region, and the feeling that economic forces are arrayed in favor of the affluent Europeans and Americans to the disadvantage of the Arabs, Turks, and Iranians.

Disenchantment with external influences is enlarged by feelings of shame, deprivation, and manipulation at the hands of more powerful external forces.

Opportunities for Change

Not all indicators of change have a downside, however. Positive trends include the following:

- Middle Eastern governments, largely ruled by autocratic oligarchies, are beginning to feel the political ground shift as populist forces urge a redistribution of power. There are some tentative moves to open political systems. In 1989, Jordan held relatively free elections for the first time in two decades, and duly elected Islamic parties were allowed to take their seats in parliament. Egypt has permitted a multiplicity of parties (with the exception of religious parties) but does maintain some controls on elections. In the wake of the 1991 Gulf War, Kuwait restored its parliament and, in October 1992, held its first election since 1986, although the franchise was extremely limited.
- Ideology, particularly that of socialist inspiration, is giving way to pragmatism. Some governments are restructuring their economies to attract Western investment and privatize state-owned enterprises. In 1989, the Arab Maghreb Union (AMU) consisting of Morocco, Algeria, Tunisia, Mauritania, and Libya was formed to enable these countries to compete economically with a more unified Europe after 1992.
- In the aftermath of the 1991 Gulf War, Arab states showed greater willingness to compromise with Israel. The virulence of the Arab-Israeli conflict abated, as exemplified by Egypt's readmission to the Arab League, despite its peace treaty with Israel; the Palestine Liberation Organization's (PLO) acceptance of Israel's right to exist; and the initiation of an Arab-Israeli peace dialogue under U.S. auspices in 1991–1992. A victory of the Labor party in Israel in April 1992 reflected a willingness by the Israeli public to be more flexible on the issue of peace with their adversaries.

This new environment presents the United States with a unique opportunity to review and reshape its strategies toward the Middle East, North Africa, and Southwest Asia. However, any rethinking of issues must be tempered by two major considerations. First, the newly emerging world order comes at a time when U.S. domestic problems demand time, attention, and resources, probably precluding any dramatic new ventures in foreign policy or grand designs to reshape the international political order. Second, the cluster of issues identified in this book, often of long duration and stubbornly resistent to change, should induce a sense of limitation on the part of policymakers. To ignore the complexity of these problems and the postcolonial psychology of the peoples of the region is to ride the tiger of self-delusion and to court policy failure.

Issues at Stake for the United States

The authors participating in this volume have been asked to examine the ways in which the new international situation will impact on U.S. interests and policies in the Middle East, broadly defined as the region from North Africa to Central Asia and from Turkey to the Persian Gulf, and to address several critical questions. What are the challenges and opportunities facing the United States in the Middle East over the coming decade? Have traditional U.S. interests changed, and if so, in what way? And what policy directions seem appropriate in a new and changing environment? To undertake this task, the authors have explored the new security environment in the Middle East from three different vantage points: the global setting, the regional setting, and transnational and subnational forces likely to affect regional stability.

The New Global Environment

The volume begins at the global level with an examination of the two traditional focuses of U.S. policy in the region—the Soviet threat and access to oil resources.

The most dramatic change in the international environment has been the collapse of the Soviet Union and the end of the cold war. What will these developments portend for Russia, the chief legatee of the former Soviet Union, as it disentangles its bureaucratic and military structures from those of its former dependencies in the Caucasus and Central Asia? How will the latter buffer zone affect Russia's relations with regions to the south? Will Russia continue its cooperation with the United States, evident in the 1991 Gulf War and in the Arab-Israeli peace process? Or can the United States expect renewed, though less dangerous, competition with its former adversary in this region? Above all, will Russia be willing and able to contain weapons proliferation if such containment comes at its own economic expense? Melvin Goodman explores these issues and what they will mean for

Russia and for the Middle East as Moscow maps a new relationship with the United States and its neighbors to the south.

Access to the region's oil resources at reasonable prices has long been recognized as a major U.S. interest, one it shares with the international community. As the 1991 Gulf War demonstrated, this global security interest can be threatened by the political volatility of the region. What role will Persian Gulf oil play in the international economy in the coming decade? Will the West, especially the United States, be more or less dependent on this resource? And how can the interests of consumers and producers best be protected, while assuring more reliability in oil flows? William Ramsay addresses the challenges of mutual interdependence between the West and Middle East oil producers, laying out the parameters of future relations. As he makes clear, Western economic interests will remain vitally engaged in this region for the coming decade.

The Regional Security Environment

Next, three authors look at the shifting balance of power in the Middle East and Southwest Asia and the potential for peaceful resolution of endemic conflicts. No regional conflict has been more enduring than that between the Arabs and Israel. Arab-Israeli wars have broken out with monotonous, if tragic, regularity once in every decade since the end of World War II—in 1948, 1956, 1967, 1973, and 1982. William Quandt weaves his way deftly through the multiple layers of controversy underlying this conflict to show that the legacy of war may slowly be giving way to conflict resolution in this arena. The outcome is not yet clear, but a settlement acceptable to all parties would fundamentally affect the prospects for regional peace and the balance of forces in the region. Conversely, failure to achieve such an outcome would adversely affect almost all U.S. regional interests and raise the threshhold of military conflict.

The second arena of recent wars has been the Persian Gulf, which has undergone an eight-year war between Iran and Iraq (1980–1988) and a short but intense war between Iraq and a coalition of thirty-four states in 1991. What are the prospects for a permanent peace between Iran and Iraq? between Iraq and Kuwait? Will this area, so essential to the world's economic prosperity, find ways to peaceably settle boundary disputes, ideological struggles, and ambitions for hegemony and control over pricing and production of oil? Or will these issues continue to keep the region tense and the United States involved, with an ever growing political and military presence? As Phebe Marr indicates, Desert Storm failed to settle the underlying causes of conflict in the Gulf, leaving the region's future highly uncertain. Crisis management may be the best the United States can achieve while it works to reduce endemic tensions.

Nothing is more likely to affect the regional balance of power more seriously than proliferation of weapons of mass destruction and advanced delivery systems. This is one issue that may have been adversely affected by the collapse of the Soviet Union and by the 1991 Gulf War. Russia and the newly independent states of the former Soviet Union, some in possession of nuclear weapons, may be unable to control their spread to the Middle East region. The Gulf War, with its dramatic demonstration of the effectiveness of high-technology weapons, may have given renewed impetus to demand for such technology. The need for effective regimes of constraint is clear. How likely are such regimes to evolve? What direction should arms control take? What role will sales of conventional weapons play in the regional balance over the decade? Will they stabilize the balance or undermine constraint regimes? William Lewis addresses these questions and the ways in which technology restraint regimes need to be changed for long-term effectiveness. As he indicates, failure to better constrain proliferation will not only affect the regional balance but may also make any future conflicts, including those potentially involving the United States, much more lethal.

Social, Economic, and Ideological Issues

Lastly, authors examine an array of transnational and subnational forces likely to destabilize the Middle East but at the same time to open new possibilities for positive change. These forces may present the United States with its most demanding challenge in the decade ahead: how to encourage positive change while reducing the potential for disruption and violence. Three critical problem areas are addressed in this volume.

First is the issue of potentially worsening economic conditions throughout areas of North Africa, the Middle East, and Southwest Asia. Thomas Naff shows how the current population explosion will press on scarce resources in the states of the Mediterranean rim, already burdened with debt and structural economic problems. A decline in water resources may become critical in several states in the course of the decade, adding to economic burdens. The chapter addresses several policy relevant questions. How will these trends affect the stability of key states of the region, on whom the United States depends for support and facilities? How can resources inequalities and deficiencies be ameliorated in an era of global austerity?

And what role can the United States, with its own financial deficit, play?

No force is more explosive or more likely to lead to domestic eruptions and regional instability than emerging ethnic and sectarian consciousness. The sudden creation of eight new states on the northern rim of Southwest Asia (two Christian and six Muslim) has given impetus to the drive for self-determination on the part of numerous minorities within the Middle East region to the south. Current territorial disputes in the former provinces of the Soviet Union show the potential destructiveness of this trend, of which Yugoslavia is the grimmest reminder. No post–cold war trend has more potential to change the shape of the region or the distribution of power than the drive for ethnic self-determination. It also has strong potential to bring Western and U.S. intervention—military and nonmilitary—as the example of postwar Iraq demonstrates. Abdul Aziz Said tackles the multiple and complex issues involved in this question and what the answers will mean for U.S. policy. Said focuses, above all, on two key questions: How much emphasis should the United States give to human rights and self-determination in its vision of the new world order? And how much emphasis should it give to geostrategic concerns and regional stability, without which at least some U.S. interests cannot be maintained?

Finally, John Esposito addresses the new ideological challenges of the post–cold war era in the Middle East. The decline of Arab nationalism and other intellectual orientations of Western origin have opened the field to new concepts, long in gestation. Chief among these is Islamic revivalism. This multifaceted force is seen by some as a threat to Western values, by others as an indigenous attempt to reform Muslim society. Whatever the view, Islamic movements are likely to challenge existing regimes, including some that support U.S. and Western policy in the region. What should be the attitude of the United States toward these movements? Is there potential for cooperation with some revivalist elements, and if so, how? What aspects of these movements may genuinely threaten Western interests? And what options does the United States have in meeting the challenge? At the same time, the United States confronts a new opportunity in the impetus for democracy slowly spreading its influence in the region. How will the incipient movement for more open societies interact with the Islamic revival? Above all, how should the United States address conflicts between "democratic change" and "geostrategic security interests"? These concerns and the paradoxes they raise are explored and carefully balanced in a chapter that integrates both ideological trends.

U.S. Policy Requirements

In her conclusion, Phebe Marr assesses the complex and varied trends outlined in the volume and places them in a policy context, indicating where the United States will face opportunities and where it must address challenges to the status quo. In a rapidly changing, multifaceted region, no single strategy is likely to be successful. In seeking to establish some policy directions, the concluding chapter addresses three fundamental questions. How have U.S. interests been affected by post–cold war transitions in the international and regional security environment? How much leadership will the United States be willing and able to exercise in an era of austerity and economic readjustment at home? To what extent must the United States fashion a new set of priorities, and what are these likely to be in a region with a lengthy historical memory, adjusting to an era of profound and wrenching change?

1

Moscow and the Middle East in the 1990s

Melvin Goodman

The replacement of the Soviet Union by the new Commonwealth of Independent States (CIS) has launched a major debate about the future of international relations. The debate turns in part on perceptions of the commonwealth, which is not a state but a fig leaf for an unwieldy association of republics that must determine responsibility for its borders, its treasure, its army, and its military assets. The agreements that formed the commonwealth sidestepped many of these matters, as well as the most serious issue confronting the eleven member-states—the collapse of their joint economy. Until the leaders of the republics, particularly those in Russia and Ukraine, deal with these issues, they will provide few clues to the new foreign and national security policies of the commonwealth.

The leaders of the commonwealth will be preoccupied in a face-off over all of these issues during the next several years. They have agreed to coordinate economic and foreign policies, but the non-Russian legislatures have pledged only "consultation" in foreign policy and not "coordination." The three largest republics (Russia, Ukraine, and Kazakhstan) have differed publicly over important national security issues, including protection of borders and control of military assets. Ukraine is opposed to the joint guarding of the commonwealth's external borders and its leaders have proclaimed that it will only participate in a commonwealth if the commonwealth remains a loose association and not a new state.

States in the Middle East and the Persian Gulf have been quick to respond to the loss of the Soviet Union as a major benefactor and to the decline of Russia's geopolitical influence. Syria permitted the United States to try to broker a peace settlement with Israel at the Madrid talks and allowed Syrian Jews to emigrate. Damascus has even entered an unprecedented direct dialogue with Israel over the Golan Heights. Iran decided to release the hostages it was holding who were U.S. citizens. Israel appears to realize that the end of the Soviet "threat" increases U.S. influence in the region, including its leverage over Israeli decision making. The end of the cold war also made it easier for the United States to assemble an Arab coalition in Desert Shield and Desert Storm.

Gorbachev's Legacy

Former President Mikhail Gorbachev was responsible for more changes in the international arena over the past decade than any other member of his generation. He recognized that the arms race with the United States was pushing the Soviet Union to bankruptcy and creating no political opportunities in the international arena. He pursued a strategic retreat that ended Soviet ties to Eastern Europe and to major clients in the Third World. Gorbachev reduced Soviet risk taking on behalf of Iraq, Libya, and Syria and removed thousands of Soviet advisers from the Middle East.

As the commonwealth begins to debate issues of national security and foreign policy, the new Russian national interest will gradually become clear. It certainly appears that the Slavic leaders of the commonwealth in Russia, Ukraine, and Belarus will pursue Gorbachev's strategic retreat from competition with the United States, Central Europe, the Sino-Soviet border, and the Third World. The "civil crisis" in the commonwealth will make this retreat irreversible in the near term and will return arms control and disarmament to the centerpiece of relations with the United States. The new Russian military force will be less threatening to East and West and will be under the supervision of elected civilians for the first time in history.

Gorbachev and former foreign minister Eduard Shevardnadze were responsible for repudiating past Soviet foreign policies and for seeking greater stability and predictability in the global arena. They also changed the entire decision-making process for the formulation of national security and foreign policies and, by incorporating more modest goals, ingratiated the Kremlin leadership with the international community. These changes ended conflicts between East and West and contributed to Gorbachev's place in history, but they could not save him from the changes unleashed at home.

The new leaders of the commonwealth, particularly those in Russia and Ukraine, will try to continue these policies, and time will tell whether their differing perceptions of national interest will hinder the formation and scope of a commonwealth foreign policy. Russian president Boris Yeltsin has shown that he is impetuous and mercurial but capable of compromising on sensitive military and strategic issues. Nevertheless, he is facing a Russia-first opposition, led by his vice president, who opposes conciliation. The vice president of Ukraine has warned on several occasions that his state's efforts to control Russian military assets have created an "explosive situation and [that] it is time for Russia to stop being a cow milked by anyone who feels like it."[1] The head of the Russian parliament also has taken a hard line on nationality, economic, and security issues with the non-Russian republics. Continued violence in Armenia, Azerbaijan, and Georgia will lead to increased conservative pressure on Yeltsin to avoid concessions of the so-called "small dictators" in the non-Russian republics. These internal problems, as well as the opposition from disaffected members of the communist party and the military, could complicate Russia's efforts to pursue a conciliatory policy with its neighbors in the Middle East and to make sure that proliferation problems are kept under control, especially on the southern border.

The Soviet economic crisis was a major reason for the strategic retreat from the Third World, particularly the reduced involvement in the Middle East. For the first time since the Second World War Soviet petroleum output was declining, with even high-level defense industry managers complaining about disruptions in their enterprises and losses of skilled workers. The consumer's lot has continued to worsen and, as the commonwealth tries to organize, problems have remained from a system now declared to be bankrupt. If predictions of food shortages prove correct, there could be additional violence. In another dramatic change, Russia has become a recipient of significant aid from the Third World, including the oil-rich Persian Gulf states.

After 1985, the Soviet Union moved to soften policies in the international arena, particularly the hard line toward Iran, Israel, and Pakistan. When Eduard Shevardnadze was appointed foreign minister in July 1985, one conciliatory proposal followed another. The decision to withdraw from Afghanistan was announced in 1988 and, during that same year, the Soviets cooperated privately with the United States, moving to resolve conflicts in Africa, Asia, Central America, and the Persian Gulf.

Soviet efforts to shrink its military role in the Third World was part of Gorbachev's campaign to reduce emphasis on military power. Since 1985 there has been a decline in the status of the military, a reduced role in decision making, and a reduction in defense spending and procurement. Top military leaders were removed in 1987. Another purge took place after the failure of the coup in August 1991.

Moscow reduced the military role of its forces in the Middle East and the Persian Gulf, showing no interest in extending deployments in distant areas and limiting the mission in out-of-area waters to reconnaissance. The Soviet Union did not try to replace bases lost in Egypt and Somalia in the 1970s or upgrade the poor facilities that naval vessels used in Yemen and Syria. Interest in the negotiation of naval confidence-building measures with the United States and the inclusion of naval forces in both strategic and conventional arms control negotiations strongly suggested that the Russians were going to rely on disarmament agreements to blunt the superiority of the U.S. Navy and could not afford a naval competition.

Military assistance to the Third World has dropped sharply, particularly to the Middle East and the Persian Gulf, in part due to a decline in purchases of weapons systems and to emphasis on less expensive spare parts and ammunition. The increase in Third World debt and the cease-fire between Iran and Iraq were also factors in the decline of weapons agreements with client states. Syria's need to invest in its economy will reduce opportunities for Russian transfers, and the drop in revenues for oil producers in the Middle East could contribute to reduced weapons purchases in the 1990s. In addition to reducing military activity and assistance, the Russians will be extending less economic aid to former clients in the Third World.

The Gulf War and Soviet-U.S. Teamwork

During the initial stages of the 1990 Gulf crisis, Moscow temporized in supporting U.S. diplomatic initiatives and the accompanying buildup of coalition forces. On several occasions, the Soviet government dispatched a senior official to Baghdad in hopes that it could garner international kudos for its attmpt to secure a negotiated settlement. Following the war, Moscow pressed Iraq to comply with UN inspections and with international safeguards to end Baghdad's nuclear, chemical, and biological weapons programs.

Izvestia commentator Aleksandr Bovin observed that had this crisis occurred before 1985 the Soviets would have adopted a position of friendly neutrality and reacted negatively to the appearance of U.S. forces.[2] For its part, he said, the United States would have accused the Soviets of supporting aggression in indulging the terrorist regime in Baghdad. Instead, Moscow supported U.S. political and diplomatic goals, condemning the invasion, suspending military deliveries to Baghdad, and demanding unconditional Iraqi withdrawal.

The Soviets justified their abandonment of Iraq on both moral and security grounds, indicating that they would protect the centrality of relations with the United States. Gorbachev called the Iraqi invasion a violation of "everything the world community now pins its hopes on as it seeks to put civilization on the track of peaceful development."[3] An authoritative commentator, Stanislav Kondrashov, explained that "sacrificing relations with another dictatorship" confirmed Moscow's commitment to "abandoning confrontation with the West . . . particularly with the United States."[4] In return, the United States agreed to acknowledge the linkage between ending the Gulf crisis and resolving Arab-Israeli tensions. A Soviet-U.S. joint statement in January 1991 indicated that efforts to resolve regional issues would be expanded after the Gulf crisis ended. By seeking Soviet partnership in his Middle East initiative in the summer of 1991, Secretary of State James Baker fulfilled the U.S. commitment. Moscow's decision to deploy two warships in the Persian Gulf in September 1992 was a strong indicator of Yeltsin's willingness to support continued U.S. initiatives against Iraq.

Moscow's "New Directions" in the Middle East

Over the past several years, Moscow has pursued increasingly flexible policies with respect to a wide variety of regional issues and has aired differences with Arab clients such as Libya and Syria over terrorism, military parity with Israel, and political relations with Israel. Moscow's emphasis on its domestic economy and the need to improve East-West relations will continue in the 1990s and will dictate a continued emphasis on cooperation over conflict. Soviet behavior during the war in the Persian Gulf indicated that Moscow wants to stay on the road of continued security cooperation with the United States, the key international policy associated with *perestroika*. President Yeltsin's preoccupation with internal instability will provide the United States with far greater freedom to pursue its interests in the Middle East.

An Opening to Israel

As Galia Golan of the Hebrew University in Jerusalem has noted, Moscow's moves toward an opening to Israel in 1985–1986 represented a "new direction" in Soviet policy and a deliberate effort by Gorbachev to broaden Soviet options in the Middle East.[5] Gorbachev was the first general secretary to pursue expanded ties with Israel and to offer concessions to enhance Moscow's regional flexibility and international credibility. Moscow had broken diplomatic relations with Israel in 1967 during the Six-Day War in response to Arab pressure and to bolster its own credibility lost during Israel's lightening success against Soviet-supplied Arab opponents. The move, however, put Moscow at a disadvantage vis-à-vis the United States in terms of mediating the Arab-Israeli conflict and contributed to the stagnation of the Soviet political position in the Middle East.

On taking office in 1985, Gorbachev made it clear that Soviet, not Arab, interests would dictate Moscow's foreign policy agenda, even in areas in which it had previously deferred to clients. He moved immediately to expand the diplomatic dialogue with Israel, sanctioning informal meetings in Paris and Washington between Soviet and Israeli ambassadors in summer 1985 and allowing Poland and Hungary to arrange the establishment of interests sections in Israel, then sanctioning full diplomatic relations.[6]

In another step to lay the groundwork for the restoration of diplomatic ties with Israel, the Soviet delegation at the United Nations decided to abstain rather than vote to expel Israel in 1991 during the annual Arab exercise to drive Israel from the UN. This was a significant step in the USSR's move away from reflexive alignment with the radical Arab states, particularly Libya and Syria, and marked the end of Moscow's role in the campaign to delegitimize Israel within various international organizations. In April 1992, the Russian vice president, Aleksandr Rutskoi, visited Israel and met with Yitzhak Shamir, then prime minister.

The Issue of Soviet Jewish Immigration

In a gesture to both Israel and the West, the Soviet Union allowed Jewish emigration to increase dramatically. Over 28,000 Soviet Jews were allowed to leave in 1987 and 1988, indicating a shift in policy that was probably aimed more at Soviet relations with the United States than with Israel. More than 70,000 Jews left the USSR in 1989, marking the highest level of Jewish emigration since the creation of the state of Israel more than forty years ago, and more than 200,000 left in 1991. These developments led President George Bush to announce that the U.S. restrictions on trade, originally legislated to retaliate against Soviet constraints on emigration by its citizens, especially Jews, would be lifted when the Soviets legalized their new emigration policy, and that he would endorse most-favored-nation (MFN) trade status for the USSR.

Virtually all Arab states have expressed outrage at the accelerated immigration of Jews from the former Soviet Union into Israel, but Moscow continues to insist that Russia will allow free emigration of its citizens. Although the overwhelming majority of immigrants has settled within Israel's pre-1967 borders, Arab officials have expressed concern that the wave of immigration will increase Jewish settlement in East

Jerusalem and the West Bank. Arab concern is focused on the potential impact on the indigenous population, countering higher population growth among Palestinians and possibly fueling their flight to Jordan. Arab leaders realize that Moscow's willingness to increase Jewish emigration during the worst violence of the *intifada* was a strong indication of Gorbachev's determination to pursue its national interests regardless of Arab sensitivities.

In 1991, six years after the resumption of the diplomatic dialogue between the Soviet Union and Israel, the two sides reestablished diplomatic relations, thus fulfilling Gorbachev's pledge to restore ties in the context of a cooperative role with the United States in resolving regional conflicts. Moscow had prepared the way for diplomatic ties by agreeing to an exchange of consulates general in 1990 and by retracting support for the UN resolution that equated Zionism with racism. Also in 1990, Gorbachev used the fiftieth anniversary ceremony memorializing the Nazi massacre of Jews at Babiy Yar in Ukraine to condemn "venomous sprouts" of anti-Semitism.[7] Gorbachev agreed to direct flights from Moscow to Israel for emigrants, which Yeltsin has also permitted.

Improved Ties with Egypt

Shortly after coming to power, Gorbachev signaled his eagerness to improve relations with Egypt, whose gradual move back into the Arab fold was consistent with Moscow's efforts to encourage a more united Arab approach to the conflict with Israel. Moscow particularly encouraged the resumption of ties between Egypt and Syria in 1990, which served the Soviet goals of giving more legitimacy to Cairo's efforts to stabilize relations in the Middle East and end Damascus's diplomatic isolation.

Under Egyptian President Husni Mubarak, there was only glacial improvement in Soviet-Egyptian relations until 1987. Mubarak permitted the Soviet ambassador to return to Cairo in mid-1985, but allowed little other progress. A major obstacle to improved relations was disagreement over repayment terms for Egypt's large military debt to the USSR. Since 1977 Egypt had refused to make payments, and Moscow had made such payments a precondition to delivery of spare parts for Soviet-made military equipment and to improved commercial relations.[8] In 1987 Moscow agreed to Egypt's terms for repayment, including a six-year grace period and generous terms for the twenty-year period of repayment.[9] Soon after this agreement, the two sides signed new bilateral economic agreements, renewed discussions of military supply, and reopened consulates.[10]

Distancing Moscow from Arab Radicals

Since April 1987, when Gorbachev explicitly told Hafiz al-Asad that there could be no military solution to the Arab-Israeli conflict (an implicit rejection of Asad's efforts to achieve strategic parity with Israel), the Russians have made it clear that their, and not Arab, interests would dictate Moscow's foreign policy agenda. This new approach has caused considerable concern among those Arab leaders who had depended on Soviet political, economic, and military support. These leaders are unhappy with Moscow's flexibility on the peace process, its expansion of contacts with Israel, its policy with respect to Jewish emigration, and its reduced willingness to subsidize arms sales.

Several radical Arab states have modified their policies and moved to bolster their regional positions, at least in part because of their shifting perceptions of Russian reliability. Syria's decision to restore relations with Egypt in 1990 was the most dramatic manifestation of this trend. Libya has improved ties with Egypt and has sought closer ties to its Maghreb neighbors. South Yemen announced unification with North Yemen and is improving relations with Oman.

The PLO is concerned about the future Russian and Eastern European commitment. The communist regimes of Eastern Europe had staunchly supported the PLO, providing it with money, weapons, training, and political support. The PLO is unhappy about Jewish emigration into Israel and the cooperation of East European states in facilitating the migration. The PLO is also displeased by improving relations between Eastern Europe and Israel and can no longer count on Eastern European support for its positions at the United Nations. Russian and Eastern European economic assistance will decline in the 1990s and, as a result, Moscow will have even less leverage in the region.

"New Directions" in the Persian Gulf

The Iran-Iraq War

The decade-long Iran-Iraq War complicated Soviet efforts to establish and maintain good relations with both Tehran and Baghdad. Throughout the war, the Soviets pressed for a rapid end to the hostilities and actively supported Resolution 598 of 1987 that called for an end to the war. They equivocated about imposing sanctions provided for in the resolution because they did not want to antagonize Iran.

Moscow backed UN efforts to mediate a settlement of the conflict, alternately putting pressure on Tehran and Baghdad to resolve their differences. In 1990 the Soviets proposed that a meeting of the Soviet,

Iranian, and Iraqi foreign ministers be held in the USSR in order to facilitate the mediation.[11] Iran and Iraq welcomed the initiative and held direct talks in Geneva in July 1990, their first since the cease-fire in 1988.[12]

The cease-fire, Moscow's withdrawal from Afghanistan, and the death of Khomeini in 1989 have led to improved Russian-Iranian relations. Moscow's patience during the worst of Iran's anti-Soviet activities—stopping shipment of natural gas, closing the Soviet consulate at Rasht, expelling Soviet embassy personnel—and the more pragmatic approach to Iran adopted when Shevardnadze replaced Gromyko as foreign minister have paid off.

In January 1989, six months before his death, Ayatollah Khomeini sent a conciliatory message to Gorbachev (his only written message to a foreign leader), praising the Soviet leader for "confronting realities" and revising ideology.[13] Shortly thereafter, Shervardnadze became the first Soviet foreign minister to visit Iran in seventy years. The visit of Majlis Speaker (now president) Hashimi Rafsanjani to Moscow in June 1989 gave new impetus to the bilateral relationship because a number of economic and commercial agreements were signed. Tehran will purchase machinery, plants, and technology for its economic reconstruction; Moscow will receive renewed deliveries of natural gas.[14] Subsequent agreements provided for tourist exchanges, expanded cultural ties, and cross-border travel.

The most dramatic document signed was a Declaration of Principles that included a Soviet agreement to "cooperate with the Iranian side with regard to strengthening its defense capability."[15] The declaration did not indicate what military equipment Moscow might be prepared to deliver, but Gorbachev confirmed that a basic decision to sell arms had been made in response to a question from a Supreme Soviet deputy. The Soviet president defended such sales as part of the USSR's overall arms policy and said they did not conflict with efforts to secure a more peaceful international climate. A foreign ministry spokesman stated in March 1990 that the goal was the restoration of military ties that existed before 1982, and later in the year Moscow began delivery of MiG-29 fighter aircraft.[16] As a result, Moscow became Iran's leading arms supplier in 1990–1991, compared with no deliveries to Iran from 1984 to 1987. Iran has become the largest hard-currency purchaser of Russian military equipment in the Third World, which has led to increased Arab demands for U.S. sales to the Persian Gulf states.

Courtship of the Conservative Gulf States

As elsewhere in the Third World, the Russians have tried to improve relations with the conservative states of the Gulf in a variety of ways.

The rhetoric of "new thinking" combined with active diplomacy and a generally more responsible position with respect to Gulf issues helped to improve Moscow's image. Moscow has benefited from a shifting perception among Persian Gulf states about the nature of the Russian threat. Prior to the Iraqi invasion of Kuwait, these states viewed Iran as the greatest threat to their stability and, because of the reduced U.S. naval presence in the Persian Gulf, they remained uncertain about the durability of the U.S. commitment to their interests—particularly the professed need for more sophisticated military equipment.[17] Moscow fostered a positive shift in Gulf perceptions through its withdrawal from Afghanistan, its low-key military posture during the Iran-Iraq war, and efforts to mediate the conflict between Tehran and Baghdad.

Since 1985 Russian contacts with all of the conservative Gulf states have intensified and relations with most have expanded. Oman and the United Arab Emirates (UAE) established diplomatic relations with the USSR in fall 1985, and Qatar established relations in 1988. Soviet relations with Oman have not progressed appreciably, but the former USSR and the UAE have had a number of contacts and have reached several agreements. Abu Dhabi has extended a loan to Moscow, discussed the purchase of weapons systems, and permitted Soviet naval vessels to visit UAE ports.[18] A Russian military delegation visited the UAE in April 1992 as part of an effort to increase arms sales to the Persian Gulf for hard currency.

The Soviet agreement to lease three oil tankers to Kuwait in 1987 was significant because it marked the Soviet Union's first participation in the Gulf in a security role. It was followed by the U.S. decision to reflag 11 Kuwaiti tankers and protect those vessels with more that 30 combatants in the Persian Gulf. The major U.S. buildup in the region was an action that Moscow failed to anticipate and led Shevardnadze to criticize his senior leadership in 1988 for failing to "predict the mass American presence in the Persian Gulf."[19] Moscow's preoccupation with reducing the U.S. naval presence in the Gulf during this period highlighted the USSR's weak position there. U.S. military successes in the Persian Gulf have led to increased Russian efforts to use naval arms control to limit Washington's presence in the region.

One tactic Gorbachev used to advance Moscow's interests with the Gulf states was to offer to cooperate with the Organization of Petroleum Exporting Countries (OPEC) to stabilize oil prices and keep production down. The Soviets indicated such willingness during visits to Moscow by the Iranian and Saudi oil ministers in the 1980s; the latter's visit had particular importance because it represented one of the few visits by a Saudi official since diplomatic relations were broken over fifty years ago. Moscow's need for Western technology and financing for its own oil reserves should limit Russian competition with the United States in the Gulf. Most of the former Soviet republics will remain dependent on Western assistance for the near term due to the inefficiency and waste of their energy industry.

The decline in Russian oil production will encourage continued cooperation with OPEC, including possible efforts to cooperate on sales and pricing to European consumers. Russia's acting oil minister, Vagit Alekperov, announced that he expected Soviet oil production to reach the lowest levels in sixteen years, averaging less than ten million barrels a day in 1992.[20] Russian exports are expected to drop to two million barrels a day, down from about three million barrels in 1990, which means significant losses in hard currency. Moscow presumably will look for arrangements in the Middle East to trade weapons systems for petroleum with Iran and Saudi Arabia.

Russian contacts with Saudi Arabia expanded in the wake of the Iraqi invasion of Kuwait and led to the reestablishment of diplomatic relations. Prior to the Persian Gulf War, Saudi Foreign Minister Saud al-Faysal visited the USSR, ostensibly as head of a Gulf Cooperation Council (GCC) delegation, and a Soviet foreign ministry official, Vladimir Polyakov, visited Riyadh in return, carrying a message from Gorbachev and becoming the first Soviet to pay an official visit to Saudi Arabia in more than fifty years.[21] Saudi Arabia hosted a meeting between Soviet Deputy Foreign Minister Yuly Vorontsov and Afghan *mujahidin* (freedom fighters) in 1988, and Vorontsov subsequently met with King Fahd—becoming the first Soviet representative to meet with a Saudi king in fifty years. In March 1990 Polyakov visited Riyadh again—this time to explain Soviet policy on Jewish emigration.[22]

Differences between the two sides continue, however. The Saudi purchase of an intermediate-range missile system from China in 1988 angered Moscow, as did the rapid Saudi recognition of the Afghan interim government in 1989. The Saudis were unhappy with the Soviet sale of SU-24 aircraft to Libya and with Soviet criticism of the Saudi purchase of Tornado aircraft from Great Britain. The Saudis were critical of Moscow's treatment of its Muslim population, exacerbated by recent events in Azerbaijan and Tajikistan, and the conservative religious establishment in Saudi Arabia is a continuing barrier to improved ties with Moscow.

The Impact of the Dissolution of the Soviet Bloc

The changes sweeping the commonwealth and the non-Soviet members of the former Warsaw Pact are having a major impact on the

Middle East, particularly on Moscow's client states and the Palestine Liberation Organization, which can only look forward to a decline in political, economic, and military support from the Kremlin. The region itself must be redefined, with the emergence of six Islamic states in Central Asia and the Caucasus. Just as Israel and the more moderate Arab states with ties to the West believe that Western economic resources will be diverted to Eastern Europe, the more radical Arab states and the PLO are anticipating a steep decline in the assistance they have been receiving from the Soviets since the mid-1950s.

New governments in the non-Soviet states of the former Warsaw Pact have already changed policy toward the Middle East. All of Moscow's East European allies except Romania severed relations with Israel in 1967 as a gesture of solidarity with both Moscow and the Arab states, and now all of these states have established full diplomatic relations with the Israeli government. East European arms deliveries to the Middle East declined in 1989, as did Soviet deliveries, largely because of reduced sales to Iran and Iraq, and Czechoslovakia is moving to convert many of its military factories to consumer production. Czech armored vehicles and artillery had been highly sought after in the Middle East. The PLO, in particular, stands to lose a major source of both weapons and training for its military forces, and more extremist Palestinian groups will lose training bases in the former East Germany and Poland. Syria, according to the London-based International Institute for Strategic Studies, lost 1,000 Soviet military advisers in 1989 and additional advisers in 1990.[23]

The Islamic Factor

The creation of the commonwealth means that, for the first time since the Bolshevik Revolution, Russia will not share a border with the Islamic states of the Near East and the Persian Gulf. An independent Azerbaijan, Kazakhstan, Turkmenistan, Uzbekistan, Kyrgyzstan, and Tajikistan will find Russia, Iran, Saudi Arabia, and Turkey competing for influence in a region that holds vast energy resources and nuclear weapons and facilities. Russia's main concerns will be the secular influence of Turkey and the Islamic influence of Iran. Except for the Tajiks, who are ethnically Persian, the former Soviet Islamic belt is formed of Turkic peoples: Azeris, Kazakhs, Kyrgyz, Turkmen, Uzbeks, and others. But pan-Turkism is a cultural force that has no role as a regional political movement. The surge in ethnic violence in the Central Asian Republic of Kyrgyzstan in 1989 occurred on the day of Gorbachev's return from a summit meeting in Washington and confronted the president with yet another domestic crisis. The violence produced more than one hundred deaths and one thousand injuries and climaxed another round of confrontations in Central Asia over grinding property and allocations of land and water.[24] Yeltsin has sent Russian troops to Tajikistan because of fighting there that has caused more than 1,000 deaths in 1992.

About six million Azeris live on each side of the Azeri-Iranian border, and Moscow and Tehran have indicated that they have no interest in exploiting instability and separatism in the region.[25] The Iranians have signaled publicly that they will not take advantage of Russia's domestic problems and have indicated that "extreme nationalism" would serve the interests of neither Russia nor Iran.[26] Presumably some Muslims would be willing to capitalize on the Azeri situation to spread the Islamic revival in the region.

The emergence of five new Islamic states in Central Asia (Kazakhstan, Uzbekistan, Turkmenistan, Tajikistan, and Kyrgyzstan) will complicate Russian decision making in the region. These new states are politically and economically vulnerable and could contribute to further disintegration within Russia itself. There are more than ten million ethnic Russians in the region, about a fifth of the overall population of fifty million. These states are aware of their weaknesses and were the strongest supporters of a "union" of republics in the wake of the coup attempt in August 1991. They were most supportive of the commonwealth that was formed in December 1991 after the dissolution of the Soviet Union. Reports of rising Islamic revivalism are exaggerated, but Islamic political activists are beginning to challenge governments in Uzbekistan and Tajikistan.

Russia will remain a major factor in the region, and all of these states have some kind of defense agreement with Russia. Kyrgyzstan is the only former Soviet republic that has not created its own army, signing a treaty with Russia in February 1992 to provide for defense cooperation. There are more than 20,000 commonwealth troops on the territory of Tajikistan, and in May 1992 Kazakhstan joined with Russia and four smaller states of the commonwealth in a common defense treaty. Uzbekistan and Turkmenistan have signed separate bilateral security accords with Russia, and Turkmenistan has agreed to allow Russia to help create its own armed forces. The continued presence of Russian troops on these territories, however, could appear to be a foreign occupying force to the Islamic states of the Middle East and the Persian Gulf.

This region has long been considered a "tragic experiment" in Soviet rule, with numerous ecological nightmares, the lowest rate of high school graduates, and the least fluency in Russian among the former Soviet Union's major ethnic groups. The average Central Asian infant mortality rate is nearly twice the Russian average and, among rural people, more than twice. Mothers in Central Asia die far more often in childbirth than their counterparts in Russia. Leaders of key Muslim states in the Middle East and the Persian Gulf merely had to look across the border for evidence of the failure of the communist system.

Religion always has been a major factor in the political calculations of the ruling elites in Central Asia, and now outside forces have complicated the politics of Islam in the region. Russian leaders are particularly leery of the Islamic competition for influence in the region among Iran, Turkey, Saudi Arabia, and Pakistan. There are also reports that Afghan guerilla leader Gulbuddin Hikmatyar, is arming Muslim groups in Tajikistan and that Afghan guerillas have been involved in the fighting in the southern part of the country. It will be difficult for Russia to stabilize political developments in Central Asia without stabilizing events in Afghanistan and seeing an end to the Afghan civil war.

Issues for the 1990s

Moscow will continue to be preoccupied with its own internal restructuring in the years ahead. In order to focus on its domestic problems, it will prefer a relaxed international environment and stable bilateral relations with the West, particularly with the United States. The Third World will decline in importance, and Third World conflict situations should pose fewer problems for Russian decision makers. Moscow will certainly give priority to calming regional tensions and preventing escalation that could lead, in the worst case, to confrontation with the United States.

Moscow's interests will be best served in the 1990s by movement in the Arab-Israeli peace process and regional arms control. For progress in either area, it needs U.S. support. Over the near term Moscow will concentrate its efforts on improving bilateral ties to all states in the region and on seeking a role in the peace process. In order to promote the process, the Russians have become more flexible on some issues important to the United States and Israel, and even the establishment of an independent Palestinian state (conceding the possibility of federation with Jordan).[27] Yeltsin has become far less partisan on all of these issues than was former Soviet leader Leonid Brezhnev, who resented Washington's domination of the peace process in the 1970s.

Moscow can be expected to present a wide array of measures for UN participation in resolving regional conflicts in the 1990s to limit the possibilities for Russian-American friction. Since 1987 Moscow has favored a central role for the UN in conflict resolution, advocating greater use of UN military observers and peacekeeping forces to separate warring parties and mediate disputes. Moscow paid arrears in contributions to the UN and it is gradually paying past assessments for peacekeeping. Moscow proposed withdrawal of all foreign fleets from the Persian Gulf in 1987 and the creation of a UN fleet, but this had more to do with the fact that there were only a few Soviet warships in the Gulf compared to thirty from the United States.[28]

Moscow favors the use of the permanent members of the UN Security Council as guarantors of regional security and in 1989 cosponsored its first UN resolution with the United States. Thus far the Russians have found a broad consensus at the UN for a more active role by the secretary general in resolving conflicts and cooperating with regional organizations to create an environment for negotiations. Conflicts between countries could be contained in this fashion, although ethnic violence and international terrorism will be more difficult to resolve.

Moscow's interest in avoiding conflicts in the Middle East has been heightened by the need for peacekeeping forces closer to Russia's borders, particularly in Central Asia and the Caucasus. Russian paratroopers and armored cars are patrolling the streets and valleys of two regions of Georgia, enforcing a shaky peace between the Georgian army and rebel separatists. The Russian Fourteenth Army patrols the banks of a river separating the Moldovan army from the militia of the Trans-Dnester region, which is populated by Russians and Ukrainians. Russian negotiators have already mediated ineffective cease-fires in Georgia with Ossetian and Abkhazian minorities, as well as in Moldova. And in Central Asia, Russian troops have fought with Tajik guerrillas from neighboring Afghanistan who are trying to assist their Islamic brethren in a deepening civil war in Tajikistan.

The conflict in Tajikistan is essentially political, but it also has strong connections to Islam and traditional rivalries. The influence of radical Islamic factions in the opposition has been rising, and these factions have been receiving support from Islamic revivalists in Afghanistan and Iran. Afghanistan, which has a large Tajik minority, has provided weapons and training to the opposition, and there are insufficient Russian troops on the Tajik-Afghan border to stop arms smuggling. Neighboring Central Asian states, including Uzbekistan, Kazakhstan, and Kyrgyzstan, fearful of the spread of turmoil across their borders, have requested Russian assistance. These states issued a joint statement in September 1992, warning that the "southern borders of the Commonwealth must not be violated and that the escalation of the civil war in Tajikistan, which is threatening the security of our nations and upsetting political stability in the region, must not be permitted."[29]

Crisis Prevention

Moscow's interest in limiting its military presence in the region and reducing the risk of Russian-American competition is even more immediate than is the longer-term search for diplomatic settlements. During Mubarak's visit to Moscow in May 1990, Gorbachev announced that the USSR would be willing to "limit" its arms sales to the region on the basis of "reciprocity" and listed arms reduction to the level of "defense sufficiency" as a major component of any Middle East peace settlement.[30] This marked the first time that any Soviet leader explicitly offered to limit Moscow's arms sales in the Middle East, although Shevardnadze stated in Cairo in 1989 that the region's "military potential" far exceeded its "real economic and demographic weight."[31] Russian officials and legislators have questioned the effect of Moscow's arms sales on regional stability and have criticized the arms policies of Iraq, Libya, and Syria.

The reduction in Russian arms sales to the Middle East is another sign of interest in toning down commitments to client regimes and reviving discussion of managing competition in the Third World. Russia may try to reduce arms in the Third World to the level of "defense sufficiency." If so, Moscow may seek a political declaration with the United States to establish limits on Russian and U.S. arms transfers to foreign countries. Russia also wants to join the Missile Technology Control Regime (MTCR) to support the international effort to limit missile systems in the Third World.

In the 1980s the USSR led in the delivery of combat aircraft, surface-to-air missiles, naval combatants, tanks, and artillery to the Middle East.[32] Since 1985 Soviet deliveries to the Third World, particularly to the Middle East, have fallen, and in 1990 the United States became the biggest supplier of arms to the Third World. The value of arms deliveries to Libya fell from $9 billion during 1981–1985 to $3.5 billion during 1986–1989. Arms deliveries to Syria fell from $10 billion to $5.5 billion and to Iraq from $28 billion to $18 billion during these same periods.[33] Russia continued to be a major supplier to eight of the top ten arms recipients in the Third World, but all of them except Iran received fewer arms in 1991 than in previous years. However, questions have arisen in the United States regarding the ability of the Russian and other commonwealth governments to control special arms transfer agreements informally arranged by their military establishments, as well as by hard-pressed managers of industries producing military equipment. Both of the latter are anxious to acquire hard currencies to supplement funds provided by civilian government ministries.

Moscow's experience in previous regional confrontations has been that its clients have pressured it for direct combat support that it has been unwilling to provide. Crisis management could become more difficult and time increasingly urgent as regional states acquire more sophisticated and lethal weaponry. It is particularly ironic that the key states in these regions are acquiring intermediate-range ballistic missiles just as the United States and Russia have agreed in their own intermediate-range nuclear forces (INF) treaty to eliminate such weapons from Europe.

Russian Military Role

Russian retrenchment in the Third World does not mean that Arab states will lose all access to Russian weapons. In a speech to the Nineteenth Party Conference in 1988, Primakov emphasized that the USSR had "in no way given up its sympathies or its actual support for the forces of progress" and that it was a "firm opponent of any attempts to export counter-revolution to countries where progressive forces have come to power."[34] Thus Moscow will continue to use its military assets to protect gains in Iran and Syria.

Russian arms transfers will remain a fact of life in the Third World, particularly in the Middle East where exchanges for hard currency to Iran and Libya will finance some aspects of Moscow's economic modernization program. Libya purchased SU-24 fighter bombers in 1989. Older Soviet equipment predominates in many Third World arsenals. Some reductions in sales to the region have been offset by transfers to Iran (e.g., MiG-29 fighter aircraft and self-propelled artillery).

Conventional arms agreements in Europe will likely lead to the addition of thousands of combat aircraft, attack helicopters, tanks, light armored vehicles, and field artillery pieces to Third World inventories. Arms control measures and unilateral reductions will lead to lower prices, attracting such debtors as Egypt and Iran. Iran needs to improve its defensive capabilities against Iraq, and India needs to upgrade armor in the event of hostilities against Pakistan. Conversely, military transfers to such economically troubled areas as Yemen will be scrutinized for savings as more resources are needed at home. The conventional forces treaty for Europe could lead to the availability of U.S. equipment for such clients as Israel, Egypt, Morocco, and Tunisia.

Moscow presumably hopes that assistance to Iran will counter recent signs of an indirect and unacknowledged—but moderate and unprovocative—dialogue between Washington and Tehran. The emergence of Hujat al-Islam Hashimi Rafsanjani as first among equals in Iran's leadership is worrisome to the Russians because of his willingness to improve relations with the West and his support for resolving differences with the United States. The removal of Mir Husayn Musavi, whose office of prime minister was eliminated, was a further setback because of his support for ties with Russia and Eastern Europe and his opposition to normalizing relations with the United States. Moscow has been successful in concluding military and economic agreements with Iran, including joint exploration for oil in the Caspian Sea, but presumably realizes that Tehran cannot resolve its economic problems without access to Western technology and capital. Iran has become the largest hard-currency purchaser of Russian military equipment and, over the past several years, has spent $5 billion on tanks, missiles, and aircraft from China, North Korea, and Russia.

Implications for the United States

Since the failure of the Soviet coup in the summer of 1991 and the dissolution of the Soviet Union itself several months later, Moscow has reduced reliance on military influence in the Middle East and the Persian Gulf in order to pursue cooperation with the United States on a broad range of issues. In addition to virtually providing carte blanche to Washington in the Gulf, the Russians exchanged diplomatic relations with Israel and improved bilateral relations with the conservative Arab states. In return for Israeli willingness to attend a peace conference, Moscow reestablished full diplomatic relations with Israel in October 1991. Russia has urged moderation on all sides in Lebanon; publicly discouraged Libyan, Palestinian, and Syrian use of terrorism; and refused to provide military parity for Syria in its rivalry with Israel.

Soviet condemnation of terrorism in the Middle East and the Persian Gulf was a strong indicator of a new policy toward the region under Gorbachev. The turning point took place in 1986, when Moscow condemned the Palestinian seizure of a U.S. airliner that resulted in the deaths of more than twenty persons. A TASS statement declared that "there can be no justification for this act, and those who committed the crime, no matter what motives guided them."[35] The Palestinian attack on a Greek cruise ship in 1988 and the bombing of a civilian Israeli bus were described as "terrorist" acts by Foreign Ministry spokesman Gennady Gerasimov.[36] Moscow even cooperated with the Israeli government in 1989, following the hijacking of a Soviet airliner to Tel Aviv, and Deputy Director of the KGB Lt. Gen. Vitaly Ponomarev noted KGB willingness to work with other intelligence services on such matters. Yeltsin specially authorized KGB cooperation with the Central Intelligence Agency (CIA) in order to prevent or resolve acts of terrorism, and talks have begun between leaders of the CIA and the KGB.

Russia has reduced its military activities in the region, particularly military support for clients. There has been a decline in the operational tempo and presence of naval forces and aviation in the Middle East over the past several years: a significant number of military advisers have been withdrawn, naval deployments in the Mediterranean have been slashed, and joint exercises with Arab navies have been reduced. Declining arms sales will mean further cuts in the advisory presence, and Moscow announced in May 1990 that it would limit arms sales even further if the United States were willing to show restraint in this area. A Russian general officer has called for "radical reduction" in arms sales and an "embargo" on dual purpose weapons in order to limit the "threat from the south."[37]

Yeltsin wants the United Nations and the Security Council to play a central role in conflict resolution in the area. Moscow has paid its assessment for the International Force in Lebanon (UNIFIL) and the peacekeeping forces in the Golan Heights. Yeltsin has reaffirmed Gorbachev's call for a UN role in verifying regional arms agreements, investigating international terrorism, and establishing standards for human rights. The Soviets endorsed UN Resolution 598 to end the Iran-Iraq War and campaigned for a revival of the Military Staff Committee to implement a series of resolutions dealing with the Iraqi invasion of Kuwait. Yeltsin has been extremely supportive of a broad consensus at the United Nations for a more active role by the secretary general in resolving conflicts and cooperating with regional organizations to create an environment for negotiations as well as international efforts to rid Iraq of nuclear, chemical, and biological weapons.

Moscow almost certainly will continue to give high priority to maintaining a relaxed international environment and expanding international economic relations and will refrain from efforts to undermine U.S. positions by capitalizing on regional instability. A foreign ministry official wrote in 1990 that if Soviet interests "clash with American interests, we must seek a resolution jointly. In other cases, American interests must not trouble us."[38] To the best of its ability, Moscow will continue to pursue political solutions to regional tensions and will encourage its clients to take moderate positions so as not to jeopardize broader interests.

The Middle East and Persian Gulf will retain their importance to Moscow because of their proximity, their wealth, and the dangers posed by chronic tensions. While progress in negotiations has reduced the danger of war, the Arab-Israeli conflict remains intractable and, in the absence of a settlement, the situation will remain volatile. The Arab states are no match for Israel, but the proliferation of nuclear and chemical weapons in the region increases the potential danger of any minor clash.

In spite of the reduced danger of global confrontation, crisis management may become more difficult and time increasingly urgent as regional states that have acquired sophisticated and lethal weaponry may feel less constrained by the fear of outside involvement; the Iraqi invasion of Kuwait, albeit a miscalculation, is a case in point. The advent of new political thinking does not mean that all U.S. and Russian interests will coincide. As Stanislav Kondrashov has warned, the interests of the two countries are not the same:

> America wants to dominate a region where there is so much oil, where Israeli interests . . . are still more important to it than Saudi interests, and which lies strategically close to the Soviet Union. What has changed in these principles of U.S. policy? It still relies on force and on assurances that force will be used in the interests of peace and stability. There are no grounds for doubting the sincerity of these assurances, but Washington reserves the right to determine what the interests of peace and stability are. Despite the level of cooperation reached between Washington and Moscow, the policies of the two nations are not and cannot be identical.[39]

New political thinking does mean, however, that Moscow no longer believes the expansion of its military presence in the Third World will give it greater political security or that Moscow must counter every U.S. move. Unlike Brezhnev, Yeltsin and the new Russian leaders are not willing to pour arms into areas of friction. Rather, just as Gorbachev advocated collective efforts to defuse conflicts, Yeltsin has continued these efforts.[40] His primary rationale for supporting regional settlements is to ensure that local conflicts do not "engender confrontation" or increase tensions between the major powers. This will remain a key Russian objective for the future as Moscow seeks to rebuild its shattered political and economic structures. As a result, the United States will have increased access and leverage in the region.

Prospects for the 1990s

In the final analysis, Yeltsin does not believe that a greater military presence in the Middle East and Southwest Asia assures greater political security for either Russia or its clients. Unlike Brezhnev, he favors sending more arms to those Third World states that can afford to pay for them and less to those who cannot. As long as the Russian economy remains in crisis, with output declining at an accelerating rate, inflation out of control, and the former republics engaged in a fierce political struggle, Moscow will have to pursue conciliatory policies on its borders. If this trend continues in the 1990s, it will significantly alter Russian delivery patterns. Countries with access to hard currency such as Iran and Saudi Arabia will receive more attention from Russian arms merchants and those with limited access such as Egypt and Syria will receive less.

Yeltsin, unlike Brezhnev, is not willing to pour unlimited amounts of arms into areas of friction in the Middle East. In 1987 his predecessor, Gorbachev, supported the idea of collective efforts to "defuse" conflicts "in all the planet's hot spots" and favored a greater United Nations role in this regard.[41] Gorbachev's support for regional settlements through the UN, as in Afghanistan, or U.S. mediation, as in Angola, was justified as a means to make sure that local conflicts do not "engender confrontation" between the powers.[42] The deputy director of the African Institute wrote in 1988 that military assistance has not created reliable allies and regional conflicts have not ended in clear victories.[43] And at the United Nations on the anniversary of Pearl Harbor in 1988 Gorbachev reminded his audience that: "The bell of each regional conflict tolls for all of us. This is particularly true because these conflicts are occurring in the Third World which even without this has many troubles and problems on a scale that cannot fail to concern all of us."[44]

The Russian emphasis on cooperation with the United States in the Middle East is the best way for Moscow to protect its interests in the region, which points to additional diplomatic cooperation in the 1990s. Moscow shares Washington's avowed desire for arms limitations for the region and is particularly concerned with the problem of nuclear proliferation.

Russian support for UN Resolution 678 to limit Iraq's nuclear and chemical weapons capabilities is a harbinger of support for limits on nuclear proliferation in the Third World. Iraq's ability to develop a plutonium-processing program without detection indicates that the international regimes to control proliferation such as MTCR and the London Suppliers Group are inadequate. Moscow would like to join these groups, and feels it is necessary to develop regimes for control of such advanced conventional weaponry as cluster bombs, precision-guided munitions, and cruise missiles.

Just as the Cuban missile crisis in 1962 convinced the superpowers that it was necessary to get the "nuclear genie back in the bottle," Iraq's invasion of Kuwait may revive the notion of a collective security regime and open a window of opportunity for the United Nations to create such a regime. It is no accident of history that in the wake of the Cuban missile crisis the United States and the Soviet Union signed the Partial Test Ban and Hot Line agreements. Soviet political commentator Fyodor Burlatsky remarked that the Cuban missile crisis was a "bad thing with a very good result . . . the first step toward new thinking about each other."[45] The Persian Gulf will mark a similar contribution toward not only crisis resolution but also crisis prevention if Third World leaders with global ambitions realize that a new era of Russian-American cooperation will limit the opportunities for threatening regional stability.

The peace conference launched in 1991 will be another test of Moscow's professed concern with persuading Syria to adopt a more flexible position toward talks with Israel. Moscow's behavior thus far indicates willingness to assume the role of middleman between Syria, on the one hand, and Israel and the United States, on the other. Moscow's internal instability—both political and economic—has reduced Russian leverage in the Middle East, however, and the United States should find it easier to arrange Moscow's cooperation for the ongoing U.S.-inspired peace process. Moscow must realize that Damascus did not agree to negotiate with Israel because of Russian pressure, but that the Syrians had to improve relations with Washington because of the collapse of the former Soviet Union, its erstwhile benefactor. As long as cooperation with the United States remains at the top of Moscow's international agenda, it remains likely that the Russians will be willing to cooperate politically and diplomatically with Washington. And until the Russians get back on their feet and a Russian nationalist policy comes to dominate thinking in the Kremlin, the United States will have a relatively free hand in the Middle East.

One of the greatest risks to stable Russian-American relations in the Middle East and the Persian Gulf is Washington's propensity for overplaying its hand vis-à-vis Moscow. There will continue to be a great deal of hard-line and conservative opposition to Yeltsin and other reformers. As a result, aggressive U.S. submarine patrolling near Russian territorial waters, resistance from Washington to legitimate Russian arms sales to Turkey and conservative Arab states, and efforts to block the sale of sophisticated Russian rocket engines to India's space commission will increase right-wing pressures on Yeltsin's government. U.S. interests would be best served by careful efforts to give Russia advance notice of Washington's military deployments in the region and to coordinate efforts to contain Saddam Husayn.

If the 1991 Gulf War was a test case of future Russian-American relations, then it appears that the Yeltsin government is committed to conflict resolution and prevention. For the first time since the Suez crisis in 1956, the United States and Russia did not back different clients in a Middle East conflict, and for the first time since the Six-Day War in 1967, Moscow did not offer diplomatic and political protection for an Arab client. Boris Yeltsin's continuing commitment to the international coalition in the Gulf indicates that Moscow will continue efforts to reinforce its relations with the West, particularly with the United States.

The creation of the Commonwealth of Independent States in

December 1991 launched political shock waves in Eurasia that brought radical changes in global politics. Moscow's political and economic weakness will create greater dependence on Western assistance and will reduce its presence and influence in the Third World, particularly in the Middle East. The Russians will not be a major factor in the region for the near term and presumably will continue to support cooperative measures with the United States to resolve conflicts in the region between Arabs and Israelis. As a result, the United States will have a freer hand in its own dealings in the Middle East, but it will have to monitor closely Russian efforts to transfer weapons systems for hard currency, particularly with Iran and the conservative Arab states of the Persian Gulf.

The sudden last-minute cancellation of Yeltsin's trip to Japan in September 1992 indicates, however, that the Russian government will protect its strategic interests and that the emergence of Russian nationalist forces has exaggerated the importance of strategic concerns. Yeltsin may be forced to compromise with the worst elements in his government, just as Gorbachev did in 1990 and 1991, even if it leads to a loss of economic assistance from the United States and other Western countries. Many Russians continue to regret the loss of the empire and their urgings could lead to Moscow's efforts to come to the defense of Russian minorities throughout the commonwealth, particularly in Central Asia against Muslim majorities.

The uncertainty of developments in Central Asia and the Caucasus will demand that Yeltsin and his immediate successors closely monitor events in Iran and Afghanistan. Russian arms supplies to Iran that are designed to buy Tehran's cooperation on border issues could lead to problems with the United States. And Russian military clashes with Afghan forces would bring harsh reminders of the Soviet invasion of 1979 and could lead to complications with Washington. Moscow paid a terrible international price for its intervention in Afghanistan, but faced with the alternative of militant Islamic influence in Central Asia, the Russian military may be needed to protect the borders of the commonwealth. Russia clearly requires stability and progress in the Middle East, as well as the East-West relationship in general, but there are many independent variables that will create difficulties for the leadership in Moscow.

Notes

1. *Pravda*, February 23, 1991, p. 5; *Izvestia*, April 29, 1992, p. 3.
2. *Izvestia*, April 11, 1991, p. 5.
3. *Pravda*, September 11, 1990, p. 5.
4. *Izvestia*, August 15, 1990, p. 3.

5. Galia Golan, "Gorbachev's Middle East Strategy," *Foreign Affairs* 66, no. 1 (Fall 1987), p. 41.

6. *Davar* (Israel), February 14, 1987.

7. TASS, October 17, 1990.

8. Karen Dawisha, "The Soviet Union in the Middle East: Great Power in Search of a Leading Role," in *The Soviet Union in the Third World*, E. J. Feuchtewanger and Peter Nailor, eds. (New York: St. Martin's Press, 1981), p. 126.

9. Middle East News Agency (MENA), Cairo, March 23, 1987.

10. TASS, October 26, 1987.

11. TASS, January 10, 1990.

12. Youssef M. Ibrahim, "Iran-Iraq Talks Produce Progress on Ending Long Confrontation," *New York Times*, July 4, 1990, p. 1.

13. Tehran Radio, January 8, 1989.

14. Tehran Domestic Service, June 13, 1989.

15. TASS, June 22, 1989.

16. TASS, March 1, 1990.

17. Kuwait has long had diplomatic relations with the former USSR and often has served as a proponent of Soviet interests in the region. Moscow has a large embassy in Kuwait and has had an arms supply relationship with Kuwait since the early 1970s. Bahrain, Oman, and the United Arab Emirates established diplomatic relations with the Soviet Union in 1985.

18. *Krasnaya Zvezda*, October 25, 1988.

19. *Vestnik Ministerstbva Inostrannykh Sel SSSR*, August 1988, no. 14, pp. 27–46. Foreign Minister Shevardnadze's report to the Foreign Ministry.

20. Steven Prokesch, "Soviets Estimate Oil Production Will Drop in 1991," *New York Times*, August 31, 1991, p. 7.

21. TASS, February 22, 1988.

22. Ibid.

23. *Kuwait KUNA*, March 6, 1990.

24. Youssef M. Ibrahim, "Arabs Fear End of Cold War," *New York Times*, March 6, 1990, p. 1.

25. The cold war can be dated to the Soviet refusal in 1945 to withdraw from Iranian Azerbaijan, where Stalin created two puppet republics along the Soviet and Iraqi borders. President Harry S Truman's suggestion of the use of force led to a Soviet withdrawal, and Iran reneged on its promise of political and economic concessions to the Soviets in the region. This marked the first of a series of Stalin's failures to support liberation struggles in the Third World. See Alvin Z. Rubinstein, *Moscow's Third World Strategy* (Princeton: Princeton University Press, 1988), pp. 82–84.

26. *Tehran Times*, January 8, 1990, p. 3.

27. *Pravda*, February 24, 1989, p. 3. Foreign Minister Shevardnadze's speech at the headquarters of Egypt's National Democratic Party on February 23, 1989, contains the most extensive description of the Soviet leadership's views on the modalities of negotiations on an Arab-Israeli peace settlement.

28. David Shipler, "Soviet Links Iran Embargo to U.N. Force," *New York Times*, December 17, 1987, p. 5.

29. Tass, September 29, 1992.

30. *Pravda*, May 16, 1990, p. 5.

31. *Izvestia*, February 24, 1989, p. 3.

32. Richard F. Grimmett, "Trends in Conventional Arms Transfers to the Third World by Major Supplier, 1982–1989" (Washington, D.C.: Congressional Reference Service, 1990), p. 63.

33. Ibid., p. 7. The Middle East and South Asia is the largest Third World arms market, accounting for two-thirds of total value of arms transfers from 1986–1989. More than one-third of these deliveries come from the former Soviet Union.

34. *Pravda*, July 2, 1988, p. 5.

35. *Pravda*, September 7, 1986, p. 5.

36. TASS, October 5, 1988.

37. Major General Vadim Makarevsky, "The Threat from the South," *New Times*, August 21–27, 1990, p. 12.

38. Andrey Kolosov, "Reexamining Policy in the Third World," *Mezhdunarodnaya Zhizn*, April 1990, no. 4, pp. 37–45.

39. Stanislav Kondrashov, "Together Against the Aggressor. What Then?" *Izvestia*, August 15, 1990, p. 5.

40. *Pravda*, September 17, 1987, p. 3.

41. *Pravda*, September 17, 1986, p. 5.

42. Mikhail Gorbachev, *Perestroika: New Thinking for Our Country and the World* (New York: Harper and Row, 1987), p. 176.

43. *Izvestia*, February 4, 1988, p. 5.

44. *Pravda*, December 8, 1988, p. 1, Gorbachev's speech at the forty-third UN General Assembly.

45. *Izvestia*, September 11, 1990, p. 5.

Suggested Reading

Campbell, Kurt M., and MacFarlane, S. Neil, *Gorbachev's Third World Dilemmas*, London: Routledge, 1989.

Duncan, Raymond W., and Ekedahl, Carolyn McGiffert, *Moscow and the Third World Under Gorbachev*, Boulder, Colo.: Westview Press, 1990.

Golan, Galia, *Soviet Policies in the Middle East*, Cambridge: Cambridge University Press, 1990.

Goodman, Melvin A., *Gorbachev's Retreat: The Third World*, New York: Praeger, 1991.

Goodman, Melvin A., *The End of Superpower Conflict in the Third World*, Boulder, Colo.: Westview Press, 1992.

Rubenstein, Alvin Z., *Moscow's Third World Strategy*, Princeton: Princeton University Press, 1990.

2

Oil in the 1990s: The Gulf Dominant

William C. Ramsay

With their low production costs and vast reserves of crude oil, the countries of the Persian Gulf will take an even more dominant position in the world energy supply picture in the 1990s than they did in the 1980s. They will also continue to expand current efforts to purchase and build refining and marketing assets overseas, attempting to secure markets for their crude in the consuming countries.

For the United States and other Western economies, this means that our energy dependence on the countries in the Persian Gulf will grow for both crude oil and refined products. In return, the Gulf countries are becoming more dependent on the Western economies for their economic stability and growth. But this deepening interdependence may be insufficient to ensure our energy security, as Saddam Husayn's invasion of Kuwait on August 2, 1990, vividly showed. Fortunately, or unfortunately for policymakers, consumers felt little impact from the recent Gulf crisis. It may, therefore, be difficult to put issues of energy security such as those noted above to a public who are unconvinced that a problem exists.

Energy, in all its forms, is vital to the United States. This country is remarkably dependent on oil as a source of energy, particularly as a transportation fuel. The security of the U.S. supply of oil is, therefore, vital to our continuing economic and military strength. For years our foreign, economic, and military policy has been influenced by the importance of oil supplies from the Persian Gulf, and will continue to be.

Concentration of Market Power in the Gulf

The last decade saw new non-OPEC crude oil suppliers enter the market and take a substantial portion of OPEC's market share (Brazil, for example, expanded production by 227 percent from 1980 to 1989, and Denmark saw a 1,817 percent jump in the same period). In 1980, OPEC provided over 45 percent of world oil production; in 1989, 38 percent of the world's oil came from OPEC. By contrast, the 1990s are likely to see market power in the hands of five or six OPEC producers. Only Saudi Arabia, Iraq, Kuwait, the United Arab Emirates, Venezuela, and possibly Iran will be left within a few years with either excess capacity (the ability to increase production substantially with little or no additional capital investment) or a substantial potential to develop such capacity. Indeed, it is conceivable that by the middle of the decade only Saudi Arabia, Iran, and Venezuela will be left with enough room to meet growing world demand. Reconstructed Iraq and Kuwait will probably not have much spare capacity until late in the decade. The two war-torn states will produce as much oil as possible to generate revenues needed to rebuild and to pay war expenses.

About 66 percent of the world's known recoverable oil reserves are located in the Persian Gulf; only 2.6 percent are found in the United States and 1.9 percent in Western Europe (Figure 2.1 and Table 2.1).[1] The big five Gulf producers together have enough oil in the ground, once developed, to supply the market for at least another century at current rates of production. More importantly, Persian Gulf producers account for almost all of the world's post-Gulf crisis excess production capacity—most of this in Saudi Arabia.

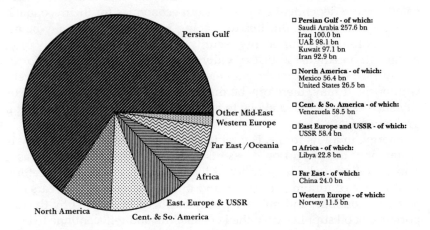

FIGURE 2.1 Estimated World Crude Oil Revenues. On January 1, 1990, the total of estimated reserves was over one trillion barrels. *Source:* U.S. Department of Energy/Energy Information Administration, *International Energy Annual 1989* (Washington, D.C.: Government Printing Office), Table 35, p. 21.

TABLE 2.1 Estimated World Crude Oil Reserves by Region (in billions of barrels)

Region	Barrels
Persian Gulf	
Saudi Arabia	257.6
Iraq	100.0
UAE	98.1
Kuwait	97.1
Iran	92.9
North America	
Mexico	56.4
United States	26.5
Central and South America	
Venezuela	58.5
Eastern Europe and USSR	
USSR	58.4
Africa	
Libya	22.8
Far East	
China	24.0
Western Europe	
Norway	11.5

Source: U.S. Department of Energy/Energy Information Administration, *International Energy Annual 1989* (Washington, D.C.: Government Printing Office), Table 35, p. 21.

We cannot expect major new oil finds in the future that would reverse this trend. Oil production is peaking or has peaked in the major fields of the United States, the North Sea, Canada, and Mexico. Indeed, crude oil output by non-OPEC producers will likely decline for the third straight year in 1991—largely due to a continued plunge in production from the former Soviet Union.

As the Persian Gulf producers add more oil reserves and capacity over the next decade, world output will become even more concentrated in the region. Over the next five to ten years the Persian Gulf's share of total world crude oil production may range between 45 percent and 50 percent (currently about 26 percent).[2]

Good or Bad for Consumers?

At least initially, this concentration of market power into the hands of a few Mideast producers may be good news for consumers.

Those few countries with spare capacity are also those most interested in moderating future oil prices to preserve their long-term markets. The steady decline in oil prices after 1981—especially the 1986 price collapse, when prices fell almost 50 percent from 1985 levels—forced large OPEC producers to realize two things: artificially maintained high prices harm oil's long-term competitiveness vis-à-vis other energy sources, and they encourage the development of non-OPEC oil supplies.

As the Gulf producers' influence over OPEC grows along with their share of OPEC output, and as OPEC gradually evolves into little more than a Gulf influence bloc, we should see a continued push by these big producers for moderate OPEC pricing policies. Iraq had a chance during summer 1990 to take over OPEC price leadership from the Saudis, but Saddam Husayn destroyed his nascent ability to move prices upward within OPEC when he invaded Kuwait.

Now it is once again the Saudis who will lead the way. The informal OPEC production agreement of March 1991 was a clear victory for a self-assured Saudi Arabia and for moderate Saudi price policies. This newly confidant Riyadh emerging from the 1991 Gulf War firmly put OPEC "have nots" on notice that Saudi Arabia and other high-reserve OPEC producers will no longer pay for their socioeconomic problems. The Saudis gained not only moderate prices but also a bigger relative share of OPEC output for big OPEC producers and an equitable sharing of the burden of OPEC price support. The result is that artificially high oil prices and OPEC's quota allocation scheme, for the immediate future, will not be used as a primary means of wealth transferal from both big producers and consumers to small producers with large populations and heavy external debt. Gulf countries are not unaware that this will exacerbate income disparities, but they seem uncertain as to how, or even if, this can be dealt with.

Even traditional OPEC member Iran, which previously favored price increases, is now supporting moderate prices to encourage growth in world oil consumption. While Iraq searches for an economic comeback, Iran is trying to cement its new postwar position as OPEC's and the Persian Gulf's second biggest oil power. Iran, however, will need to moderate its behavior and rejoin the community of nations before it can attract the Western credit, equipment, technology, and markets it needs to begin putting its long-neglected economic house in order. With foreign assistance Iran plans an output capacity expansion to 5 million barrels per day (mmb/d) by 1993 (probably an overly optimistic figure) from its current 3.5 mmb/d capacity.[3] The political uncertainties of doing business with Iran remain: It is not certain how far the desire for policy moderation and outreach to the world community extends within its own society and power structure.

Downstream Investment: Further Inducement to Moderation

Downstream investments by key producers continue to be a further inducement for the OPEC producers to moderate price increases over the longer term.[4] By integrating downstream, OPEC countries ensure international markets for their crude oil, and they acquire an interest in continued world economic growth unhampered by energy price hikes. Consumers, then, gain somewhat more reliable supplies of crude and refined products. The world oil market is undergoing a major transition back to a fully integrated industry that may, in time, resemble the pre-OPEC "Seven Sisters," the seven major international oil companies that initiated and developed Persian Gulf oil fields before the 1960s. The primary difference this time is that OPEC states are among the biggest players. In the early 1980s high-reserve OPEC countries moved into petroleum refining and marketing in consumer countries, trying to stop losses of their share of the oil market in those countries. Major OPEC producers now seek to have most of their future annual oil output destined for their own downstream facilities—either at home or abroad.

Although OPEC's own refinery capacity and downstream presence can be expected to grow in all major markets, the numbers are still small. Product exports from the Gulf now total about 2 million barrels per day without Iraqi and Kuwaiti capacity, compared to an estimated export capability of 3.2 mmb/d in January 1990. Venezuela, with about 3 percent of Free World refining capacity at home and another 1.2 percent abroad, is OPEC's downstream leader. Before Saddam Husayn's destruction of Kuwait's oil sector and the allied bombing of Iraqi refineries, about 8 percent of the Free World's refinery capacity lay within the Gulf states.[5]

The Gulf producers' ownership of and active participation in foreign refineries is limited, so far, to Kuwait and Saudi Arabia, representing less than 1 percent of the Free World's total capacity. Kuwait controls about 1 percent of Western Europe's refining capacity, and equity participation by Saudi Arabia in U.S. refineries now represents about 2 percent of the total operable U.S. refining capacity.

OPEC National Oil Companies: Poised for Growth

According to a 1990 *Petroleum Intelligence Weekly* survey, four OPEC national companies now rank among the top ten oil companies in the world on the basis of oil and gas reserves, production, product sales and refining capacity. With the 1989 start-up of Star Enterprises, a 600,000 barrels per day (b/d) (crude) U.S. joint venture with Texaco, Saudi Aramco became the largest oil company in the world. This was the first, and probably far from the last, Saudi move toward international integration of its industry. Indeed, the Gulf crisis has spurred producers' interest in capturing more value added for their crude and in trying to fill the market void left by Kuwait's sophisticated export refineries.

Saudi Arabia is not only upgrading its present domestic refinery capacity but is also reportedly exploring a deal with three Japanese companies and Caltex Petroleum Corporation to build two refineries, one in Japan and one in Saudi Arabia. Similar projects are being explored in Korea and Western Europe.

Albeit troubled by management and cash woes, Iran's National Iranian Oil Company (NIOC) follows right below Venezuela's Petróleos de Venezuela, Sociedad Anónima (PDVSA) to rank as the number five oil company in the world. Iran is emerging from its years of enforced isolation to actively pursue refinery joint ventures or processing deals, both at home and abroad, with such diverse countries as Pakistan and Romania. Tehran is currently talking with prospective foreign partners, for example, for a large joint venture export refinery at a newly established free trade zone on Qishm Island at the mouth of the Persian Gulf.

Number ten, Kuwaiti Petroleum Corporation (KPC) has gone several steps further than its OPEC colleagues, perhaps a portent of things to come. KPC markets its own products through four thousand wholly owned gas stations throughout Europe (under its Q-8 logo), is involved in exploration and development around the world, and has its own fleet of oil tankers.

The Gulf War may also force cash-strapped high-reserve producers to accept foreign participation upstream as they try to accelerate plans to increase their production capacity. It is a lesson that many small producers learned during the lean years of the mid-1980s. With the Iranian government publicly calling for international cooperation in both offshore and onshore oil/gas development, Iran could just be one of the best bets within OPEC over the next few years for equity participation upstream by foreign firms. The Iranians are already talking with numerous foreign firms about possible joint ventures in oil and gas production off the coast of Iran in the Persian Gulf. The upshot here is that OPEC national oil companies are already operating in U.S. and Western markets, and those operations are growing. From a policy perspective, this will enhance U.S. energy security. To shut off oil supplies to the West, Gulf states will be damaging their own economic interests.

Development: A Two-Way Street

The United States and Europe will continue to attract Gulf investors by the sheer size of their markets, despite the short-term prospects of relatively stagnant energy consumption. These regions will also provide the money, technology, and managerial know-how for the Gulf region's upstream capacity expansion. But Japan and the Far East will become increasingly important both as markets and as sources of financial and technical resources. Saudi Arabia is focusing on Japan, but Thailand, South Korea, Indonesia, and other rising newly industrialized countries (NICs) may also be very good prospects for Gulf downstream investment. The latter are experiencing the world's fastest growing oil demand. These countries are also opening their doors to foreign firms interested in helping them become major refining, petrochemical, and distribution centers for the fast-growing areas of Southeast Asia and the Pacific Rim. Backed by large oil reserves and marketing expertise, the Saudis (and previously the Kuwaitis) are competing with the majors in the Indochina and Pacific Rim products market. As often as not, they are coming out winners.

Wither Russia?

Prospects for increased trade and economic activity between the Gulf states and the former Soviet Union (FSU), China, and Eastern Europe are uncertain at this point in time. All of the former centrally planned economies (CPEs) are in deep economic trouble. Their energy problems—inefficiency, waste, unreal pricing, misallocation of resources—are symptomatic of their larger woes. The FSU will likely never become a net importer of energy, but other former CPEs may have to compete in world markets for other supplies (including Gulf oil) if exports from the states of the FSU drop off due to falling production.

Persian Gulf states may play a role in restructuring the energy economies of these countries. Gulf producers have the money, the expertise, and the trading instincts to shape energy developments. They also have the oil to replace lost FSU supplies to Eastern Europe. As the economies of the FSU states are rebuilt, perhaps Gulf efforts to expand into Eastern Europe and the former Soviet Union will be rewarded, both in developing domestic production and refining facilities and in increasing exports from the Gulf. Iran and Kuwait have already shown interest in Romania and Hungary, and Iran has also made several diplomatic and economic overtures to its northern neighbors. But the degree of the job is enormous. Given the disparity of the political and economic scale between the former Soviet Union and China and the Gulf states, the Kuwaitis and others might seek to share the risks with others, including U.S. companies, should really big opportunities arise in these areas.

It might be argued that the Gulf states would rather watch Russian oil production languish (Russia is the predominant producer of the FSU) and replace it with their own oil on world markets. This would be shortsighted, however. Given the existing oil infrastructure and massive reserves in the FSU and the rest of the region, it will be much less expensive to refurbish and rehabilitate that than to build new pipelines, refineries and the like, let alone develop the new production capacity needed to meet the loss of Russian production. Whoever secures an ownership stake in FSU oil facilities will likely earn a substantial financial return in the long run.

Kuwait's Lessons for Its Neighbors

Before the Gulf crisis, only Kuwait among the Gulf producers could process over half of its annual crude oil output through its own domestic and foreign refining interests. But Kuwait's economic survival during Iraq's occupation of its territory, due to its extensive downstream operations and its portfolio of investments overseas, has provided a powerful lesson for crude-dependent countries. In early 1990 Saudi Arabia processed only about 38 percent of its crude output, compared to Kuwait's 57 percent and Venezuela's 114 percent. But once Gulf producers corner the world crude oil market, we can expect them to try to do the same in products—if not in this decade then in the next.

An intense period of international oil mergers and acquisitions may be expected in the future as producers seek to cover possible losses in upstream operations with refinery profits. The international companies who survive in what is likely to be an increasingly volatile world market will be those—either state-owned or privately held—with just this sort of flexibility. Gulf oil producers may have the advantage via their control over the growing crude trade and because they have the funds to invest in new export refineries designed to meet environmental concerns. This may provide for some tough trade and investment issues, similar to concerns over Japanese holdings of U.S. real estate, but the economic reality of the situation will likely overcome nationalism.

Growing World Appetite: The Cost of Industrialization

These producers leading the trend downstream recognize that the oil market of the 1990s will continue to be product-led (that is, led by jumps in demand for products such as gasoline and petrochemicals), fueled by the world's growing taste for oil. It is well known that the United States has a prodigious appetite for oil and that domestic production has fallen. Approximately 58 percent of the increase in gross U.S. crude and petroleum product imports since 1985 has come from the Persian Gulf. Put another way, nearly one-half of the Gulf's output increase since 1985 has been due to rising U.S. import needs.[6] Gulf suppliers provided approximately 6 percent of U.S. total oil imports and about 2 percent of U.S. oil consumption in 1985. The Gulf producers—primarily Saudi Arabia and Iraq—provided more than 30 percent of U.S. imports in 1990, representing an almost equal amount of U.S. consumption (Table 2.2). Only these countries had the additional capacity to meet the United States' rising needs.

TABLE 2.2 Increase in U.S. Oil Imports by Source from 1985 to 1990 (in percentages of imports)

Country	1985	1990
Persian Gulf		
Iraq	1.44	8.72
Kuwait	0.12	0.78
Saudi Arabia	4.12	20.28
Other Gulf states	1.94	0.78
Total	7.62	30.56
Rest of the world		
Angola	3.25	4.00
Canada	14.62	10.91
Colombia	0	2.38
Mexico	22.34	11.69
Nigeria	8.75	13.30
United Kingdom	8.68	2.63
Venezuela	9.56	11.30
Other	25.18	13.23
Total	92.38	69.44

Source: U.S. Department of Energy/Energy Information Administration, *Petroleum,* June 1991 (Washington, D.C.: Government Printing Office), Table 5.3, pp. 8–15.

    In 1988 Saudi Arabia passed both Canada and Venezuela to become
the biggest supplier to the United States of crude oil and oil products.
That year Saudi Arabia provided over 15 percent of U.S. oil imports—
five times what it supplied in 1985. From a Saudi perspective, the
United States now takes 20 percent of their annual crude and products
output.
    Even with stagnant 1989 U.S. oil demand and negative demand
growth in the first half of 1990, the United States remains the biggest
energy market in the world, consuming one-quarter of the world's total
oil output each year. Twelve percent goes directly into U.S. automobile
tanks.[7] In response to sliding oil prices since 1983, the United States
has become complacent. Gasoline lines have disappeared—replaced
by the illusion of permanent, cheap abundance. The results? Fuel efficiency gains have flattened since the oil price collapse of 1986, and
U.S. oil consumption has risen by 11 percent since 1983—coming after a
19 percent drop in oil usage during 1979–1983 (Figure 2.2).[8] Combine
these facts with a 15 percent drop in domestic crude oil production, one
can see why annual net imports have risen 66 percent since 1983.
Imports grew almost 10 percent from 1988 to 1989 alone as Alaska's oil
field production began to decline, and despite a 2.5 percent drop in
demand, imports continued to grow in the first half of 1990 by 8.7
percent over the same period.[9]
    Unless these trends are reversed—by legislated alternative fuels

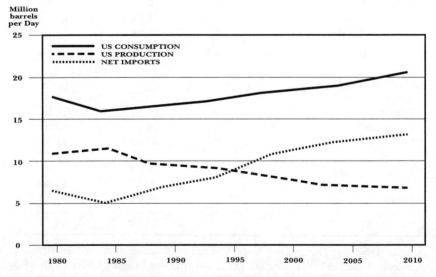

FIGURE 2.2 Petroleum Balance Sheet 1980–1990, with Projections to 2010

use, consumption taxes, renewed conservation initiatives, or by a sustained price spike—the United States will remain the Gulf producers' major growth market. And recent history, including the Bush and Reagan administrations' quite vocal opposition to oil import fees and consumption taxes, let alone new regulation, seems to mitigate against these factors.

And the Rest of the World?

The United States is not alone. The rest of the world is also absorbing OPEC's excess barrels at an unparalleled rate. Europe is behaving much as the United States is at the moment, with sluggish demand growth but at a higher level of historic import dependency. European member countries of the Organization for Economic Cooperation and Development (OECD) now import 64 percent of their oil, with 45 percent of imports coming from the Persian Gulf.[10] Foreign oil will continue to account for close to 100 percent of Japanese consumption, 65–70 percent from the Gulf. Fueled by deregulation of the domestic gasoline market and by nuclear plant problems, Japanese demand grew about 5 percent annually during 1988 and 1989.

In absolute terms, the OECD markets will remain the most important for Gulf producers' economic well-being as the century draws to a close. But world energy demand growth, before the Gulf crisis increasing at an underlying rate of 1–2 percent per year, will be driven elsewhere—fired by 4–5 percent demand increases in the NICs of the Far East and in the lesser developed countries (LDCs). Moderate oil prices help fuel rapid economic growth in these areas that, in turn, leads to greater demand for oil. And the countries with big reserves, concerned about the long-term prospects for their crude, will try to keep production high and prices low to ensure that rapid growth. If prices remain stable, for example, countries such as Thailand and Korea may see annual double-digit energy demand growth for much of this decade.

New Clouds: Developments in Eastern Europe

OECD net oil imports from the former Soviet Union generally increased throughout the 1980s. Most of this was crude oil, up 80 percent from 1980 to 1988. But production problems came to a head in 1989 resulting in a 13 percent decline in Soviet crude exports to the OECD. Since that time, production has fallen even more rapidly and is predicted to average 7.4 mmb/d in 1992. Further cuts in oil exports from the FSU could hasten the return to a seller's market.

Constraints on future oil production in the former Soviet Union are many. The new nations lack modern equipment and effective management methods. Their oil-sector infrastructure is either poorly developed or worn out, and their refineries need a complete overhaul. Many of their historically most productive fields are in decline and are located in areas troubled by civil unrest. The economies of the FSU states are some of the most fuel-inefficient in the world, and prospects for improvement are dim.

Further complicating the FSU oil situation is that domestic demand for oil will rise as the consumer sector gets more attention. The number of cars, for example, is growing rapidly. Large imports of refined products could be required in the future unless their low refinery utilization (76 percent in 1985) is drastically increased.[11] Thus, the FSU—if domestic demand is not to suffer—must cut back exports as output declines.

Events in Eastern Europe could also put pressure on future oil supplies. Indeed, securing adequate oil supplies may be one of Eastern Europe's main economic problems in the future. Already the states of the FSU have begun settling all accounts with socialist countries in convertible currency, raising the cost of Russian and Ukrainian oil to East European countries and sending Eastern Europe into Free World markets to compete for Gulf barrels. A return to market economies in Eastern Europe and eventual economic rebirth there will spur oil demand in that region as it has in the Third World.

Future Oil Supplies: No Sure Thing

What do these longer term trends mean for consumers? More importantly, what are the implications for U.S. energy security interests? To some extent, as already noted, increased producer-consumer interdependence decreases the likelihood of a major disruption of oil flows by OPEC for political reasons. There should be a greater recognition by producers that a strongly aggressive price position would only lower the profitability of the whole oil industry, including their share of it. Even with a market position bolstered by increased world dependence, Gulf producers will act to keep prices low to ensure that the billions of barrels of oil within their control retain their value for many years to come, rather than to raise prices and force consumers to again increase efficiency and search for new sources of energy.

But there is no "sure thing" regarding oil. There are just too many imponderables in the years ahead that will affect how oil is made available to the world market—for example, political instability within major producing countries; environmental concerns;

transportation infrastructure fatigue; OPEC capacity expansion; East European oil demand; developments in the former Soviet Union; growing import needs among dynamic LDCs; major new oil finds and technological advances; and changes in producer-country investment climates.

One of the biggest "ifs" for the 1990s is how big Gulf producers will behave as their share of the world market expands. The inescapable fact is that the world's major oil supplies lie in a historically unstable part of the world. We must keep in mind that, on balance, developments in the Persian Gulf are ruled not by oil but by politics. The Iraqi invasion of Kuwait is only the most recent indication that the Persian Gulf states are far from being a cohesive group. Gulf countries obviously march to their own national agendas and rarely fall neatly into either moderate/conservative or militant/radical categories. Disputes over deep-seated religious divisions; fundamental differences in economic, social, and political institutions; and borders that have never been clearly defined by international agreement will crop up from time to time to help flame long-standing disputes. This is as true for the 1990s as it has been since the fall of the Ottoman Empire.

Even without the Gulf crisis, the military buildup throughout the Gulf was expected to intensify throughout the 1990s, adding immeasurably to regional volatility. Disputes over oil and gas fields straddling two or more countries, such as the vast Rumaila field shared by Kuwait and Iraq or the offshore North Dome gas field claimed by both Qatar and Iran or even Qatari-Bahraini territorial disputes over half-submerged islands offer continuing opportunity for tension. The competing political and leadership aspirations between oil giants Iran, Iraq, and Saudi Arabia for influence over Gulf politics have already been a major factor in shifting Gulf political alliances and disputes.

Only the Latest Example: Iraq Versus Kuwait

The Persian Gulf crisis clearly pointed to the deep diversity of national agendas within the Gulf region. Iraq's short-run revenue needs were bound to clash with Kuwait's long-term revenue maximization strategy. Kuwait, unlike its more oil dependent neighbors, could afford a lower return on crude exports now to stimulate flagging world oil demand. By having followed its own national oil-depletion agenda, Kuwait arguably contributed to the lowering of Iraq's early 1990 oil revenues by 20 percent compared to 1989 levels.

Iraq has only one major source of foreign exchange, oil. Saddam Husayn needed expanding oil revenues for his political ambitions, which required keeping key elements of Iraqi society contented with economic growth while denying the growth of democratic institutions. Oil sales were also Saddam Husayn's ticket to international legitimacy. Growing oil revenues were needed for reconstruction of an economy devastated by eight and a half years of war, for jobs for a young population, and for new weapons to protect the hostile Iranian border. Thus, by threatening Kuwait, Husayn was acting in his own perceived self-interest.

The initial thrust of Saddam Husayn's threats was to lead OPEC's "have nots" in a revolt against OPEC domination by moderates. Charging Kuwait and the UAE (and implicitly Saudi Arabia) with damaging the interests of other producers, Husayn struck a responsive chord with low-reserve, indebted producers in and outside OPEC. His stature within the region and among oil producers worldwide had been enhanced no matter how uncomfortable others may have been with his tactics.

Looking to the Future

Had Husayn stopped there, the U.S. view of the oil market and the security of oil supplies in the 1990s might be far different today. With a successful July 1990 OPEC ministerial completed, Husayn would have made it much harder, but ultimately not impossible, for OPEC price moderates to control future price and output policies of the group. In a real sense, he had given price increasers an unexpected second wind, advancing by several years an upward price trend already expected this decade. Iraqi saber rattling seemed here to stay as a new element of OPEC and Gulf meetings for the next several years. The United States might have been paying more for U.S. oil if "Saddam the Enforcer" had managed to keep OPEC cheaters in line, probably somewhere around $25 per barrel (bbl). Supply worries and energy security would still have remained on the back burner for most consumer countries and governments.

It also seemed likely that once Iraq was able to expand its productive capacity enough to give Saddam Husayn the flexibility of maximizing revenues by over-producing like its southern neighbors, the price increasers might well have lost their leader to the opposing camp. Indeed, immediately before the Gulf crisis, some analysts were giving the chance of a severe supply shortfall of Mideast oil in the 1990s a probability of less than 1 percent.

By invading Kuwait, Saddam Husayn put in question consumers' sense of long-term security, and not just of energy supplies. The economic, political, and strategic balances in the Mideast and with the West all fell prey to Saddam Husayn's attempts to assert regional hegemony over the Gulf region. It became clear that with such men as Saddam Husayn, petrodollars, which the Saudis and other major producers have used to improve their own welfare and to help fuel international economic expansion for the past twenty years, could easily have become terrorist petrodollars as Saddam Husayn and his supporters used their oil gains to fuel both their own aggressive acts and those of terrorists everywhere.

The United States and the UN family of nations took a major, and undeniably painful, step to restore security relationships within the region. The allies succeeded in keeping an unprecedented amount of oil wealth, and thus power, out of the hands of a man who had proven time and time again that he could not be trusted.

False Sense of Security?

The United States may have succeeded in stopping Saddam Husayn's aggressive tendencies; however, risks for consuming nations not only remain but could also grow in the years ahead. With world demand for OPEC oil in 1992 around 23 mmb/d (expanding at about 2 percent annually) and OPEC sustainable output capacity around 26.0 mmb/d, the day may be approaching when world demand could outstrip most producers' physical capacities.[12] As more Gulf oil is tied up in the region's own export refineries and petrochemical plants, less crude will be available for spot sales worldwide. Even before the Gulf crisis, the United States was already seeing short-term squeezes— perceived or real—on the world's dwindling supplies of product-rich sweet light crudes, which add to increasing price volatility throughout the world market. Within a few years, the United States could experience enough supply tightness to invite repetition of the steep price climbs of the 1970s and early 1980s.

The reasons are visible. Continued low oil prices (both before and after the Gulf Crisis) are accelerating U.S. dependence on oil imports by diminishing price incentives for new exploration and development and are reducing momentum for conservation. The economies of the NICs and LDCs are growing with little, if any, thought to fuel efficiency, to building stocks, or to finding alternative energy sources. Eastern Europe is not now, and probably will not be for years to come, in an economic position to invest in energy security.

At the same time, environmental issues and even labor disruptions limit coal use. Hydroelectric power is limited by lack of investments over the last decade. Fear of nuclear Armageddon and the NIMBY (Not In My Back Yard) complex have halted development of nuclear power generation in all but a few countries. Natural gas may be the only major energy resource left to tide the United States over until economic alternatives can be developed. And the United States may be bumping up against limits here as well.

Lessons of the Gulf Crisis

One of the major lessons of the Gulf crisis is that high levels of oil imports need not imply vulnerability to disruptions in its flow. Diversified world supply, increased government stocks (in particular the U.S. Strategic Petroleum Reserve) and quicker response mechanisms to oil supply disruptions have greatly reduced threats of physical cutoff.

Over the past decade, member countries of the International Energy Agency (IEA) have been assiduous in their efforts to prepare for potential supply disruptions. What developed was a close consultative process that was to prove, once and for all, its usefulness during the Gulf crisis. The IEA oil-sharing system was gradually improved over the past decade, becoming available for use in the event of a major, prolonged supply disruption. Recognizing the potentially serious impacts of even small disruptions, however, the IEA more recently has developed procedures for the rapid, multilaterally coordinated drawdown of oil stocks to counter a disruption regardless of size. These procedures, which were in place and ready to go at the outbreak of hostilities on January 15, 1991, involve a rapid stockdraw, supplemented by other measures such as fuel switching and demand restraint, and these measures should substantially offset any anticipated interruption of physical oil supplies.

After months of intense preparation and market analysis, IEA members on January 11, 1991, agreed that as soon as the Persian Gulf hostilities began the IEA would release 2.5 mmb/d of oil on the world market, 80 percent of this by release of strategic stocks and the remainder by conservation.

The strong bilateral ties that the United States has with key producer countries, furthermore, proved essential to covering the gap left by the August 6 UN embargo of 4.3 mmb/d of Iraqi and Kuwaiti crude oil exports. Within a few short months, Saudi Arabia and virtually every producer worldwide had responded to the U.S. call to increase their production to the maximum possible to prevent an extended and serious dislocation of the global economic system. It was an unprecedented commonality of interests between producers and consumers of oil. At no time in the post–World War II period have nations worked so closely together to prevent an economic disaster in the making, one that was clearly not in the interests of either consumers or producers, big or small.

The result was a crisis that limited actual physical shortages to all but a few spot shortfalls in some markets. Consumers neither waited in long gas lines, were subjected to rationing, nor were forced to pay astronomical price increases. Since it all worked so well, it will be difficult to convince consumers that energy security is an ongoing area of concern.

Price Effects Bedevil Crisis Management

But the fact that oil prices climbed to over $40 per barrel in mid-October 1990—not because of any actual shortfall but because of the expectation of future supply disruptions—showed how vulnerable the global oil market has become to price dislocations due to wild swings in speculative demand. As imports rise and become concentrated in the Middle East, consumers become increasingly subject to the price effects of a disruption, either deliberate or accidental, in a volatile world oil market that responds instantly to world events. Indeed, the disruption need be nothing more than a perceived threat to cause a price crisis.

Should Gulf countries expand their worldwide refinery capacities to the point of influencing downstream prices and supplies, risks to economies will be magnified. In addition, the Gulf already is known to have 30 percent of the world's proven gas reserves.[13] As they continue to explore this figure will grow, so that by the turn of the century Gulf nations could also control much of international gas trade as well.

The integration of world energy markets means price shocks no matter how quickly alternative supplies can be mobilized. The United States may avoid future gas lines such as those occurring in 1974, but not the price rises. World events reverberate quickly through highly developed spot, forward, and futures markets that have sprung up over the last decade in New York, London, Singapore and elsewhere. Often the fear of a squeeze on one of the world's market crudes is enough to send the market into panic-buying. Alaska's oil spill in the spring of 1989 and subsequent United Kingdom North Sea accidents, for example, did not cause any serious supply problems, but fears of a shortfall were enough to send prices for the U.S. benchmark, crude West-Texas Intermediate, soaring 26 percent between March 20 and April 20, 1989. It is not surprising, therefore, that fear of Iraqi attacks on essential Saudi oil fields and transportation systems led consumers and refiners around the world to horde or build up sizable precautionary inventories during fall 1990.

The more oil-intensive the U.S. economy, the more vulnerable the United States is to oil price gyrations. At pre-Gulf crisis 1990 net import levels, every dollar per barrel increase in the price of crude oil represents a $6.1 million per day surcharge on the U.S. economy and financial transfers to oil suppliers. Yet even if the United States imported not one drop of oil, the interdependence of Western market economies is such that a disruption of oil supplies to heavily import-dependent Western Europe and Japan would have a negative impact on U.S. export earnings, prices, and overall production and employment levels.

Preparing for Uncertainty

But did consumer governments manage the Gulf crisis too well? If oil prices remain lower in the next few years than might have been the case under a Husayn-led resurgence of OPEC higher price policies, will consumers' false sense of security even grow?

Although producers are likely to be more realistic in their actions than they have been at times in the past, the lesson of the Gulf crisis is that the unpredictable and the unexpected can occur. It is our good fortune that key producer and consumer interests currently coincide. Consumers must keep in mind that producers are following their own self-interest at present by supporting moderate price growth aimed at increasing both global oil demand vis-à-vis other fuels and OPEC's share of the world oil pie. The United States cannot assume that this unprecedented postwar commonality of interests will always exist—that short-term political or economic pressures within the Persian Gulf will not arise once again to put OPEC on a high-price course.

The United States should not, however, be lulled into thinking that energy policy alone or some magical level of import dependency will be a protection against future supply disruptions or price shocks. Vigorous national energy policies can marginally trim U.S. dependency on Mideast oil, but they cannot alter the long-term facts of the growing dependency of the United States, nor will energy policy lower the probability of another Gulf crisis occurring somewhere down the road. In fact, this may all happen again. No one now knows what the Gulf will be like for the next decade. But it is clear that having won the war, the United States and its allies must also struggle to preserve the peace that has followed. Preserving the peace means the long-term stabilization of the political, economic, and strategic imbalances in the region. No one believes this stabilization will be easy or quick. Certainly the Gulf crisis fostered an anger within the Middle East that may remain for years to come.

What the United States and its allies can do is to foster those countries in the region that are at peace with themselves, that bestow their oil wealth in benevolent ways. We must collectively support those leaders who do not focus on financing regional misadventures but those who are intent on raising the welfare of their own people. Regional security ties must be strengthened. Glaring economic imbalances between the Middle East countries must be addressed by the people of the region itself as well as by the international community. A more active GCC may offer one possible and ready forum for intra-Gulf stabilization. And the Arab League may also be an active force in addressing disparities in wealth.

The United States and its allies must also return to the fostering of the interdependency of consumers and producers and must take care not to provoke a protectionist or xenophobic reaction to rising Gulf imports and investments. Besides harming relations with friendly long-term energy suppliers, this would also harm U.S. economic growth. The United States must carefully maintain and hone bilateral relations with friendly Gulf nations and keep the doors open to future Gulf downstream investments. Although others might suggest that the risks of interdependence tip the balance in favor of the alternative of energy independence, the costs of achieving that independence (if it is even possible) would be devastating to the future economic growth of the United States.

The transfers of wealth over the next decade from consumers to Arab producers generated by additional oil sales will also create export opportunities for nations with developed economies. It will be up to the United States to find ways to take advantage of this enlarged market. Just as the United States continues to welcome foreign oil and investments, it must work with oil-producing countries to address trade and investment restrictions against foreign exporters and investors. The United States hopes to work with the Gulf states through the General Agreement on Tariffs and Trade (GATT) (Kuwait is a full member of GATT and the Saudis are considering membership), the GCC, and bilaterally to remove trade and investment barriers. The United States, the European Community (EC), and Japan are all working to revitalize relations with the GCC with this in mind.

Thus, the United States has revitalized its economic dialogue with the GCC (the last bilateral discussions were in January 1991). Vast differences in trade and investment outlook make U.S.-GCC agreement difficult. For example, negotiation of a bilateral investment treaty would require the Gulf countries to drop the Arab boycott and provide "national treatment" of U.S. investors. Special and differential treatment for GCC petrochemicals would be a major sticking point in GCC-U.S. trade talks, especially in light of U.S. opposition in the Uruguay round to allowing such treatment. On the one hand, by urging the GCC countries to join with the United States in GATT and by pursuing the establishment of a formal framework for regularly scheduled bilateral talks on investment, energy, and other trade issues, it is hoped that it may be possible both to liberalize investment and trade between the two sides and to further strengthen the energy security ties to some of the United States' major oil suppliers.

On the other hand, a formal multilateral dialogue between consumers and producers, including OPEC, would be counterproductive and viewed as a step toward intervention in the market. The United States has very active bilateral discussions with a wide range of producing countries, and it is looking for ways to expand the possibilities for fruitful multilateral discussions between producers and consumers. However, these discussions are, and will continue to be, designed specifically as information exchanges, *not* as talks that would directly interfere in market decisions on price and production levels. The U.S. government will only support dialogue with producers that is informal and will not include OPEC.

The United States must continue to prepare for the oil crisis that may never come. But in a world awash in cheap oil, the public is still likely to pay little attention to energy security, and may balk at the price tag for our preparations. Yet the public must be made aware that the United States remains at risk. Here again, vulnerability, not import dependency, is the key to how well the world's economies will weather future crises. Diversified world energy supply, increased government strategic stocks, and quicker IEA response mechanisms to oil supply disruptions will remain essential tools to reduce the threats of physical cutoff. The United States must continue to support conservation and efficiency efforts as well as the Strategic Petroleum Reserve—still the best insurance against a future supply disruption; and it must continue to work with its allies in the International Energy Agency to enhance our mutual security.

Public concern over the environmental effects of hydrocarbons may help government officials. Policy remedies to reduce our vulnerability to oil price gyrations and "greenhouse gases" are the same: more natural gas and nuclear power, conservation and efficiency gains. But the United States needs to do more to make the necessary policy connections. If Saddam has done nothing else, he has forced us all to realize that complacency is not only dangerous but very costly.

Notes

1. U.S. Department of Energy/Energy Information Administration, *International Energy Annual 1989* (Washington, D.C.: Government Printing Office [GPO], February 1991 [DOE/EIA-0219(89)]), p. 99.

2. U.S. Department of Energy/Energy Information Administration, *International Petroleum Statistics Report* (Washington, D.C.: GPO, June 1991 [DOE/EIA-0520(91/06)]), pp. 34–35.

3. Marcus Wright, "Western Oil Concerns Are Negotiating with Iran to Develop Offshore Oil Fields," *Wall Street Journal*, May 30, 1991.

4. For convenience, oil operations are often divided into two categories: upstream and downstream. Upstream operations include exploration, drilling, completing oil wells, and rough processing (separating water and gas from oil). Downstream operations include transportation, refining, and marketing of crude oil.

5. DOE/EIA, *International Energy Annual 1989*, p. 54.

6. DOE/EIA, *International Petroleum Statistics Report*, p. 43.

7. Ibid., pp. 2–3, 9; and DOE/EIA, *Petroleum Supply Monthly* (Washington, D.C.: GPO, June 1991 [DOE/EIA-109(91/06)]), p. 17.

8. DOE/EIA, *International Petroleum Statistics Report*, p. 9.

9. Ibid., p. 40.

10. Ibid., pp. 39–41.

11. DOE/EIA, *International Energy Annual 1989*, p. 42.

12. DOE/EIA, *International Energy Outlook 1991* (Washington, D.C.: GPO, June 1991 [DOE/EIA-0484(91)]), p. 6.

13. DOE/EIA, *International Energy Annual 1989*, p. 99.

Suggested Reading

Askeri, Hossein, *Saudi Arabia's Economy: Oil and the Search for Economic Development*, Greenwich, Conn.: Jai Press, 1990.

Crystal, Jill, *Kuwait: The Transformation of an Oil State*, Boulder, Colo.: Westview Press, 1992.

Doran, Charles, and Buck, Stephen, eds., *The Gulf, Energy and Global Security Political and Economic Issues*, Boulder, Colo.: Lynne Rienner, 1991.

Karshenas, Massoud, *Oil, State, and Industrialization in Iran*, Cambridge: Cambridge University Press, 1990.

Lesser, Ian O., *Oil, the Persian Gulf and Grand Strategy*, Santa Monica, Calif.: Rand Corporation, 1991.

Palmer, Michael, *Guardians of the Gulf: The Growth of American Involvement in the Persian Gulf, 1833–1991*, New York: Free Press, 1992.

Yergin, Daniel, *The Prize: The Epic Quest for Oil, Money and Power*, New York: Simon and Schuster, 1991.

3

The Military Balance: Change or Stasis?

William Lewis

Political analysts and military specialists have conducted voluminous postmortems assessing the reasons for the successful prosecution of the war against Iraq and its significance for the future balance of political and military forces throughout the Middle East. The fundamental premise of U.S. policy as the war approached was that "defeating Saddam Hussein [Husayn] would discredit radicalism, strengthen moderates and enhance regional stability."[1] Concomitantly, the U.S. government anticipated that new thinking would emerge from within the Middle East on the urgency for a peaceful settlement of conflicts and the need to end the proliferation of weapons of "mass destruction."

A Two-Track Strategy

The U.S. government has embarked on a two-track strategy in an effort to diminish the potential for violence that afflicts the Middle East. The first involves broad arms control initiatives intended to restrict, if not end, the flow of advanced conventional weapons to the region; the second is directed toward the strengthening of international conventions that seek to eliminate chemical and biological weapons from the arsenals of all members of the international community and, where feasible, to further constrain Third World efforts to acquire nuclear weapons capabilities. The outlook for effective controls is uncertain at best.

The regional arms race . . . may be one of the most complex issues of all. Israel has proposed a nuclear-weapons-free-zone in the Middle East, but insists on mutual inspection by the parties and rejects reliance on an international agency or intermediary. In contrast, the Arabs insist on the Nonproliferation Treaty and International Atomic Energy Agency as the vehicles for international restraints on the Israeli nuclear program without the backdoor recognition that mutual inspection would afford.[2]

Comparable problems exist in the area of transfers, by sale or by unreimbursable grants, of conventional weapons. (See French sales to the region [Table 3.1].) Controlling the spread of advanced conventional weapons is problematic for several reasons: (1) It is a buyer's market; (2) Western and communist world suppliers are pressed for hard currencies and foreign purchasers to maintain their defense industries in the wake of the cold war's demise; and (3) the number of Third World supplier sources has grown over the past two decades thus adding to competition for market shares. Not surprisingly, suppliers, both private and governmental, are anxious to realize unit cost savings by increasing the export of their products abroad.

The United States has put forth several arms control plans to dampen the urge by nations in the Middle East to acquire advanced conventional weapons as well as to acquire chemical, biological, and nuclear (CBN) weapons capabilities. President Bush, on May 13, 1991, using the Gulf War as the basis for a departure of U.S. policy on chemical weapons, underscored support for the Conference on Disarmament then in progress in Geneva by announcing several unilateral measures to accelerate negotiations to ban such weapons. These included

TABLE 3.1 French Weapons Transferred to Iraq, 1981–1988

Weapon	Type of Weapon	Number Transferred
Mirage F-IC	Fighter/Interceptor	143
AMX-30 Roland	Antiaircraft vehicle, missile armed	105
AM-39 Exocet	Antiship missiles	734
ARMAT	Antiradar missiles	708
AS-3OL	Antiship missiles	1,200
HOT	Antitank missiles	1,600
Milan	Antitank missiles	4,800
Roland-2	Surface-to-air missiles	1,050
R-530	Air-to-air missiles	257
R-55 Magic	Air-to-air missiles	534

Source: Office of Technology Assessment, from data in Stockholm International Peace Research Institute, SIPRI Yearbooks, 1970 through 1990, *Armaments and Disarmament.*

formally forswearing the use of chemical weapons "effective when the convention comes into force," the assurance that the United States would destroy all such weapons within ten years of the convention's coming into force, and a proposal that all parties "refuse to trade in chemical weapon–related materials with states that do not join in the convention."[3] This action was followed by an announcement on the part of a constellation of major suppliers of chemicals (fertilizers, etc.) to Third World nations—the so-called "Australia group"—that they intended to strengthen efforts to monitor and control sales to reduce the likelihood that their products would be used for "illicit purposes."

Control or limitation of conventional arms transfers to the Middle East have also been proposed in several forums. The prime minister of the United Kingdom has recommended the establishment of an international register, presumably under United Nations auspices, to track arms sales.[4] On May 29, 1991, President Bush called for a freeze on acquisition, production, and testing of new surface-to-surface missiles (SSMs) in the Middle East. He also proposed extensive consultations among major suppliers with a view to securing an agreement on "collective self-restraint" in making advanced weaponry available to nations in the region. (In addition, the president linked his initiative with a proposal to ban production of nuclear weapons in the area and a call to place all nuclear facilities under the safeguards of the International Atomic Energy Agency.) Not to be outdone, the government of France has called for international arms sale registries to assure a "reasonable balance" of Third World defense requirements, the registries serving to monitor attempts to upset regional arms balances.

The ultimate sanction in arms control has been imposed against Iraq in the wake of the Gulf War. Under UN Security Council auspices, Iraq is required to destroy all its CBN stocks and production capabilities. In addition, the Security Council voted a total arms embargo on June 18, 1991, under which all member states are required to report to the secretary general measures taken to insure that their citizens and corporations do not supply Iraq with military material, including technology and machinery that might be used for military purposes.[5]

Despite the best exertions of the United States and other involved suppliers, the appetites of Middle Eastern governments for ever more advanced weaponry is not likely to diminish during the decade of the 1990s. The Gulf War merely served to mask the fact that during the onset of the crisis and in its immediate aftermath the region experienced continuing conflicts and crises that were emblematic of the inherent instability of the Middle East. These ranged from civil wars in Ethiopia and Somalia, to the overthrow of a Chadian regime hostile to Libya's Colonel Muammar Qadhafi, to occasional military collisions between Moroccan troops based in the western Sahara and *Polisario* guerrilla forces. Elsewhere, Lebanon was beset by internal violence, as was Mauritania; the situation also continued to deteriorate in the West Bank, Gaza, and along the Iraqi border with Iran and Turkey. Where governments, through structural reforms, sought to cope with rising public discontent—notably in Algeria, Morocco, Tunisia, and Jordan—political power remained in delicate equilibrium as the Gulf War came to a conclusion.

The inherently brittle nature of the region, together with the conclusion of the cold war, paradoxically, have produced a dynamic that virtually assures the failure of efforts to end arms competition. Leaders are likely to adopt self-help strategies to fill the void of an assured superpower benefactor. Several factors come increasingly into play:

- The transformation of the international security architectures of Europe and Asia will add to the impulse of arms producers to take advantage of the Middle East market.
- The search of governments in the region for security insurance can be vouchsafed in only one of three ways: (1) collective security arrangements with an external "power"; (2) resolution of disputes through peaceful negotiation; or (3) acquisition of weapons that provide, cognitively, a clear deterrent edge. (No external "power" is prepared to provide unlimited security guarantees.)
- Of importance is the dynamic associated with the proliferation of weapons of mass destruction (CBN) and the increasingly sophisticated conventional weapons that are approaching the CBN threshold in terms of lethality.
- Also important is the example set by the United States in applying high technologies in defeating soundly the Iraqi military establishment. Without an external benefactor, self-reliance will impel nations to acquire modern, high-technology capabilities.

Diffusion, rather than concentration, of military power is clearly a prospect in the immediate future, a portent that will in all probability produce significant change in the security environment of the Middle East. Despite rhetoric from European leaders and the United States, there is little reason to believe that governments in the region will be "guided" by external exhortations. As one specialist in the field has observed: "A technological approach to stalling weapons proliferation will never by itself be an effective retardant, because it does not treat the incentives to proliferate."[6] Moreover, the U.S.

initiative to control conventional weapons proliferation lacks credibility. In addition to special dispensations for favored friends and allies in the region, the U.S. government proposes to be guided by the following deliberately ambiguous criteria relating to a code of supplier conduct: restrictions on arms that add "sophisticated new military capabilities" in the area; that increase a nation's ability to project its military power outside its borders; that contribute to regional imbalances or encourage competitive military buildups; and that place an "undue burden on the political stability of recipient states." These criteria are shopworn and boilerplate, and if fully adopted, they will erode the credibility of U.S. efforts to constrain arms buildups in the Middle East.[7] They suggest a diplomatic holding operation while those in Washington and other interested parties attempt to establish new political-military balances in the region. For their part, governments in the area, ineluctably, will seek to avoid externally imposed constraints and will attempt to gain advantage from the acquisition of advanced military technologies (see Table 3.2). Other motivating factors include a mixture of traditional rivalries, and, in some instances, the impulse to achieve regional hegemony.

In the following sections we examine the role of various technological and weapons systems in upsetting the region's military balance, as well as alternative arms control strategies that might be adopted.

Technology on Demand

The post-Gulf War sorting out process has both a political and a military dimension. The first involves a combination of political-military realignment and efforts on the part of various nonregional parties to help resolve long-standing local conflicts. On the purely military level, various security specialists—including the U.S. defense analytical community—have been conducting intensive "after action" studies. Not surprisingly, these analyses and interpretations reflect the special interests of the governments and specialists most directly concerned; some skewering or distortions are to be anticipated. A number of strategic planners within the U.S. defense community have already concluded that the Gulf experience was sui generis and the future structure and deployment of U.S. forces should not be predicated on the outcome of previous military operations in that region.

What has drawn the attention of most analysts has been the role of advanced technologies in determining the war's outcome. From the U.S. perspective, the war demonstrated that high technology is preferable to its less advanced counterpart, indeed, that the U.S. defense community should be encouraged to develop even more

TABLE 3.2 Arms Transfer Deliveries to the Third World, 1983–1990 Agreements with the Leading Recipients (in millions of current U.S. dollars)

Rank	Recipient	Agreements Value 1983–1986
1	Saudi Arabia	21,819
2	Iraq	20,490
3	India	9,261
4	Iran	8,940
5	Syria	7,235
6	Vietnam	6,700
7	Cuba	6,685
8	Egypt	5,812
9	Angola	5,155
10	Libya	5,030
		1987–1990
1	Saudi Arabia	68,495
2	Afghanistan	10,920
3	Iran	9,990
4	Iraq	9,965
5	India	7,505
6	Egypt	7,040
7	Cuba	5,921
8	Angola	5,775
9	Vietnam	5,680
10	Syria	5,590
		1983–1990
1	Saudi Arabia	57,323
2	Iraq	30,455
3	Iran	18,930
4	India	16,766
5	Afghanistan	14,235
6	Egypt	12,852
7	Syria	12,825
8	Cuba	12,606
9	Vietnam	12,380
10	Angola	10,930

Source: U.S. Government Arms Control and Disarmament Agency, *Annual Report* (Washington, D.C.: GPO, 1992), p. 32.

sophisticated technologies for deployment later this decade. The former Soviet military establishment shares the same perspective, but reportedly confronts the need to reexamine its long-held doctrine emphasizing the use of infantry and armor supported by massed artillery. In Iraq, coalition air dominance and ground mobility largely neutralized Baghdad's command-and-control systems and offset the seeming numerical advantage held by Iraq in armored vehicles, tanks, and artillery pieces.[8] This should have a profound effect on future planning by Saddam Husayn or his successors.

Israel, even with an unacknowledged nuclear arsenal, is compelled to reevaluate the deterrent value of its weaponry. Baghdad, using a 1950s missile system, was able to attack major urban centers in Israel, compelling its population to don gas masks in anticipation of chemical attacks, to enter bomb shelters, or to flee into the neighboring country-side. Ironically, although Western technology today is directed toward accuracy of delivery systems and limited "collateral" damage, governments in the Middle East are prepared to acquire SSMs capable of mass terror. This presents the United States and other potential suppliers with an inescapable dilemma, whether to restrict technology transfers and hence permit indiscriminate use of obsolescent SSMs or to enhance accuracy in the hope that governments will restrict targeting to adversary military installations.

Israel has decided to embark on a dual-track strategy—to invest additional resources in civil defense while speeding its "Arrow" tactical air defense research program (with U.S. financial and technical support). Israel's defense planners, operating on a worst-case basis, are compelled to assume that other Saddam Husayns are in the wings prepared to accept the costs associated with total war. As one Israeli defense analyst has noted: "If the effort to arrive at broad-based political settlements in the Middle East—which must include arms-control arrangements—should fail, it will no longer be possible to speak of conventional deterrence, for this will have been the last major war in the Middle East to have been fought with conventional weapons."[9]

The perspectives and felt needs of most Middle Eastern governments differ markedly from those of their Western counterparts. They perceive their military requirements in terms of a threat horizon that is "tous azimuths." Turkey feels itself potentially threatened by several neighbors, notably Iraq, Iran, and Bulgaria; Syria evinces concerns over Lebanon, Turkey, Israel, and Iraq; similarly, Saudi Arabia must fashion its security strategy in terms of a shifting power balance involving Iran, Iraq, Yemen and, given its religious responsibilities, several others. Jordan feels itself surrounded by a number of potential adversaries. As a result, all seek to secure an added measure of security through external benefactors. For its part, the United States is prepared to serve as the supreme military arbiter in the Gulf region if its prerequisites can be met—"homeporting" of naval units, joint military maneuvers on a regular basis, sale of advanced weapons systems, and prestockage of U.S. military equipment at local bases. Gulf "allies," however, will insist on the acquisition of military-related technologies that will afford them a special edge vis-à-vis potential rivals. The Saudis already seek to diversify the sources of their military supply, paradoxically, to demonstrate reduced dependence on the United States.

During the decade of the 1990s, a wide assortment of military technologies are expected to come onstream in the West and to be eagerly sought by customers and clients in the Middle East. On the drawing boards or already to be found in production are: Fuel Air Explosives, a Precision Location Strike System, and the Sadarm Cluster Projectile. These meet three essential requirements for conventional war fighting effectiveness—range enhancement, accuracy, and explosive power— that affords field commanders the ability to destroy an enemy's massed armor division with a single projectile.[10] Although these systems will not all be readily transferred to the Middle East, other second-generation technologies are available and promise to enhance local military capabilities. Key among them are Global Positioning Satellite (GPS) receivers, originally designed to provide geographic location data for U.S. military forces. Such receivers can now be linked to SSMs, thus improving appreciably their accuracy. If they had been available to Iraq during the Gulf War, the Scud and its derivative could have achieved a target accuracy of between 5 and 10 meters.[11] Thus U.S. supply depots, command-and-control centers, and massed military formations would then have come under direct missile attack.

Recognizing that technology—both military and dual-use—is a critical security factor in an international environment that is undergoing dramatic transformations, Middle East governments will almost certainly seek to bolster their deterrent and war-fighting capabilities with the following acquisition priorities clearly in mind:

- Linkage of civilian and military requirements to reduce procurement and operations costs, as well as to overcome Western technology transfer restrictions;
- Renewed emphasis on improvement of advanced surveillance and early warning systems (including space monitoring), secure command-and-control, and advanced intelligence and data processing;

- Force multipliers such as cruise systems;
- Systems that enhance probability-kill exchange ratios (terrain control, night vision, etc.);
- Missile defense systems.

We can also anticipate that many Middle Eastern governments will seek new technologies to upgrade older-generation systems while attempting to improve the absorption and performance levels of their professional military personnel, and will seek to adopt the innovative strategies needed to insure effective performance of the acquired technologies under wartime conditions.

Advanced Weapons: Missiles

Prior to the onset of hostilities on January 17, 1991, one of the principal concerns of coalition military commanders was the perceived likelihood that Baghdad would launch chemical weapons attacks against allied forces. U.S. commanders were fearful that their early warning procedures and protective gear would prove ineffective—and that a regime that had used such weapons against Iran as well as its own Kurdish population would be disposed, in extremis, to violate the 1925 Geneva Protocol prohibiting such use. Several Western leaders, somewhat belatedly, awakened to the threat and warned of a stern retaliatory response.[12] In the end, chemical weapons were not used by Saddam Husayn for several reasons: (1) they had limited military utility against coalition forces from a tactical point of view; (2) defensive measures were taken by coalition forces; and (3) there was a threat of an escalatory response.

As the Gulf War evolved, the more effective Iraqi military weapon proved to be its inaccurate, but difficult to locate, mobile Scud missiles. Chemical and nuclear weapons were irrelevant—as long as U.S. forces were involved. However, Iraq's use of Scuds against Israel represented a political statement, one freighted with far-reaching implications for garrison state regimes.

The deterrent effect of Israel's nuclear arsenal was brought into question by Saddam Husayn's missile attacks on Israel's civilian population centers. Recourse to a nuclear response by Israel would have produced a fire storm of international criticism and would have destroyed the cohesion of the coalition forged by the U.S. government. Moreover, Iraq's mobile SSMs would likely have survived the riposte and, if armed with chemical or biological warheads, might have inflicted heavy casualties in Israel's urban centers. Indeed, the 1990–1991 war has raised questions in some quarters about the intimidating or deterrent effect of nuclear arsenals. For some observers, it is felt that missiles armed with chemical or conventional warheads might well serve in the future as a counterdeterrent—that is, raise the human and material costs associated with crossing the nuclear threshold in conflict situations.

The introduction of ballistic missiles of increased range and accuracy, together with efforts to develop home-grown, chemical-biological weapons systems, has led Western observers to reexamine the calculus traditionally used to weigh the balance of military forces in the region. Although population size and density, technical competence, tanks, aircraft, and artillery continue to be of importance, the ability to evade early warning systems, invade adversary airspace, and inflict punishment both on civilian populations and on military formations with "terror" weapons has assumed greater specific weight. Missiles have become the "force multipliers" of choice.

The next ten years could be the most dangerous for the security and stability of nations in the Middle East. Paradoxically, at a time when North Atlantic Treaty Organization (NATO) member states and the former Soviet Union are engaged in negotiations intended to codify the end of the cold war through the reduction of lethal weaponry, the trend in the region to the south favors the accumulation of new weapons systems. Security concerns in Europe are now shifting away from the East-West axis to the volatile Middle East. As one former director of the United States Arms Control and Disarmament Agency observed during an international conference held in April 1989:

> In the West, and certainly in the United States, we have not determined what we need and what outcomes we desire from arms control. A complicating factor in assessing desirable outcomes is the problem of proliferation of weapons and delivery systems outside the Warsaw Pact and NATO. As NATO and the Warsaw Pact grandly move forward to talk about conventional force reductions in Europe, other countries are shopping around for modern missiles and chemical and nuclear warheads to fit on these missiles. What kind of world will we have ten years from now if the Pact and NATO have achieved a first round reduction and approximate parity in Europe, but five, six, seven, or eight smaller nations have achieved worldwide notoriety because of the possession of a small number of nuclear weapons?[13]

Although Turkey's neighbor, Bulgaria, remains a traditional source of distraction, it is Iraq, Syria, and, to a lesser extent, Iran that pose the greatest potential threat to Turkey's territorial integrity. Similarly, Greece and Italy, along with Turkey, must view with some trepidation the proliferation of modern delivery systems amongst states along the southern reaches of the Mediterranean rim. None of these NATO member states possesses the early warning, air defense, or retaliatory capabilities necessary to give them confidence that they can deter the "over the horizon" threat emanating from the Middle East and North Africa. In like manner, the senior echelon of military planners in Moscow is compelled to address the rapidly evolving military realities in what it has designated "the greater Middle East." The area includes three nuclear armed states—India, Pakistan, and Israel—and others that have embarked on comparable programs, as well as nations accumulating intermediate-range ballistic missiles and new generations of strike aircraft. Not to be ignored by Moscow is the rising tide of the Islamic revival, both within the Central Asian republics and in Middle Eastern countries at the borders of the former Soviet Union. Like the United States and other Western nations, Moscow has yet to fashion a comprehensive strategy to deal with the changing military balance in the "greater Middle East." Moreover, Moscow and several of the former Soviet republics may be losing control over military exports initiated by local military entrepreneurs and black marketeers.

To the casual observer, the missile factor is unique or new to the region. In reality, neither SSMs nor chemical weapons are recent arrivals in the Middle East. The armed forces of Syria and Egypt have been supplied by Moscow with short-range SSMs since the mid-1970s. Egypt is known to have used its chemical weapons against Yemeni forces in the 1960s. More recently, Colonel Qadhafi of Libya approved extensive use of chemical weapons during his early 1980s attempt to annex Chad. What has made the region an arena of even greater volatility has been the changing nature of these systems and the mounting number of states with ready access to them.[14]

By the mid-1970s, Egypt, Iraq, Israel, Libya, and Syria had ballistic missiles in their inventories. Three more countries—Iran, Saudi Arabia, and Yemen—have since acquired such missiles. The multiplicity of foreign sources of supply willing to make their products and technological know-how available to nations prepared to offer hard currency for acquisition rights has meant that virtually any country in the Middle East with a wish to include missiles in its inventory can readily meet this goal.

Until recently, the majority of states in the Middle East were compelled to rely on nonregional sources for their SSMs. As the 1990s began, several states were in a position to manufacture their own systems, albeit with the assistance of foreign advisers, engineers, and technicians. Amongst the Arab states, Iraq had seemingly achieved dramatic breakthroughs, having deployed and utilized the 650-km range al-Hysayn and 900-km range systems in the war against Iran. Israel has countered with the 500-km range Jericho I and 1,450-km range Jericho II. These achievements have not been confined to the Middle East (see Table 3.3). Given the interrelatedness of missile research in the Third World—including joint projects and shared technology—the impetus for interregional collaboration has grown over the past decade. Iraq's attempted partnership with Argentina to develop the Condor II ballistic missile—designed to carry a 1,000-lb warhead 900 km—was an example of such collaboration, one which ultimately aborted as a result of U.S. pressures on Argentina.

Barring significant improvement in their guidance systems, existing intermediate-range SSMs will serve as "terror weapons" when linked with conventional warheads. There is ample precedent for such use. Precisely when the United States and Moscow were concluding a treaty banishing intermediate-range, nuclear-tipped missiles in 1987–1988, "The War of the Cities" involving missile attacks on Tehran, Baghdad, and Basra was in progress. For the first time since Adolph Hitler vented his frustrations in "V" bomb attacks against defenseless British urban centers, missiles were once again bombarding civilian population centers. According to the most reliable count more than 800 missiles were launched by both sides with Iraq's extended range Scud-Bs causing large-scale evacuations from Tehran and producing the 1989 cease-fire between Iran and Iraq. From Saddam Husayn's perspective, the Iraqi objective in the war was to attain better peace terms than likely would have been available had he not been in a position to launch indiscriminate missile attacks against the Iranian capital and center of the Islamic revolution. Saddam Husayn was proved prescient in his estimate of the situation.

There is little consensus among Western military specialists about the ultimate utility of Saddam Husayn's use of Scuds during the 1991 Gulf War. Husayn, if he remains in power, will almost certainly contend that, despite defeat in Kuwait, his efforts have placed in doubt past Arab sentiment concerning Israel's invulnerability and military invincibility. Strategic parity with Israel is no longer a problematic goal, particularly if Arab governments acquire a second-strike SSM capability with chemical or conventional warheads that ensure an ability to overwhelm any future Israeli air defense systems.

Lessons Learned

Saddam Husayn and other Arab leaders learned some important lessons in the wake of the Israeli raid on the Iraqi Tammuz nuclear reactor in June 1981: first, the need to avoid transparency—that is, to

TABLE 3.3 Third World Ballistic Missiles

Country	Missile	Range (km)	Warhead (lbs)	Status
Argentina	Condor I	100	880	under development
	Condor II	900	1,000	under development
Brazil	MB/EE-150	150	1,100	in testing
	SS-300	300	2,200	in testing
	SS-1000	1,200	2,200	r & d
	MB/EE-350	350	NA	r & d
	MB/EE-600	600	NA	r & d
Egypt	Frog-7	70	1,000	used in 1973 Arab-Israeli War
	Scud-B	300	1,100	deployed
	Saqr-80	80	450	deployed, replacing Frog-7
	Improved Scud	300	2,200	Production planned
	Badr-2000	900	1,000	under development
India	Prithy	150–300	1,100–2,200	test fired 1988
	Agni	2,500	2,000	test fired 1989
Iran	Frog-7	70	1,000	used against Iraq
	Scud-B	300	1,100	used against Iraq
	Oghab	40	660	used against Iraq
	Iran-130	120	NA	used against Iraq 1988
Iraq	Frog-7	70	1,000	used against Iran
	Scud-B	300	1,100	used against Iran
	al-Husayn	600	420	used against Iran 1988
	al-Abbas	900	NA	test fired 1988
	Condor II	900	NA	under development
	Fahd	250–500	1,000	r & d
Israel	Lance	110	600	deployed
	Jericho I	500	680	deployed
	Jericho II	1,450	NA	test fired 1987
Libya	Frog-7	70	1,000	deployed
	Scud-B	300	1,100	used against Lampedusa 1986
	Otrag	490	NA	under development
North Korea	Frog-7	70	1,000	deployed
	Scud-B	300	1,100	deployed (produced in N. Korea)
South Korea	Korean SSM	180–250	NA	deployed
Kuwait	Frog-7	70	1,000	deployed
Pakistan	HATF I	80	1,100	test fired 1989
	HATF II	300	1,100	test fired 1989

Continues

TABLE 3.3 Continued

Country	Missile	Range (km)	Warhead (lbs)	Status
Saudi Arabia	CSS-2	2,200	4,500	deployed
South Africa	Unknown	NA	NA	test fired July 1989
Syria	Frog-7	70	1,000	used against Israel in 1973
	Scud-B	300	1,100	deployed
	SS-21	120	1,000	deployed
Taiwan	Ching Feng	120	NA	deployed
	Sky Horse	960	NA	r & d
North Yemen	SS-21	120	1,100	deployed
South Yemen	Frog-7	70	1,000	deployed
	Scud-B	300	1,100	deployed
	SS-21	120	1,000	deployed

Sources: Congressional Research Service Report for Congress, February 9, 1989; *The Military Balance* 1988–1989 of the International Institute for Strategic Studies; *World Military Exports and Arms Transfers* 1988 of the U.S. Arms Control and Disarmament Agency; testimony before Congress, and 1989 press reports.

conduct advanced weapons program development as clandestinely as possible; second, to diversify dependency by multiplying external sources of supply and following multiple-track development efforts; finally, to wed these efforts with mobile missile systems. Future progress by other regimes will diminish crisis stability. Given Israel's existing preemptive or first-strike strategy, the proclivity of SSM-armed Arab nations will be to adopt "Launch on Warning" (LAW) or even more hair-trigger "Auto-Launch Response Mode" (ALARM) crisis postures. The emphasis in these circumstances will be on survivability of retaliatory, or second strike, capabilities so that Israel or any other potential adversary will not be in a position to dictate the terms of a cease-fire.

The ability of Middle Eastern nations to absorb technologies of state-of-the-art sophistication varies widely, but the progress registered by India may be instructive:

India has a major missile development program that includes both short- and medium-range missiles. The short-range model, the Prithvi/tactical missile, can carry a 2,200-pound warhead for 150 kilometers or a 1,100-pound warhead 300 kilometers. It was tested successfully in March 1988. In May 1989, India successfully tested a long-range Agni missile over the Bay of Bengal, with a 2,000-pound payload, a range of 1,500 kilometers, and an inertial guidance system run by an on board computer. The Agni can strike at any target in Pakistan and many in China with what Indian officials suggest will be considerable accuracy. An Indian spokesman said the goal of India's program is to build a missile that is able to hit a target 1,500 miles away with precision. India denies any intention of arming the Agni with a nuclear warhead, but it has that capability.[15]

Barring peaceful resolution of disputes or effective international safeguards, the experience of the United States over the previous two decades suggests that it might be reasonable to anticipate a SSM progression from conventional through chemical-biological to nuclear warheads; in short, a combination of horizontal and vertical proliferation of weapons of mass destruction may be seen in the decade immediately ahead.[16]

War is an excellent tutor for nations that feel imperiled by more powerful neighbors, and many governments in the Middle East have digested the lessons of the Gulf War. The most important is that conventional armaments alone are not an effective equalizer. Rather, the nation with accurate SSM delivery systems has both an equalizer and a potential advantage over most of its adversaries. Given our experience in other Third World regions, we can anticipate the technological evolution of SSMs along a heightened lethality curve during the coming decade involving: (1) extended geographic reach as a result of new importations from China, North Korea, and other sources; (2) improvement in precision as differential GPS and advanced inboard systems are introduced; (3) acquisition of ballistic and cruise systems to saturate and overwhelm such defenses as Patriot and "Arrow"; and (4) movement from liquid to solid fuel and cruise/Remote Pilotless Vehicle (RPV) systems to facilitate rapid fire, low flight trajectory capabilities, and diminished detectability. Longer ranges will be achieved by producing multiple-stage SSMs. At the same time, radar detection and early warning by defenders would be complicated in advanced SSMs with warhead separation from boosters at early launch stage. At present, Scuds in Middle East inventories involve booster and warhead marriage throughout much of flight, enhancing their early detection and acquisition by radar.

The introduction of such advanced systems will have several significant consequences for military planners in the region. Most critically, it will expand their security defense zones geographically, as was demonstrated by Iraq's missile attacks against Israel. The improved SSMs will provide attacking forces with substantial target flexibility, ranging from military targets to population centers. The systems will be available for follow on use—to dissuade adversaries from engaging in retaliatory responses. Most important, the introduction of these systems will compound difficulties within the U.S. government in its efforts to establish a calculus for determining the appropriate military balance in the Middle East.

To appreciate the inherently destabilizing nature of SSMs, one must view the problem within the context of the strategic culture of the Middle East. The procurement of new generations of SSMs is conducted within the framework of militarily value-maximizing strategies. The search for military advantage is predicated on a perception of a regional environment that is inherently threatening and conflict-ridden. Uncertainty is fed by mistrust on the part of adversaries, each perceiving the other's actions negatively and its own positively. Thus, the field of competition is zero-sum, with little sensitivity to each other's legitimate security needs or the benefits to be derived from accommodation and collaboration. This psychology produces an action-reaction syndrome that, in turn, serves as a catalyst for the existing arms race. The strategic military balance, therefore, is viewed in the framework of constant disequilibrium. For military chieftains in the region, SSMs, cruise missiles, and space-launched vehicles inevitably are viewed as future military trump cards needed to ensure a measure of military advantage vis-à-vis potential adversaries.

Chemical Weapons

Building an arsenal of chemical weapons (CW) presents no prepossessing challenge for most nations in the region. Many of the older toxins such as mustard gas, cyanotic gases, and nerve agents can be manufactured in the same center, using compounds also assigned to fertilizers and insecticide production. The basic components are available on the open market, most often from West European countries with lax export regulations.

Libya is a classic example of the ease with which CW capabilities can be acquired. The country's head of state since 1969, Colonel Muammar Qadhafi has made strenuous efforts to acquire an indigenous CW capability since the mid-1980s. Initially, he received small stocks of chemical weapons directly from Iran, which were used intermittently and apparently unsuccessfully against Chadian forces opposed to Qadhafi's efforts to annex their country. Concerned over his dependence on Iran as a source of supply, the colonel determined in 1987 that Libya should establish its own CW production capability and selected Rabta—30 miles south of the national capital of Tripoli—as an appropriate manufacturing site. Its prime advantages were remote location, defensible position, and close-in transport networks.[17]

Iraq, however, before 1991 commanded the most extensive CW-biological weapons inventory in the Middle East. Having initiated its program in the 1960s, Baghdad decided in 1974 to build its own facilities to manufacture toxins. By early 1989 the Saddam Husayn regime had produced several thousand tons of chemical agents. Iraq then appeared to have an annual production capacity of approximately 700 tons. The primary agents manufactured were mustard gas and two nerve agents, tabun and sarin.[18] However, as already noted, CW affords governments possessing them limited military advantage.

The Cycle of Lethality

The government of Israel has been placed in a particularly delicate security position as the proliferation of nonconventional weaponry by its neighbors takes place. Since the late 1960s the regional military balance has quite perceptibly tilted in Israel's favor. The Israeli advantage has been the result of superior planning and tactics, the availability of relatively sophisticated weapons systems—largely U.S.-supplied—and technically skilled personnel able to offset numerical disadvantages vis-à-vis Arab neighbors through an ability to wed professional military competence with human resourcefulness. Moreover, whenever and wherever threatened, Israel has seized the strategic advantage through preemptive initiative. This was amply demonstrated in 1981 when the Israeli air force attacked and severely damaged the Iraqi nuclear reactor at Orsirak. Throughout, the Israeli Defense Force has retained the trump card of nuclear weapons, thus compelling Arab adversaries to confine their military planning to conventional and unconventional warfare.

The military and psychological equilibrium began to shift as the decade of the 1980s came to closure, however. The discovery of Chinese CSS-2 sites under construction in Saudi Arabia startled Israel, the United States, and several West European governments.[19] Suddenly an Arab country—despite vast oil resources and a growing conventional weapons inventory, but hitherto not considered an important player in the Middle East power equation—had the ability to strike any urban center in the region with little or no warning. Israeli defense specialists had estimated that Arab states would not acquire an intermediate-range missile system until the mid-1990s. Iraqi technological achievements in the same field, together with Baghdad's chemical weapons arsenal, further disturbed Israeli leaders, who now realized that a reprise of the Orsirak reactor venture could produce a painful retaliatory response. Apocalyptic arguments soon surfaced in

Jerusalem and Tel Aviv about Israeli vulnerabilities, arguments which remain in the wake of the 1991 Gulf War.

Closer examination of the changing military balance led Israeli specialists to conclude prior to 1990 that apocalyptic visions were premature. They believed that the following factors needed to be taken into account:

- The new military technologies being introduced into the Middle East represented generational changes rather than asymmetrical transformations—after all, ballistic missiles and chemical weapons had been in the hands of adversaries for more than twenty years.
- Chemical weapons did not represent an effective offset to Israel's nuclear arsenal, given the imponderables associated with climate and weather conditions as well as the availability of protective clothing for civilian populations.
- Although adversaries had achieved deep-strike capabilities, their capacity to integrate such capabilities into effective war planning had yet to be demonstrated by Israel's adversaries.

Today there is growing concern in the wake of the 1991 Gulf War about the implications of the transfer of state-of-the-art technology to Arab military establishments—both "frontline" and those geographically removed. As one specialist has observed:

> Military forces in the Middle East will remain dependent on imported high technology equipment. Even if they are able to manufacture some sophisticated systems, they will remain dependent on the transfer of underlying technologies from the United States, Western Europe, or the Soviet Union.
>
> This dependence on foreign systems and technology, though moderated by domestic arms production, means that the character of the future battlefield in the Arab-Israeli conflict will be determined in part by the nature of the world arms trade in the coming years.[20]

Particularly noteworthy has been the accelerating processes of horizontal and vertical arms escalation over the past decade. Most observers of the Middle East military scene assumed that, from a cost-benefit point of view, the priority of the overwhelming majority of states in the region would be the continued acquisition of conventional weaponry (horizontal escalation). Moreover, they assumed that the momentum of acquisition would slow as a result of declining oil revenues and as competition grew for scarce financial resources by civilian sector ministries. Reality has intruded rudely on such presumptions. From 1983–1987, the Middle East became the principal recipient of arms exports worldwide, accounting for 48 percent of the total (see Table 3.2). Although the demand could be attributed in part at least to local conflict situations, other factors had also come into play: (1) the need to replace obsolescent weaponry; (2) the felt imperative to compensate for seeming advantages by neighboring states or, conversely, to intimidate or otherwise influence the policy choices of the latter; or (3) a decision to shift away from dependence on such major suppliers as the United States and the Soviet Union. Whatever the felt need, the consequence has been to build two potentially different and unrelated battlefield situations, one involving conventional armaments, the other SSMs, chemical, and related systems. The latter involves vertical escalation—both systemically and spatially—since new generations of missiles offer the opportunity to bypass the land battlefield and available air defenses. The Patriot missile defense system has not thus far proved leakproof. However, the United States and others expect to improve point and area air defense systems over the coming decade. Point defense relates to airfields and storage sites; area air defense relates to cities and other large centers of military and civilian concentration.

The acquisition of state-of-the-art missile systems poses a wide range of new threats to the already tenuous stability of the region; most immediately and directly: (1) the distinction of weapons acquisition for purposes of deterrence as opposed to war-fighting tends to become blurred; (2) prospects for maintaining crisis stability during periods of tense interaction become attenuated as a result of refusal by states in the region to pledge "no first use"; (3) the ability of adversaries to confine hostilities to the purely military sector is placed in doubt; (4) nations contemplating wars of attrition must now examine costs of abbreviated "total" wars; and (5) the concept of "winning" undergoes alteration when the human costs associated with war rise exponentially.

Deterrence, in particular, is increasingly problematic as conventional weapons in Middle East inventories become more lethal in terms of probability-of-kill ratios and intensity of exchange. For example, well-directed SSMs of abbreviated range could have the same devastating impact as low-yield tactical nuclear weapons, thus threatening fixed command-and-control centers, logistics installations, or massed tank or infantry formations. Similarly, airfields and port installations might be interdicted by hard-target "kill" missiles or, alternatively, remote-controlled attack aircraft outfitted with terrain guidance systems. Under such circumstances, the initial advantage would repose with an adversary prepared to conduct a crippling first strike with such conventional weapons—under conditions in which a retaliatory nuclear response would only generate massive casualties on both sides. In brief, it is not unreasonable to anticipate that the so-called "red line" of military strategy between conventional and nuclear warfare—as well as between deterrence and actual war fighting—will begin to lose relevance. The majority of missile sales include a mix of SSMs, surface-to-air, and other systems, as was evidenced in French sales to Iraq during its war with Iran (see Table 3.1).

Given these circumstances, competitive acquisitions of unconventional and conventional weaponry will continue over the coming decade and beyond.

Existing Strategies

Received wisdom in the United States and elsewhere tends to address arms control strategies either from a *supply-side* perspective or, in the traditional argot of the economist, a *demand-side* approach. Strategies to induce restraint in the proliferation of systems have generally been directed toward the establishment of control regimes by supplier nations. The demand side concentrates on diplomatic initiatives that resolve underlying issues leading to conflict in regions such as the Middle East. As part of conflict resolution, emphasis is placed on the establishment of confidence-building measures of the type and range laboriously put in place by the United States and the Soviet Union in the midst of the cold war.

Arms control is an appropriate mechanism to inhibit conflict according to observers of the Middle East scene. But arms control in and of itself is likely to yield only short-term results. There exist too many suppliers and too many competitively priced systems in the international marketplace to effectively shut off arms and technology transfers. As we have learned elsewhere, multilateral restraint regimes encompassing comprehensive compliance and verification measures are exceedingly difficult to bring into place. In the case of the former Soviet Union, governments are experiencing difficulties in controlling sales initiatives by military entrepreneurs and managers of defense industries hard-pressed for foreign currencies.

Overlooked by many proponents is the increasing globalization of military production and technology. The migration of defense industries across national boundaries, as well as the nomadic character of skilled manpower, both serve to undermine efforts to erect fail-safe restraint regimes. Providing impetus to globalization are declining budgetary resources for production of defense items in major arms-producing states and the resultant need for corporations to compensate by forming international cooperative ventures to assure market shares for their products. Global economic forces thus compel the fashioning of transnational arrangements that make weapons manufacturers almost autonomous actors in the international marketplace—actors that increasingly view corporate interests as separate and superior to the interests of their parent nation-states.

Hitherto, the United States, when addressing supply-side strategy, has opted for a dual-track approach. The first has involved the establishment of a Missile Technology Control Regime (MTCR) embracing, inter alia, the United States, Canada, the United Kingdom, West Germany, France, Italy, and Japan. The MTCR agreement (signed in 1987) did not enjoy the status of an international treaty; it was concluded in the expectation that the signatories could slow, if not end, the flow of missile technology and weapons systems to such volatile regions as the Middle East. The second track has involved U.S.-led efforts to organize and implement an international convention outlawing the production, storage, or use of chemical weapons in time of armed conflict.

Both approaches have serious deficiencies. The MTCR was flawed from its inception both in conceptual design and in application. The regime failed to include such supplier nations as the former Soviet Union and the People's Republic of China, as well as such potential suppliers as Israel, Brazil, and Argentina. Moreover, the MTCR did not provide for effective monitoring of signatory compliance; nor was provision made for sanctions against nonsignatory governments unwilling to abide by the MTCR guidelines. Finally, the MTCR adherents apparently fell into the quantitative-qualitative trap. A technological (or qualitative) arms race differs from its quantitative counterpart in that each side seeks to introduce advanced weapons to escape the high costs associated with accumulating less sophisticated conventional weapons. The presumption held by the MTCR signatories has been that a leap into qualitative systems acquisition could be controlled as accumulations of conventional weapons in the Middle East grew—in part because nations in the area would direct their energies toward absorption of the newly acquired conventional weapons systems.

The restraint regime has developed other significant weaknesses, and there is little likelihood that its founder will overcome the majority of these infirmities. The interface between civilian and military technology applications, the multiplicity of commercial suppliers (involved in competition for market shares), and the absence of effective monitoring and sanctions have all served to erode the MTCR.[21] In addition, the United States has witnessed the emergence of local production complexes with substantial support from nonarea sources. External dependence is now diminishing. India and Israel have recently developed missiles without foreign assistance. Finally, the restraint regime lacks credibility when its principal organizer and sponsor, the United States, is prepared to countenance Israel's transmission of U.S.-acquired guidance systems and related technology to South Africa and China. However, the proliferation specter, although real, should not be exaggerated. Particularly daunting for most Third World nations remains the process of wedding missiles with CW-biological warheads. The technical challenge is both complex and time consuming. Involved are special metallurgy requirements to encase the warheads within missile systems. The latter must be integrated with launch vehicles that, in turn, must be prepared for deployment at fixed sites. These requirements are even more demanding where mobile intermediate-range systems are to be linked.[22]

The second major initiative undertaken by the U.S. government has been directed toward the negotiation of a multilateral chemical weapons convention (CW Convention). President Bush requested that all Middle Eastern states become party to the convention and that they undertake confidence-building measures before the actual signing of the convention. The separate Biological Weapons Convention (that came up for review in 1991) and the envisaged CW Convention suffer from an obscure, but important, omission. Both ban development, but fail to mention research.[23] In addition, the chemical treaty negotiated at the Conference on Disarmament in Geneva calls for cessation of chemical weapons production and the destruction of all existing poison gas stockpiles within ten years of the treaty taking effect. With forty nations involved, the target date for destruction could run well into the twenty-first century.

Experienced U.S. officials now acknowledge that formal pledges that restraint will be observed by signatories to international treaties or conventions are no longer considered to be sufficient for an effective CW or missile control regime. Other strategies are clearly needed to deal with the rapidly changing military balance in the Middle East.

A Multitiered Strategy

As every student of national security policy is aware, the balance of military power in any geographic region is relative and dynamic. Every nation's status and influence changes in accordance with shifts in its position in that balance. Moreover, under constantly changing circumstances, military capability assures varying degrees of political potency. Nevertheless, a military establishment that is capable and that disposes of credible power is the cornerstone of most nations' security. Israel has used its perceived military power—conventional and nuclear—in defining its relationship with Arab states in the Middle East. Iraq sought to organize its military and foreign policies around the same criteria. In developing a triad of conventional weapons, missiles linked to CW, and aspirations for membership in the nuclear weapons club, Iraq was not only seeking to emulate Israel but to demonstrate as well its claim to Arab world leadership. Saddam Husayn apparently concluded that a nation whose relative power is perceived to be growing can be more assertive—can be taken more seriously by neighbors—and can have greater potential influence over regional affairs. Ultimately, he acted on such assumptions vis-à-vis Kuwait. This psychological dimension in evaluating relative military capabilities in the Middle East is all too frequently overlooked.

Saddam Husayn, several years prior to the invasion of Kuwait, publicly declared that Arabs needed a nuclear and chemical weapons inventory to establish a "balance of terror" vis-à-vis Israel in order to prevent the latter from unilaterally establishing a "red line" against Arab governments and using its nuclear arsenal for purposes of intimidation. In his view, Israel's nuclear weapons have been fashioned to pursue a strategy of "compellence," one intended to deny Arabs military equivalency and to compel Arab acceptance of Israel's annexation of the West Bank, Gaza, East Jerusalem, and the Golan Heights. A key element in Israel's strategy is to organize an international consortium to deny Arabs the technology necessary to achieve military parity with Israel. Within this analytical framework, deterrence is an invention of Israel and the United States, one that "cheats" Arabs by consigning them to inferior status. Not mentioned was the potential provided by CBN weapons in the hands of Saddam Husayn to intimidate fellow Arab rivals and Iran.

A significant problem for U.S. national security policy planners is the absence of a well-defined military "doctrine" on the part of most governments in the region. Israeli "doctrine" has been clearly defined over the past two decades: (1) deterrence, in the form of threatened destruction of adversaries, as enunciated in public statements; (2) adoption of preemption strategies when armed conflict appears imminent; (3) research to improve active defense capabilities; and (4) passive defense measures in the civilian, noncombatant area. For Iraq, Libya, Syria, and Saudi Arabia, military "doctrine" appears to be situational and amorphous. Most, if not all, have acquired missile systems with Israel in mind as their primary target. Prestige, other Arab rivals, and the operational requirements of local military commanders have been additional compelling considerations. Available information suggests that past missile-CW "doctrine" in Syria and Iraq represents a last resort approach rather than one intended for a first strike against Israel or other targets. This may be changing. Israel, as already noted, has established a "red line," making clear that use of such weapons by adversaries would generate a devastating riposte by Israel, against both military and civilian targets.

The concern of most U.S. arms control specialists is that a crisis control regime has *not* been established in the region, nor have traditional adversaries been inclined to fashion confidence-building arrangements to stabilize future crisis situations. This lacuna might be perceived by U.S. policymakers as a "window of opportunity." To take advantage, the U.S. government should begin to develop a broad strategic design, one that is multilayered and multidimensional.

- The existing control strategy involving missile technology transfers should be broadened into a UN-sponsored international convention with appropriate challenge inspection, safeguard, and sanction measures.
- Concomitantly, the United States should alter its posture on CW. The convention itself should be strengthened to vouchsafe on-site challenge inspections to ensure general compliance.
- Nations in the Middle East and adjacent regions should be encouraged to participate in a UN-sanctioned conference intended to (1) pledge immediate termination of CW and nuclear weapons research; and (2) negotiate as wide a range of arms control and confidence-building procedures as possible.

Formal pledges are likely to carry little weight in the Middle East barring a full panoply of supporting initiatives. Confidence-building might be enhanced by advance notification on the part of states in the region of planned military exercises of division-sized units and larger, accordance of observer status for foreign military attaches wishing to attend such exercises, advance notification of tests to be conducted for missiles with ranges exceeding 150 km, challenge inspections under the auspices of international agencies of facilities alleged to be producing CW or biological agents, exchange visits by senior military commanders and defense ministry personnel, and, where appropriate, courtesy port calls by naval units.

Other confidence-building initiatives might include establishment of crisis control centers in subregions such as the Persian Gulf, the eastern Mediterranean area, and the area to the west of Cairo. Several European governments—notably Spain, France, and Italy—have recommended that a Western Mediterranean Conference on Security and Cooperation, comparable to the all-European counterpart, be organized to address local disputes and to resolve outstanding human rights and associated issues. Such an initiative should receive the full diplomatic backing of the U.S. government.

Not to be overlooked in such regional undertakings would be formal pledges of "no first use" of chemical, biological, and nuclear weapons. Threatened use would constitute a "red line" in the event of heightened tensions. Similarly, Israel would be required to forsake repetition of the 1981 Orsirak attack; failure to offer such an undertaking weakens prospects for confidence-building in any regional restraint regime that might be attempted.

The policy challenges confronting the United States are multifaceted and more than regional in dimension. As the sole remaining major power with global influence, U.S. policy objectives in the Middle East must be fashioned with U.S. interests and needs—notably in Europe and Asia—in mind. However, our goals and purposes in the Middle East can easily be diluted by policy imperatives elsewhere. Moreover, U.S. policy practitioners are generally inclined to deal with violations (noncompliance) on a case-by-case basis. Such an approach, if endorsed by the president, can only serve to undermine the credibility of U.S. policy in the Middle East.

In summary, the decade immediately ahead will be a testing period for arms control policies and strategies currently fashioned by the United States and other industrialized nations. Clearly, governments in the Middle East will not accept restraints that provide rivals— both existing and future—with what are felt to be unfair advantages. Barring peaceful settlement of disputes, these governments will perceive a military balance that is equitable only if it is tilted in their favor or if risks are shared by all. Advanced technology, both in regard to conventional weapons and weapons of mass destruction, will be the criteria for measuring military parity in the region. Given this perspective, the concept of deterrence will lose its potency, particularly if conventional weapons technology approaches the threshold of lethality associated with tactical nuclear weapons, as this author believes likely. In this respect, existing arms supply restraint strategies are likely to slow the process of technology diffusion but may not effectively seal it off.

The U.S. government will confront some difficult choices in simultaneously urging restraint on supplier nations and Middle Eastern customers while itself making conventional weapons available to clients in the region. In the six month period following the conclusion of the 1990–1991 war with Iraq, the United States agreed to transfer $6 billion worth of arms to the region, more than four times as much in dollar terms as the United States provided in 1984–1988. West European governments are likely to look askance at U.S. requests that they adopt a posture of self-denial while U.S. weapons sales to selected clients mount dramatically. Attempts to maintain a balance between arms sales and arms control will be complicated by Iran's efforts at weapons modernization, the threatened proliferation of weapons of mass destruction, and the economic imperatives of other exporting nations.

Concomitantly, the U.S. government will have to establish an effective strategy to strengthen the defense capabilities of southern members of the NATO alliance and the Middle Eastern client states that feel threatened by proliferation. Although a U.S. military presence in the region will provide a measure of reassurance, proliferation confronts U.S. military units in the region with widening risks. The requirement for enhanced self-defense capability is currently under intense study by the United States and its NATO allies in the region. The prospect of early elimination of the challenge is and likely will remain in doubt during much of the decade of the 1990s.

Notes

1. Peter W. Rodman, "Middle East Diplomacy after the Gulf War," *Foreign Affairs* 70 (Spring 1991), pp. 1–18.

2. Ibid., p. 15.

3. Bureau of Public Affairs, U.S. Department of State, *Dispatch* 2, no. 20 (May 20, 1991), p. 361.

4. Alton Frye, "How We Can Contain the Mideast Arms Explosion," *Washington Post*, June 16, 1991, p. B1.

5. *New York Times*, June 18, 1991, p. 5.

6. Jed C. Snyder, "Weapons Proliferation and the New Security Agenda," in *On Not Confusing Ourselves*, Andrew Marshall, J. J. Martin, and Henry Rowen, eds. (Boulder, Colo: Westview Press, 1991), p. 271.

7. John Yang and R. Jeffrey Smith, "China Agrees to Confer on Mideast Arms Sales," *Washington Post*, June 8, 1991, p. A17. The uncertainties surrounding these criteria relate to the known vagaries that inhere in the designations "sophisticated new military capabilities," how one measures the capacity to project military power, or factors that encourage military buildups. These are, at best, slippery criteria subject to individual interpretation by weapons suppliers and consumers alike. In addition, problems associated with such criteria are compounded when addressing questions relating to dual use (civilian-military) technologies of the future.

8. Atlantic Council of the United States, Washington, D.C., *Bulletin* 2, no. 4 (April 15, 1991).

9. Ze'ev Schiff, "Israel After the War," *Foreign Affairs* 71, no. 69 (Spring 1991), p. 33.

10. Marshal Nikolai Ogarkov, then chief of the Soviet General Staff noted the *March of Technology* in May 1984 in that: "automated reconnaissance-and-strike complexes, long-range, high precision remotely controlled weapons, pilotless aircraft, and qualitatively new electronic controls systems are making many types of armaments global and are making it possible to increase sharply by at least ten times the strike force of conventional weapons, bringing it close, as it were, to the effectiveness of weapons of mass destruction." Cited in Marshall Brement, "Reaching Out to Moscow," *Foreign Policy*, no. 86 (Fall 1990), p. 69.

11. See statement of Henry D. Sokolski, "Export Control Policies and Processes," U.S. Congress. Senate. Report before the Subcommittee on Technology and National Security, April 23, 1991.

12. Paradoxically, the United States, which had the gravest concern, had failed for fifty years to ratify the 1925 Protocol. When presented to the U.S. Senate for advice and consent, it was set aside until 1975 as a result, inter alia, of the then existent Army Chemical Warfare Service, which insisted on preserving the right to deploy some chemical agents in wartime situations. In addition, the U.S. chemical industry opposed ratification of the protocol.

13. Address by Major General William F. Burns (Retired) presented to the CISA-Wilton Park Joint Conference, Weston House, West Sussex, United Kingdom, April 2, 1989. Report prepared by the Science Applications International Corporation, McLean, Virginia.

14. As Shai Feldman has observed, the best surveys and analyses of the proliferation of ballistic missiles in the Middle East are to be found in Aharon Levran, "Surface to Surface Missiles: The Threat to Israel," Memorandum no. 24 (Tel Aviv: Jaffee Center for Strategic Studies, Tel Aviv University), July 1988; and in W. Seth Carus, "Missiles in the Middle East: A New Threat to Stability." *Policy Focus* no. 6 (Washington, D.C.: Washington Institute for Near East Policy) June 1988, and "Chemical Weapons in the Middle East," *Policy Focus* no. 9, December 1988. See also Carus, "The Genie Unleashed: Iraq's Chemical and Biological Weapons Production," *Policy Papers* no. 14, May 1989; and, his "NATO, Israel, and the Tactical Missile Challenge," *Policy Focus* no. 4, May-June 1987. See also *Policy Focus* May-June 1989. For a reliable inventory of surface-to-surface launchers in the region's states see Shlomo Gazit and Ze'ev Eitan, *The Middle East Military Balance 1988–1989,* Jaffee Center for Strategic Studies (Jerusalem: *Jerusalem Post* and Boulder, Colo.: Westview Press, 1989), p. 329. According to Seth Carus, the force structures of Middle East states, including Israel's, by June 1988 included some 300 surface-to-surface missile launchers and some 1,200 missiles. This figure, however, includes short-range rockets such as the Frog-7s. In addition to surface-to-surface missiles, local inventories include antitank guided missiles (SAGGER, MILAN, HOT, and TOW); naval surface-to-surface systems SYTX (MM-38, Exocet, Harpoon, and Gabriel); air-to-air missiles (Sparrow, Sidewinder, Matra, Magic, AA-6/ACRID, AA-2/ATOLL); air-to-surface missiles (GABRIEL III, SHRIKE, Standard Arm, Maverick, Walleye, AS-9); and surface-to-air missiles (HAWK, GRAIL, SA-6, SA-8, SA-13, CHAPARRAL, Rapier, and Roland).

15. James T. Hackett, "The Ballistic Missile Epidemic," *Global Affairs* 7, no. 4 (Winter 1990), p. 47.

16. The U.S. government estimates that at least fifteen developing nations could be producing their own ballistic missiles by the year 2000. The hair-trigger effect will lead to incentives to require chemical and nuclear warheads.

17. Qadhafi has claimed that Rabta, known as "Pharma 150," is designed to manufacture pharmaceuticals. However, several characteristics suggest otherwise: (1) the facility is heavily protected with ground security forces and air defense systems; (2) its research and production staffs are kept under close security surveillance; (3) its production is treated as a classified question not open to foreign examination; (4) the structure of the production plant varies in substantial degree from most pharmaceutical plants; and (5) the Libyans have gone to great lengths to confound Western security services from using satellites to study the facility.

18. Robert Pear, "Iraq Can Deliver, U.S. Chemical Weapons Experts Say," *New York Times*, April 3, 1989, p. 8.

19. During the frenetic period, three accompanying events further shocked the Israeli public: (1) the U.S.-forced cancellation of the Lavi-fighter project; (2) the eruption of the Palestinian *intifada* in December 1987; and (3) the unanticipated agreement by Tehran to a cease-fire with Iraq.

20. Hirsh Goodman and W. Seth Carus, *The Future Battlefield and the Arab-Israeli Conflict* (New Brunswick, N.J.: Transaction Publishers, 1990).

21. For further discussion on the subject, see Hackett, "The Ballistic Missile Epidemic," pp. 48–49.

22. Absorptive capacity, in the form of trained operational, logistical, and maintenance support arrangements, also needs to be understood. For example, testing and maintenance equipment must be acquired along with the launch rocket and warhead system, as well as retrofit and refire backup systems. These, in turn, must be integrated with command-control-communications systems. Finally, to be fully operational (and credible), all of the components and elements must include in the overall system architecture appropriate early warning and air defense arrangements. The manpower, training, and support costs in these undertakings are substantial.

23. In the case of the CW Convention, the omission may not prove fatal since militarily relevant quantities cannot be produced in a research laboratory. This might not prove the case for a Biological Weapons Convention, because although production of chemical weapons requires a production plant, production of a militarily relevant quantity of biological weapons can take place in a laboratory.

Suggested Reading

Carus, Seth W., *The Genie Unleashed: Iraq's Chemical and Biological Program*, Washington, D.C.: Washington Institute for Near East Policy, 1989.
Cordesman, Anthony, *Weapons of Mass Destruction in the Middle East*, New York: Oxford University Press, 1991.

Kemp, Geoffrey, *The Control of the Middle East Arms Race,* Washington, D.C.: Carnegie Endowment for International Peace, 1991.

Nolan, Jeanne, *Trappings of Power: Ballistic Missiles in the Third World,* Washington, D.C.: Brookings Institution, 1991.

Spector, Leonard, and Smith, Jacqueline, *Nuclear Ambitions,* Boulder, Colo.: Westview Press, 1990.

ARAB-ISRAELI AREA

4

The Arab-Israeli Conflict in the 1990s: Prospects for a Settlement

William Quandt

The conflict between Israel and its Arab neighbors has ranked among the most dangerous and intractable for so long that it may be difficult to accept the proposition that its basic dimensions have significantly changed in recent years. Both the end of the cold war and the crushing defeat of Iraq in the Gulf War had a major impact on the Arab-Israeli conflict. Combined with the return of the Israeli Labor party to power in the 1992 elections, the effect of these global and regional changes has been to improve the prospects for a negotiated settlement.

To appreciate the extent of changes, one needs to compare the nature of the Arab-Israeli conflict in the late 1960s and the early 1990s. In the earlier period, Israel had emerged victorious from the June 1967 war against Egypt, Jordan, and Syria. With strong backing from the United States, Israel was then proposing to negotiate with any and all of its neighbors on the basis of trading recently occupied territory—the Sinai, the West Bank and Gaza, and the Golan Heights—in exchange for peace, recognition and security. The Arab parties were wedded to a policy of no recognition, no negotiation, and no formal peace with Israel. They insisted that Israel withdraw to the June 4, 1967, lines as a precondition for peace talks. Israel adamantly insisted that withdrawal could only be a result of direct negotiations and firm Arab commitments on peace, recognition, and security, a position supported by the United States.

The Soviet Union stood solidly behind Egypt and Syria as a reliable arms supplier. The Palestinians were just beginning to rally behind the Palestine Liberation Organization and its call for armed struggle to free all of Palestine from Israeli control. The United States, for the first time, was becoming Israel's main source of military support. Throughout the 1970s and 1980s the Arab-Israeli conflict became inextricably linked to the ongoing cold war.

By the early 1990s much had changed, in large measure because of the dramatic ending of superpower rivalry and the collapse of the Soviet Union and its East European empire. It is true that some of the same leaders were still in place and that Israel still held some of the territory—the West Bank, Gaza, and the Golan Heights—that it had captured in the 1967 war. But the broad parameters of the conflict had been dramatically changed by eight developments:

First, Egypt and Israel began serious negotiations after the October 1973 war, and in March 1979 they signed a peace treaty.[1] More than ten years later that treaty still served as a strong cornerstone for stability in the region. The Arab states that initially boycotted Egypt because of its unilateral peace with Israel had all resumed normal diplomatic relations with Cairo by 1990. The Arab League returned to Cairo in 1991 after a decade in Tunis. Peace between Israel and Egypt has meant that a large-scale Arab-Israeli war is unlikely, although not impossible.

Second, the Soviet Union reduced its involvement in the Arab-Israeli conflict beginning in 1987. Moscow had, until then, backed a fairly tough Arab position of insisting that Israel relinquish all Occupied Territories and agree to a PLO-led Palestinian state. Syria, Libya, and Iraq had been generously supplied with Soviet arms to bolster the overall Arab military position. But in 1987 the Soviet leadership signaled that it would only back a political solution to the conflict with Israel. To this end, it began to reduce arms transfers to its traditional clients and to expand diplomatic and economic contacts with Egypt, Jordan, and Israel. Increasingly, Moscow seemed to be seeking normal relations with states throughout the region, rather than privileged ties with just a few. The collapse of the Soviet Union in late 1991 reduced Moscow's influence in the region to a post–World War II low.

Third, the Palestinians, although weakened by the stance of their leaders in the 1991 Gulf crisis, continue to confront Israel with a difficult political challenge. In brief, Israel may keep the West Bank and Gaza (with their Palestinian population of more than 1.7 million) and risk becoming a binational state with a permanent underclass, or, at some risk to Israel's security and in the face of great internal opposition, Israel might relinquish control over most of the Occupied Territories in return for Arab commitments to peace. This would help preserve the Jewish character of the state. Finally, Israel may try to keep the territories and expel the Arab inhabitants, an option favored by a minority and one that is sure to result in harsh international reactions and the probable collapse of Israel's peace with Egypt. The election in mid-1992 of a Labor-led government increased the prospects of a settlement of the Israeli-Palestinian conflict built around the idea of territorial compromise.

Since the opening of the Madrid peace conference in October 1991, Israelis and Palestinians have faced each other across the negotiating table, discussing concrete proposals for an interim arrangement involving self-government for the Palestinians. This still leaves the ultimate outcome of peace talks uncertain, but at least a major procedural hurdle has been overcome.

Both Israelis and Palestinians, on the one hand, seem to feel some urgency in moving forward in the negotiations. The *intifada*, or Palestinian uprising in the Occupied Territories of the West Bank and Gaza, may be on the wane, but Israel cannot count on a cost-free occupation, even so.[2] The Palestinians, on the other hand, face the prospect of economic hardship and loss of land the longer the occupation goes on, so they too have an incentive to negotiate an agreement, provided that it puts an end to Israeli settlement activity and land expropriation.

Among Palestinians, two distinct political trends can be discerned: the mainstream, still loyal to the PLO, that is prepared to accept a "two-state" solution to the conflict and that supports the idea of negotiations with Israel; and a radical Islamist trend, probably a minority, that rejects accommodation with Israel and the whole idea of secular nationalism.

Fourth, Israel is increasingly preoccupied with the challenge of absorbing large numbers of new immigrants from the former Soviet Union. During the 1990s over one million Jews from the former Soviet Union may come to settle in Israel. For some Israelis, this could be a welcome answer to the Palestinian demographic threat. (More Arab than Jewish babies are born each year in the territories controlled by Israel.) As such, the new immigration provides a further rationale for holding on to all of the Occupied Territories. Other Israelis, however, feel that the task of absorbing the immigrants requires that Israel turn its energies inward, away from conflict with its neighbors, and thus they conclude that a peace agreement is an urgent necessity. The Knesset elections of mid-1992 showed a significant shift away from Likud, which had not succeeded in delivering services to the new immigrants. As a result, for the first time since 1977 a Labor-led coalition came to power, significantly increasing the chances for a negotiated agreement with the Palestinians and Syrians.

Fifth, the multiple arms races in the Middle East—between Israel and Syria, Iraq and Iran—insure that future conflicts will be very dangerous.[3] Unless serious arms control agreements can be reached, large quantities of U.S., European, and Russian conventional weapons are likely to be made available to states in the Middle East, more for commercial reasons than as a result of strategic calculation by the arms providers. Also, lethal new weapons systems will arrive on the scene, including surface-to-surface missiles, precision-guided munitions, chemical weapons, and possibly nuclear capabilities as well.[4] In this setting, the risk of some form of preemptive military action is likely to grow.

Sixth, Iraq's August 2, 1990, invasion of Kuwait demonstrated the complex links between Gulf crises and the Arab-Israeli conflict.[5] To rally support in the Arab world, Iraqi President Saddam Husayn had regularly threatened Israel but, in fact, his target was Kuwait. Once in control of Kuwait, he tried to establish a link between Iraq's possible withdrawal from Kuwait and Israel's withdrawal from the West Bank and Gaza. Shortly after the UN multilateral force, under U.S. leadership, took military action against Iraq on January 16, 1991, Saddam Husayn, as he had threatened to do, unleashed Scud missiles against Israeli cities. His strategic rationale, it seemed, was to draw Israel into the conflict, therefore splitting the Arab coalition ranged against him. Under U.S. pressure, Israel refrained from retaliating, a remarkable development in light of prior Israeli practice. The military effect of the Scud attacks was negligible, the economic costs were substantial, and the political significance was very great. For the first time during a Middle East war, Israeli civilians had been attacked without their government being able to do much to protect them. This may only have been possible because of the unusual circumstances of massive U.S. military involvement in the crisis, but it did nonetheless raise questions about Israeli military doctrine in future crises. On balance, however, Iraq's crushing defeat left Israel more secure than at any previous time in its history.

Seventh, Syria's position in the region has changed as a result of the loss of meaningful support from Moscow; its alignment with the United States and the conservative Arab regimes in the 1991 Gulf War; improved relations with Egypt; and because of the consolidation of Syria's preeminent role in Lebanon.[6] A politically secure but economically weak Syria can no longer aspire to "strategic parity" with Israel, Hafiz al-Asad's much-vaunted goal of the 1980s. Instead, Asad faces a choice of living with the status quo on the Israeli front or trying to make some gains through diplomacy. In agreeing to go to the Madrid peace conference to negotiate with Israel, Asad showed a realistic, pragmatic side of his policy. Along the way he was also able to improve his relations with Western countries, including the United States. During the September 1992 round of negotiations in Washington, both Syrians and Israelis reported some progress toward agreeing on the "land for peace" formula, but hard bargaining lay ahead.

Eighth, finally, the Iraqi crisis brought into focus the suppressed issue of nuclear weapons in the Middle East. As long as Israel was the only regional power with nuclear capabilities, the United States observed a discreet silence. No doubt U.S. policy was influenced by Israel's nuclear option. Large transfers of conventional arms to Israel were meant to raise the threshold for the use of Israel's nuclear weapons. One could also argue that one motive for multilateral intervention by the United States and its allies against Iraq in 1990–1991 was to ward off an Iraqi nuclear capability that almost certainly would have led to an Iraqi-Israeli confrontation sometime in the decade.[7] In short, the United States must now take nuclear matters into account in its Middle East policy. If nonproliferation efforts fail, the choices are grim: to allow regional powers to confront one another with their nuclear capabilities; to take U.S. action to disarm one or more powers; or to give green lights to regional powers to do the job. In the latter case, the United States could find itself condoning Israeli military strikes against an Arab country or Iran, a situation that would be fraught with political implications.

Threats to American Interests

With these changes in mind, how should the United States assess the threat to its interests that may be posed by the Arab-Israeli conflict in the coming decade? It is reassuring that war between Israel and some group of Arab states that could detonate a larger superpower confrontation is no longer plausible. This scenario had been the nightmare of U.S. policymakers from 1967 through the early 1980s. In fact, on several occasions there was a hint of just such a confrontation in the air, especially during the last phase of both the 1967 and 1973 wars, but also in more muted forms during the September 1970 crisis involving Jordan, Syria, Israel, and the PLO, and Israel's 1982 invasion of Lebanon.[8]

Even if we can imagine Arab-Israeli wars in the 1990s, it is difficult to see how both the United States and Russia might be drawn in. In the 1990–1991 Gulf crisis, Russia showed no signs of seeking to play a military role. Given the extent of its internal crises, it seems out of the question that Moscow will be inclined to intervene militarily in the Middle East. Even an impending Israeli defeat of Syria, for example, would be unlikely to provoke more than Russian diplomatic efforts in response.

If, by chance, the Arab side were to get the upper hand against Israel in some future war, then the United States might well feel compelled to intervene, as it did on a limited scale with Patriot missiles in the Gulf crisis, both to assist Israel and to prevent Israel from resorting to its nonconventional forces. Could such U.S. intervention in the future lead to an armed confrontation with any power from outside the region? That seems unlikely. In short, the pre–World War I Balkans analogy, which was prevalent in the late 1960s and early 1970s, no longer seems relevant, even if one can imagine some very dangerous wars erupting between Israel and Arab countries.

This reassuring conclusion is somewhat weakened by the fact that the states in the Arab-Israeli theater remain very heavily armed. The quantity and quality of arsenals on both sides are impressive. Israel possesses formidable capabilities, including nuclear weapons, missiles, precision-guided munitions, advanced command-and-control, good battlefield intelligence, and a fledgling satellite capability for intelligence gathering and communications. The Arab arsenal is less sophisticated but larger, and includes both chemical weapons and the means to deliver them to populated areas. These bristling arsenals may provide a degree of mutual deterrence, but there is always the risk that new systems, such as missiles or newer highly accurate and lethal weapons or the acquisition of nuclear weapons could tip the balance. Given the presumed advantages of striking first, there may also be a hair-trigger quality to the deterrence relationship that could be worrisome. Even in the 1980s, there were examples of such preemptive temptations as evidenced by Israel's 1981 strike on Iraq's nuclear reactor. In 1991, Iraqi President Saddam Husayn deliberately struck Israel in an attempt to alter political conditions in the region. Such calculations defy the normal assumptions of deterrence theory. How can one deter a state that is trying to provoke an attack for political reasons?

Even with Iraq's dramatic defeat in the Persian Gulf War of early 1991, a potentially dangerous conflict between Israel and some Arab states remains a possibility, though not a high probability. Syria is the most important of Israel's present adversaries, but Iraq could, in time, rebuild its military forces. If either country were on the verge of obtaining a usable chemical or nuclear capability against Israel, then the risks of war could be substantial.

The United States would find it difficult to remain on the sidelines of a large-scale Arab-Israeli war, especially if Israel were taking heavy casualties. An attempt would almost certainly be made to stop such a war at an early date and to provide Israel with defense against missiles and protection against nonconventional threats. Any Arab-Israeli war should be relatively short, since Israel could not tolerate a prolonged war of attrition. Therefore, any action envisaged by the United States, whether it involves diplomatic initiatives or arms supply, would come early in the conflict.

Terrorism and Oil as Security Problems

Two other facets of a future Arab-Israeli conflict deserve mention: terrorism and oil. The conscious resort to terror—threats to innocent civilians, hostage taking—have accompanied all of the recent conflicts in the Middle East, whether they have involved Palestinians, Lebanon, Iraq, or Iran. Despite enormous efforts, especially in the 1980s, the United States never found a satisfactory military response to the problem of terrorism. Like crime, terrorism probably cannot be eradicated, but one can hope to reduce the number of incidents and insure that terror does not dominate the political discourse. If there is no progress in resolving the Arab-Israeli conflict, it seems inevitable that political extremism will grow and that terrorism will remain a force in the Middle East. Apart from threats to individual U.S. citizens and to pro-Western regimes, terrorists might try to target oil facilities in the Gulf as a way of hitting at U.S. economic interests. A settlement that satisfied most Palestinians and Israelis would not eliminate all risks of terrorist actions, but it would be a step in the direction of bringing terrorism under control.

The specter of the oil weapon has long hung over the Arab-Israeli conflict, despite the fact that oil and Arab-Israeli politics have not been closely intermingled.[9] The exceptions, however, are important to note. As part of the Arab strategy in the October 1973 war, Saudi Arabia took the lead in orchestrating a reduction of oil output and an embargo on oil shipments to the United States. The embargo per se was not very important, but the cuts in oil production had a major impact on oil prices. The costs to the world were immense, measured in the tens of billions of dollars, slower economic growth, rapid inflation, and, for Americans, annoying lines at gas pumps.

For most of the 1980s, the United States was rather complacent about oil. Prices dropped sharply in the mid-1980s and then remained relatively stable. It was believed that markets were working to assure adequate supplies. But by 1990 several trends had emerged. First, domestic U.S. production was declining and imports were nearing 50 percent of total consumption. Second, other sources of supply, including the former Soviet Union, were beginning to decline. Third, spare production capacity around the world was shrinking, leaving Saudi Arabia and Iraq as the only countries with major potential to expand production significantly in the future.

One need not be an alarmist to note that sometime in the 1990s the Arabs may once again conclude that they have a usable oil weapon. And in some future Arab-Israeli war, there may be a concerted policy to withhold supplies in the hope of influencing U.S., European, and Japanese opinion. In short, another oil shock cannot be entirely ruled out, although it would certainly not be on the scale of the 1970s. Although different interests would govern policy considerations in key Arab capitals in normal times, in the event of an Arab-Israeli war Arab oil powers might be expected to try to coordinate their oil policies, at least for a period of time, in order to gain diplomatic leverage.

Why Peace Remains an Imperative

We can conclude from this overview that the Arab-Israeli conflict in the 1990s, although not likely to endanger vital U.S. security interests, will remain a potentially serious threat. A whole range of U.S. interests would be well served if the conflict were solved through diplomatic means. It is imperative that the Arab-Israeli conflict move toward resolution in order to avoid the dangers enumerated below.

- The Egyptian-Israeli cornerstone for regional stability could begin to crumble in the absence of further movement in the peace process. Egypt could come under pressure from other Arab states and from its own Islamic movements to curtail its relationship with Israel. If "cold peace" were to turn to "cold war" on the Egyptian-Israeli front, U.S.-Egyptian ties would also suffer.[10] U.S. access to military facilities could be restricted; joint training exercises could be suspended; and the arms supply relationship could be brought to a sudden halt.
- Political extremism, including religious revivalism, could gain ground in the absence of a settlement. This sentiment is likely to be harshly anti-American and anti-Israeli. Growing extremism may be manifested in acts of terrorism against U.S. citizens. Frustration over lack of progress in the peace process may feed Islamic sentiment, particularly among Palestinians, Jordanians, and Egyptians. The growth of such sentiment would add to the difficulties involved in maintaining good ties with Egypt in particular.

- Pro-Western regimes in the region (Egypt, Jordan, Saudi Arabia, etc.) may come under popular pressure to sever some contacts with the United States. Defense cooperation is probably the most sensitive, and therefore vulnerable, issue in the view of populist opposition leaders. But U.S. cultural and economic programs could also be targets, as they were in Iran in the 1980s. Some regimes could be toppled.
- Oil-rich countries may divert more of their money to support for hard-line regimes and for Islamic political movements as a form of insurance; they may come under political pressure to use oil production as a political weapon, as happened in 1973–1974.
- An Arab-Israeli war might be accompanied by the use of surface-to-surface missiles, chemical weapons, and even the threat of nuclear weapons. This could stimulate the desire of other nations in the region and beyond to acquire such capabilities.

Alternatives to War

In an optimistic scenario for the 1990s, continuing negotiations would lead to agreements between Israel and its Arab neighbors. Most likely, any agreements will be implemented over a period of years. In such an environment, Egypt and Israel would remain at peace. Regional issues, such as water, economic cooperation, and arms control, will also be subjects of negotiations.

These developments would create a relatively benign environment for U.S. interests in the region. But for any peace process to succeed, the United States would have to remain heavily involved in Arab-Israeli diplomacy. Left to themselves, Israelis and Palestinians, as well as Israelis and Syrians, are unlikely to take serious steps toward reconciliation.

For this optimistic scenario to be realized, the international community would be required to mobilize substantial financial resources, especially to assist with Palestinian refugee compensation and rehabilitation and to help develop the infrastructure of the West Bank and Gaza. Also, if progress is to be made on the Syrian-Israeli front, a substantial international role in creating a "buffer zone" between the two adversaries may be needed.

A more pessimistic scenario would involve the collapse of the peace process, a return to power of a hard-line Israeli government, growing influence of Islamic radicals in Jordan, Egypt, or in the Palestinian movement, and a resulting heightening of tensions between Israel and its Arab neighbors. Several possible developments, however, could lead to a sudden deterioration of the situation: A change of regime in

Jordan could tempt Israeli hard-liners to "solve the Palestinian problem" on the East Bank; large-scale deportations of Palestinians might take place; Egypt could then react by freezing relations with Israel; Syria could launch a propaganda offensive in a bid to mobilize Arab support for a hard-line stance against Israel; or Iraq, in a renewed bid for leadership in the Arab world, might once again find itself moving toward a confrontation with Israel, although it will be many years before any regime in Baghdad can afford to concern itself with Israel. In these dangerous circumstances, much would depend upon how the United States reacted. Could it contain such a volatile mixture? If war were to break out, could it be contained and could it be terminated quickly?

Some hard-line elements in Israel seem convinced that this pessimistic scenario is the best that can be hoped for. They seem persuaded that they can hold off Arab military threats indefinitely, especially now that the cold war is over. They also take heart from the likely arrival of very large numbers of immigrants from the former Soviet Union in coming years. But even the arrival of some one million Jewish immigrants from the former Soviet Union during the 1990s will not relieve Israel's need to address the Palestinian issue. It will simply mean that Palestinians will not outnumber Israelis in the territory now under Israeli control until the second decade of the twenty-first century instead of the first decade.

Divisions Within Israel

Both Israeli society and Israeli politics are deeply divided over the question of how best to deal with the Palestinian challenge. Two main schools of thought exist. One, on the left wing of the political spectrum and in charge of the government since mid-1992 is prepared to relinquish control of much of the West Bank and Gaza in favor of a Palestinian/Jordanian government if several conditions are met: The details of any agreement would have to be freely negotiated; a lengthy transitional period would have to be provided in order to test the viability of new political and security arrangements; Jerusalem would remain undivided; and Israel's security concerns would have to be allayed. A motivating consideration for Israelis of this persuasion is the concern that, within twenty years or so, the Arab population in all of the territories now under Israeli control may well outnumber the Jewish population, even if there were large numbers of new immigrants.

The members of the right wing of the Israeli political spectrum are less concerned with the demographics. They seem to believe that the new wave of immigration will help redress the balance in Israel's favor. Their key concern is to retain the integrity of Eretz Israel (the Land of Israel), for both security and ideological reasons. According to this view, the Arabs living in the Occupied Territories can have autonomy or they can leave; in either case, they will not play a role within the Israeli body politic. The most that Likud leaders seem willing to consider are steps that would result in a modest degree of self-government for the Palestinians in the West Bank and Gaza. Any role for the PLO, and any type of a Palestinian state, are ruled out.

Labor's narrow victory in 1992 does not mean that its ascendancy is assured. But for the foreseeable future, Israel is likely to be led by parties that are prepared to negotiate seriously with their Arab neighbors, and most Israelis seem prepared to make concessions in return for peace and security.

Politics Among the Palestinians

The major achievement of the PLO over the years has been its ability to forge a Palestinian consensus around nationalist symbols. As an umbrella organization, the PLO always had within it many different factions, but the mainstream has been committed to some form of Palestinian statehood since the mid-1970s. Some Arab nationalists on the left and some Islamic revivalists on the right have rejected the idea of a Palestinian state, but the mainstream has dominated the agenda.

By late 1988 PLO leader Yasir Arafat had moved the consensus position a notch further by publicly endorsing a two-state solution, that is, a Palestinian state alongside Israel. A Palestinian state was in fact declared and Arafat was named its first president. Arafat also accepted UN Resolutions 242 and 338, recognized Israel's right to exist, and renounced terrorism. This led to the opening of a U.S.-PLO dialogue.

Much of the impetus for these developments had come from the Palestinian *intifada*. When the Palestinians began to stand up to Israeli occupation they began to feel a sense of pride. In this frame of mind, it was probably easier for Palestinians to articulate the two-state strategy than it had been in the past when they had felt weak and besieged. The *intifada* also convinced King Husayn to drop Jordan's claims to the West Bank.

Within the Occupied Territories, the *intifada* resulted in a growing militancy on the part of the hard-pressed Palestinian population. Many sympathized with political tendencies that were considerably tougher than those of the mainstream of the PLO. For example, the HAMAS movement (HAMAS is an acronym from the Arabic words for

Islamic Resistance Movement, and it also means "zeal" or "enthusiasm"), which called for an Islamic state in all of Palestine was much stronger inside the territories, especially in Gaza, than it was in the PLO on the outside. Similarly, the leftist factions, which advocated armed struggle and called for involvement of the Arab states in the struggle, carried more weight on the inside than on the outside.

Despite these differing tendencies, the PLO has managed to keep a grip on the mainstream of Palestinian politics, although Arafat's personal leadership has been increasingly questioned. And if the PLO's diplomatic efforts were to fail, then challenges might become even more visible. Would the Palestinian mainstream revert to a harder line? Might Arafat be replaced? Would the leadership within the Occupied Territories replace the PLO, and would it be more militant or less militant? Might armed struggle and terrorism once again be the favored tactics for significant numbers of Palestinians?

All of these questions first came to the fore in May 1990 when a small faction of the PLO led by Abu-l-Abbas carried out a sea-borne military operation near Tel Aviv. Although there were no casualties, the United States labeled the raid a terrorist act and insisted that PLO Chairman Arafat discipline Abu-l-Abbas. Adding to the tension in U.S.-PLO relations, Washington vetoed a resolution at the United Nations that called for sending a team to the Occupied Territories to report on conditions there. In these circumstances, and with many Palestinians criticizing Arafat for having given up too much already, the PLO leadership was unwilling to meet U.S. conditions. President Bush responded by suspending the U.S.-PLO dialogue. With no movement in the peace process and no dialogue, the center of gravity in the Palestinian movement drifted toward a harder line. It was precisely in these circumstances that Saddam Husayn invaded Kuwait. Not surprisingly, many Palestinians, already frustrated by their powerlessness, saw in the Iraqi leader a potential ally. Although it condemned Iraq's occupation of Kuwait, the PLO seemed to side with Iraq as the crisis wore on, thus earning the deep enmity of the regimes in the Gulf in particular and further alienating the United States and moderate Israeli opinion. As a result, the PLO found itself in an isolated position when the Madrid peace conference convened in late 1991. The PLO was obliged to remain in the shadows at the conference, agreeing to the participation of non-PLO Palestinians within a joint Jordanian-Palestinian delegation. In the subsequent negotiations, however, the Palestinian team continued to consult closely with Arafat and it was his support that allowed them to stand up to skeptics in the Occupied Territories.

Egypt's Role

When it signed a peace treaty with Israel in 1979 Egypt changed the politics of the Arab world. By 1989 most Arab regimes had accepted the inevitability of eventually reaching some form of agreement with Israel, only if the Palestinians could be minimally satisfied with a state of their own in the West Bank and Gaza. Having patched up its ties to the PLO, Cairo emerged in the late 1980s as a player in the Arab-Israeli game once again. First it helped to broker the U.S.-PLO dialogue; then, in close cooperation with Washington, it tried to pave the way for the opening of Israeli-Palestinian talks.

It is the Egyptian establishment and not the public at large who have the most interest in playing a major role in the peace process. There is little enthusiasm in Egypt for the idea of peace with Israel, but it is an accepted fact of life. The Egyptian press and academic circles are generally quite hostile to Israel, and growing Islamic sentiment reinforces this tendency. Many Egyptians appear to be tired of the whole Palestinian issue and are much more concerned with internal affairs. But the government wants to show that its initial decision to make peace with Israel was not a mistake. It recognizes the value in Washington of Egyptian cooperation in the peace process, and it wants to avoid conditions that might strengthen the hand of hard-liners in Israel. Thus serious efforts will continue to be made to keep the peace process alive. For example, Egypt worked hard to bring Syria into the framework of peace talks and to find an acceptable formula for Palestinian representation.

Egypt's role in the formal peace process is inevitably rather limited, although Cairo serves as a useful channel for Israeli messages to other Arab leaders, and the Egyptians have undertaken to try to persuade some of the Arab parties to negotiate seriously. In addition, Egypt participates in the multilateral talks, especially on arms control. But Egypt cannot be an impartial mediator between Israel and the Palestinians, or between Israel and Syria. On substantive issues, Egypt is bound to side with the Palestinians and with the broad Arab consensus. In addition, for domestic reasons Egypt will not want to be seen to be selling out Palestinian rights. No Egyptian leader will want to get drawn into negotiations over the future of Jerusalem. Egypt does, nonetheless, have a contribution to make.

Meanwhile, U.S.-Egyptian relations will continue to depend on much more than cooperation in the peace process. Close cooperation during the Gulf crisis has contributed greatly to the overall strength of the relationship. But the most serious issues facing Egypt today involve the economic future of the country. Economic reform is essential, but Egyptians feel this must be done gradually to avoid social and political upheavals. They look to the United States for continued economic and military assistance. The United States' agreement to cancel $7 billion in military debts in late 1990 was welcomed in Cairo.

Syria, Jordan, and Iraq

Syria is the most powerful of Israel's neighbors. It has the capability to launch large-scale military operations as well as to harass Israeli forces through surrogates in Lebanon. It does not, and will not, have the capacity to defeat Israel in battle. Syria's President Hafiz al-Asad seems to understand these military realities, and the Israeli-Syrian front has been remarkably quiet over the years.

Syria may take a tough line in negotiations with Israel, but Asad seems to recognize that he no longer has a realistic military option. Syria has actively joined the Madrid peace conference and the follow-on bilateral negotiations. Direct negotiations have taken place. Syria has spoken of "total peace for total withdrawal" and Asad has expressed his view that the Golan Heights could be demilitarized as part of a settlement. None of these hints necessarily adds up to a fundamental change in the Syrian position, but Syria seems to have significantly shifted its positions in light of changes in the regional and international balance of power.

Jordan, of course, has a keen interest in how the Arab-Israeli conflict might be resolved. The Hashemite regime fears that it could be the victim of an unending Arab-Israeli conflict, especially if Palestinians are forced out of the West Bank into Jordan. But Jordan shows no sign of wanting to resume its former responsibility for the West Bank. Meanwhile, Jordan must tend to its fragile economy, manage its complicated inter-Arab relations, recover from the damage done to its diplomatic position by its support for Iraq during the Gulf crisis, and deal with the ferment unleashed by a bold, but potentially risky, experiment with elections. In short, Jordan remains a crucial but heavily constrained player in the peace process.

Iraq has generally been distant from Arab-Israeli diplomacy, but Israelis looked at Iraq with concern once the Iran-Iraq war came to an end in 1988. Initially, they noted signs that Baghdad was prepared to support the Arab consensus on negotiating a peace agreement with Israel. Saddam Husayn explicitly acknowledged Israel as a fact in the region and spoke of its security concerns. Since that time, Iraq maintained a large, battle-tested army and, by early 1990, seemed to be on a confrontation course with Israel. Iraq invaded Kuwait in August 1990. The Persian Gulf War with its Iraqi Scud missiles landing in Israel will not soon be forgotten, but the Israelis see Iraq as significantly weaker and therefore less of a threat than before the crisis. They will now keep a careful watch for signs that Iraq is rebuilding its missile or nuclear programs.

Policy Guidelines

Even the most pessimistic scenario for the Arab-Israeli conflict must stop short of a situation in which there is the danger of large-scale U.S. military engagements in the region. In addition, the "oil weapon"—even if it is used in the 1990s—will probably have less dramatic consequences for the world economy than it did in the 1970s, primarily due to the existence of larger reserve stocks and a better understanding of how the oil market operates. With reduced danger of U.S. military involvement and of oil shocks, the Arab-Israeli conflict of the 1990s will present less of a threat to U.S. interests than it did in the 1970s.

Offsetting these reassuring tendencies are the arrival of very lethal weapons on the Middle East scene—conventional, chemical, and nuclear. In the hands of states, militias, or terrorists, these can do great damage, including damage to U.S. interests. It is worth remembering that in the space of one year—1983–1984—the U.S. embassy in Lebanon was bombed twice, as was the Marine barracks, with well over three hundred killed. In addition, one of the most costly foreign policy fiascoes—the Iran-contra affair—was driven by an understandable but misplaced desire to free hostages. So, even short of the dangers of Arab-Israeli war, superpower confrontations, or disruptions in oil supplies, conflict in the Middle East region would place U.S. interests at serious risk. This means that the United States will continue to have an interest in supporting moderate regimes in the Arab world through economic and military assistance, promotion of the peace process whenever possible, and through attempts with others to curb the introduction of destabilizing military technologies such as surface-to-surface missiles and chemical and nuclear weapons.

A solution to the Arab-Israeli conflict in the 1990s would result in the reduction of threats to U.S. interests as well as significant changes in the regional political scene. A peaceful Middle East might allow a degree of political liberalization and economic reform to take hold. Spending on arms could be reduced, the region might then become less dangerous. If, by contrast, the situation deteriorates, extremists could gain ground and U.S. interests might suffer even in the absence of a full-scale war and oil embargoes. The risks in the future entail the erosion of the political, social, and economic order in the region that, ultimately, will make it difficult for the United States or other Western countries to maintain positions of influence in the region. Iran and Lebanon stand as testimony to how inhospitable such a Middle East would be for U.S. interests.

The United States still has a substantial interest in promoting an Arab-Israeli peace settlement. The odds of success in reaching an overall Arab-Israeli settlement in the coming years are better than they have been in years. Combined with serious efforts to prevent nuclear proliferation in the region and encouragement of political and economic reforms, the peace process will remain a crucial centerpiece of American Middle East policy in the 1990s.

With the end of the cold war, the Arab-Israeli conflict is no longer such a major threat to U.S. national interests. Nonetheless, it remains a source of instability and tension in an important part of the world. Therefore, U.S.-led diplomatic efforts to find a negotiated solution to the conflict will most likely continue. The process will be difficult and will require U.S. leadership, but there are some favorable signs, especially in the changes in the Syrian position. The end of the cold war has helped advance the chances for Arab-Israeli peace. Barring a turn toward isolationism, the United States should remain a full partner in the search for a negotiated settlement of a conflict that has cost the world too much already.

Notes

1. See William B. Quandt, *Camp David: Peacemaking and Politics* (Washington, D.C.: Brookings Institution, 1986).

2. On the origins of the *intifada*, see Ze'ev Schiff and Ehud Ya'ari, *Intifada: The Palestinian Uprising—Israel's Third Front* (New York: Simon and Schuster, 1989).

3. Geoffrey Kemp, with Shelley A. Stahl, *The Control of the Middle East Arms Race* (Washington, D.C.: Carnegie, 1991).

4. On Israel's nuclear program, see Seymour Hersh, *The Samson Option: Israel's Nuclear Arsenal and American Foreign Policy* (New York: Random House, 1991).

5. Joseph S. Nye, Jr. and Roger K. Smith, eds., *After the Storm: Lessons from the Gulf War* (New York: Madison Books, 1992).

6. See Alasdair Drysdale and Raymond Hinnebusch, *Syria and the Middle East Peace Process* (New York: Council on Foreign Relations Press, 1991).

7. After Iraq's defeat in the "Desert Storm" campaign, UN inspectors gained access to Iraqi nuclear facilities and were able to determine that a substantial research and development program had been put in place. Several different technologies were being experimented with to develop enriched uranium and plutonium. The UN inspectors estimated that the program could have resulted in Iraq's

acquiring a small nuclear arsenal by the mid-1990s. No other country in the region, apart from Israel, is known to be close to a nuclear capability, but one can assume that Israel and the United States will keep a close eye on Iran, Syria, Egypt, Libya, and Algeria.

8. See William B. Quandt, *Peace Process: American Diplomacy and the Arab-Israeli Conflict Since 1967* (Washington, D.C.: Brookings Institution, 1993).

9. Daniel Yergin, *The Prize: The Epic Quest for Oil, Money, and Power* (New York: Simon & Schuster, 1991).

10. William B. Quandt, *The United States and Egypt: An Essay on Policy for the 1990s* (Washington, D.C.: Brookings Institution, 1990).

Suggested Reading

Cobban, Helena, *The Superpowers and the Syrian-Israeli Conflict: Beyond Crisis Management?* New York: Praeger, 1991.

Freedman, Robert O., ed., *The Intifada: Its Impact on Israel, the Arab World, and the Superpowers*, Miami: Florida International University Press, 1991.

Presidential Study Group, *Building For Peace: An American Strategy for the Middle East*, Washington, D.C.: Washington Institute for Near East Policy, 1988.

Quandt, William B., ed., *The Middle East: Ten Years After Camp David*, Washington, D.C.: Brookings Institution, 1988.

Saunders, Harold H., *The Other Walls: The Arab-Israeli Peace Process in a Global Perspective*, Princeton: Princeton University Press, 1991.

PERSIAN GULF REGION

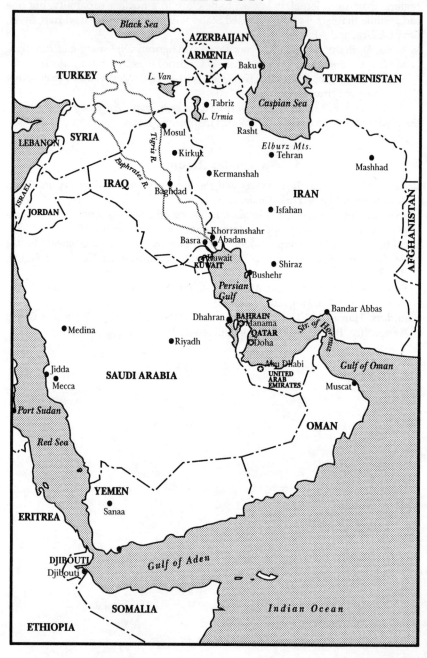

5

The Persian Gulf
After the Storm

Phebe Marr

The 1991 Gulf War may not have been as decisive an event as was originally predicted, but its results will reverberate throughout the region for the remainder of the decade. The war rolled back Saddam Husayn's aggression in Kuwait; weakened Iraq's military power; reinforced the existing state system in the region; and shored up Gulf Cooperation Council (GCC) regimes likely to support oil policies favorable to the West. But Desert Storm did not solve the multiple underlying problems that have precipitated two Gulf wars over the past decade and that are likely to shape the configuration of regional power in the future. As a result, the Persian Gulf will remain an area where instability is endemic. If some progress is not made in addressing underlying problems, war could again become a reality before the end of the decade.

Strategic Dilemmas and Political Dynamics

Compounding existing tensions are basic structural imbalances in the Gulf. A region without cultural or political cohesion, the Persian Gulf comprises countries and societies at varying levels of development and with differing resource bases that share a common body of water of critical importance to all of them. Iran, the largest and most populous state, has substantial but declining oil resources, over 1,100 miles of shoreline on the Gulf, and partial control of the Strait of Hormuz,

The views expressed in this article are those of the author and do not reflect the official policy or position of the National Defense University, the Department of Defense, or the U.S. Government.

which gives it considerable power projection capabilities. Iraq, the second largest state, has but a third of Iran's population but has greater proven oil reserves. However, it is barely a Gulf power, with less than 20 miles of shoreline controlled by Iran on one side and Kuwait on the other. Saudi Arabia and the GCC states, although controlling virtually all of the shoreline on the Arab side of the Gulf have less than a quarter of the combined population of Iran and Iraq. These microstates do not have the capacity to mount a credible military defense of their territory and are vulnerable to the superior military power of their northern neighbors. GCC strength, particularly that of Saudi Arabia, lies in its vast oil reserves (considerably larger than those in either Iran or Iraq) and its highly developed production facilities. These factors give the GCC a commanding position in influencing production and pricing of oil, and therefore, the economic well-being of the other regional states.

Not only is the balance of power in the Gulf inherently unequal but the potential for conflict also remains high. The societies of the Gulf are undergoing fundamental change in the process of modernization and their future political direction is uncertain. Societal change is taking place, moreover, within countries harboring animosities and suspicions toward their neighbors that can be traced back centuries. They also face tensions of more recent origin, arising from differences over resource allocation, conflicting ideologies, and competing national interests. These differences have led to the outbreak of war twice in the past decade. Though armed conflict is unlikely in the near term, primarily because of the exhaustion of Iran and Iraq, the most likely adversaries, existing constraints may diminish as both countries rebuild their economies and reconstitute their military forces. The sources of potential conflict are many and varied but the following are chief among them.

Arab-Persian Rivalry

The Gulf presents a genuine cultural fault line dividing the Persians to the West and the Arabs to the East. Behind linguistic and ethnic divisions lie differences of political culture and centuries of fears and anxieties that will inhibit cooperation, even under conditions of peaceful coexistence. Arab countries, including Iraq, share a common linguistic and ethnic heritage that owes much to the desert traditions of egalitarianism and pride in the Arabic of the Quran. Iran draws its heritage from its pre-Islamic Persian literary tradition, its ancient civilization, and a tradition of Persian kingship and empire. Centuries of competition in the Gulf between these two peoples remains and continues to define the limits to cooperation, as well as to shape the potential for a Gulfwide collective security system.

Unresolved Boundaries. Overlaying the age-old rivalry between the Persians and the Arabs are newer boundary disputes emanating from the establishment of the modern nation-state system in the area early in the twentieth century. Boundaries between Iran and Iraq, between Iraq and Kuwait, and between several GCC states are unresolved and fuel local tensions. Disagreement over the Shatt al-Arab boundary between Iran and Iraq was a proximate cause of the Iran-Iraq War. The border between Kuwait and Iraq is likely to remain contentious, despite the internationally sanctioned 1992 demarcation of the UN boundary commission, which Iraq has refused to accept. Iran and the UAE both lay claim to three Gulf islands, Abu Musa and the two Tunbs, which lie athwart shipping channels at the foot of the Gulf. Among the GCC states as well there are numerous boundary disputes that constrain cooperation, including a conflict between Qatar and Bahrain over the Hawar Islands, and, more seriously, between Saudi Arabia and Oman, over large parts of Omani territory.

Ideology. The very different political ideologies of the main Gulf countries will, at best, make communication and easing of tensions difficult, and, under certain circumstances, could be used as a justification for acts of aggression. The government of Iran espouses a Shiite version of the Islamic revival. Although the messianic drive of the Iranian Revolution has abated, it has not been entirely tamed. Rather, Iran's revolutionary impulse has been infused with traditional Iranian nationalism and the long-standing assumption that Iran, by virtue of its size and population, should be the Gulf hegemon. However, psychological and political appeals to Islam, with Iran as its champion, will continue to be used as an instrument of foreign policy, particularly among the Shiite populations on the Arab side of the Gulf.

Iraq's current leadership advocates a secular form of nationalism, primarily Arab in orientation. Of all the Gulf countries, Iraq is probably the most secular, which puts it at odds with the religious orientations of both Iran and Saudi Arabia. Baghdad's espousal of Arab nationalism and its bid for Arab world leadership will continue to be perceived as posing a threat to Saudi Arabian leadership and to the governments of the Gulf states.

Saudi Arabia is the leading proponent of a strict Sunni orthodoxy, often erroneously identified as Wahhabism, after its founder, Muhammad ibn Abd al-Wahhab. This orientation favors social conservatism, preservation of the status quo, and strong ties with the

United States and the West. Saudi Arabia has been assiduous in promoting its version of Islam in the Muslim world, often dubbed "American Islam" by others.

Ethnic and Sectarian Separatism. In the Gulf, as elsewhere, the emergence of ethnic and sectarian separatism also threatens regional order and stability. For example, as a separate Kurdish political structure takes shape in northern Iraq, its impact may be felt in Kurdish-inhabited areas in Iran and Turkey, increasing the potential for cross-border conflict between Iraq and Turkey, Iraq and Iran, and Iran and Turkey.

In the south of Iraq the emergence of Shiite consciousness has encouraged Iranian intervention in Iraq's domestic politics and could affect the Shiite populations in Kuwait, Bahrain, and the eastern province of Saudi Arabia. Indeed, fissiparous ethnic and religious forces are reminders of the artificiality of the nation-state concept in the Gulf and the brittleness of recently created boundaries.

Regime Survival. All Gulf states have authoritarian regimes that rest their staying power on a fragile base of legitimacy. Regime survival is the primary, if not the only, goal of many of these regimes. In an environment in which state interests clash and mutual suspicions abound, the temptation to take advantage of a rival's internal problems as a means of realizing regional ambitions often proves to be irresistible. Ultimately, such temptations threaten to produce local conflicts.

Control over Oil Production and Pricing. The oil factor was the major precipitant of Iraq's incursion into Kuwait. In an international market beset with falling oil prices, and pressed by creditors for repayment of debt, Iraq accused Kuwait and the UAE of "economic warfare" against it by producing more oil than allowed by their OPEC quotas. Competition and, ultimately, conflict over oil prices and market share may become more prevalent as Iran and Iraq confront the challenge of rebuilding their economies and as the GCC states attempt to recoup the costs of the 1991 Gulf War.

Many of these potential conflicts are crosscutting rather than reinforcing. Some governments may adopt positions on issues, such as oil quotas, that are at variance with others, such as ethnic separatism. In time, manifold conflicts, the prevailing atmosphere of tension and suspicion in the aftermath of a decade of war, and the zero-sum competitive attitude that prevails throughout the region make avoidance of war problematic. Moreover, given the dynamics of the region, conflict could embroil others, leading to a collapse not only of regimes but even of states. Such alterations in the regional balance of power are difficult to predict. We must acknowledge, on the positive side, that one of the most significant changes in the regional balance—the merger of two hitherto independent countries, North and South Yemen—occurred by relatively pacific means in 1990 and without disturbing the regional equilibrium.

To understand the nature of the changes likely to occur in the Persian Gulf, it is necessary to examine in depth the current situation of the three major actors in the Gulf—Iran, Iraq, and the GCC states. This chapter will address several overlapping questions: (1) What forces are likely to affect the distribution of power in the Gulf? (2) What are the relative strengths and weaknesses of the three major Gulf players? (3) Are these strengths and weaknesses likely to undergo significant alteration? (4) What are the foreign policy orientations of these states? (5) Are they likely to favor the status quo or to seek change? (6) If they desire change, will it generate conflict or adversely affect U.S. and Western interests in the Gulf?

Iran: The Potential Gulf Hegemon?

Iran has the potential to dominate the Gulf by virtue of its population size, its land area, its geostrategic position, and its material resources. However, Iran's potential probably will not be fully realized for much of the decade because of the profound economic and social trauma experienced during the Iranian Revolution and the eight years of war with Iraq. Following the Iran-Iraq War, Iran experienced a brief respite from the downward trend of its economic and political situation, due to several factors: First was the death of Khomeini in June 1989 and his replacement by a collective leadership dominated by more pragmatic elements, notably Ali Akbar Hashimi Rafsanjani. The new leaders emphasized economic development and declared a willingness to seek limited accommodation with the West. Second, Iran was a major beneficiary of the 1991 Gulf War, which tilted the balance of power in Iran's favor by weakening its major rival. Third, Iran has benefited from the collapse of the Soviet Union. The removal of a threatening superpower on its northern border, and the resultant establishment in its stead of a buffer zone of weak states, has altered Iran's security problems, mainly for the better.

The Economic Dimension

Even with such favorable circumstances, however, Iran has encountered difficulty in efforts to recapture its prerevolutionary economic momentum. A decade of internal revolutionary fervor and war have greatly eroded Iran's infrastructure, lowered living standards, and raised the economic and human costs of reconstruction. From 1977, Iran's peak production year prior to the Revolution, to 1989, Iran's gross domestic product (GDP) declined 15 percent—on a per capita basis, 46 percent. Living standards, as measured by private consumption per capita, declined 40 percent; and investment in the economy declined 65 percent. In the same time period, unemployment may have risen, to claim one-quarter of the work force; if disguised unemployment is added, it probably reached 40 percent.[1] War damage to factories, homes, hospitals, schools, bridges, dams, electrical power stations, irrigation works, oil and petrochemical installations, ports, and railroads was extensive and all required reconstruction.

Although the infrastructure may be easily repaired, it is not so easy to replace the lost human resources. In 1988 the Iranian government estimated that 160,000 Iranians had been killed during the war with Iraq, although the unofficial (and more accurate) toll was probably 300,000—with up to 700,000 wounded; over half the wounded were permanently disabled. Some 1.6 million Iranians, mainly from war zones, were left homeless.[2] In addition, revolution and war have depleted the population of educated and skilled workers. Due to emigration, there is a substantial shortage of college graduates, and only about one-half million technical specialists remain in the country.[3] According to one estimate, half the physicians in Iran fled the country, which led the government to employ Indian doctors to make up for the shortfall.

To these melancholy statistics must be added a rapid population growth, which is expected to double Iran's population by the year 2010 to approximately one hundred million. Unless oil revenues and profits from other productive sectors significantly increase, Iran may not be able to raise living standards appreciably. Not only is growth necessary but structural changes are necessary as well. Inflation is rife; the gap between rich and poor is growing; and many existing investments in the industrial sector will not produce increased employment for the next several years. Since the end of the Iran-Iraq War, Iran has accumulated foreign debt, which rose to $15 billion in 1991.[4] Although Iran has begun to liberalize its economic policies, private investment may be slow in arriving. Iran's need for foreign investment and inflows of technology and technocrats gives the West a measure of potential influence over Iran. If Iran does not achieve a period of sustained, high-level, noninflationary growth, it will face continued—if not rising—unemployment, inflation, poor living standards, and a repetition of the riots that afflicted its cities in 1990 and 1991. This, in turn, could threaten the stability of the regime.

Domestic Political Forces

Iran also faces a fluid domestic political environment. Worsening economic conditions could provide social and political ammunition for extremists and hard-liners inside Iran. Although "ideology has receded as a motive force in Iranian foreign policy" and pragmatists appear to have control of the reins of power, a number of episodes in 1992 were sharp reminders that Islamic militants are still contenders for power.[5] Although the militants do not dominate Parliament, they are entrenched in other sectors (with funds for patronage as well as charity). During 1992 the militants gained political influence, suggesting that Iran's messianic revolution has not yet run out of steam or the urge to export the revolution been dissipated. Militants continue to support Islamic movements, including the Hizballa in Lebanon, the Islamic Salvation Front in Algeria, and the Islamic government of Sudan. If these efforts to undermine conservative leadership groups continue, they are certain to feed tensions, not only in the Gulf, but much further afield, undercutting the more pragmatic image that Rafsanjani is attempting to project.

Ethnic Separatism

A third element that threatens to affect Iran's stability is a little-studied human fault line now emerging in the north and west. It centers around the ethnic separatism in the Islamic republics of the former Soviet Union, which continues to find expression in rebellions within the new states and in border wars that could undermine Iran's territorial integrity. Some 40 percent of Iran's population is composed of ethnic minorities; most of these—Armenians, Azeris, Kurds, Turkomans, and Baluchis—ring Iran's Persian heartland and straddle borders with its neighbors.[6] There are smaller groups of Hazars, Kazakhs, Pathans, and Uzbeks as well. Widening ties with the new states to the north could prove a double-edged sword. This would extend Iranian influence into new northern areas but at the same time sharpen the ethnic self-consciousness of Iran's own minorities.

Iran's domestic stability has already been affected by conflicts on its borders. As a result of the Afghan war, Iran hosts about two million Afghan refugees; they constitute an economic burden and could prove to be a destabilizing factor if they do not return home. To the north, Azerbaijani independence raises the prospect of Azeri ethnic nationalism spreading to Iran. Azeri separatism resulted in the establishment of a short-lived republic in that province in 1920, and it surfaced again more recently in 1979–1980 over a struggle for power among the clerics. In the northeast, Turkish ethnic consciousness could spread into Iran from the independent republic of Turkmenistan. Iran must also worry about pan-Turkism encouraged by Ankara's influence among the Turkish-speaking population. Finally, Iran has already expressed concern over the emergence of Kurdish separatist aspirations in Iraq and their spread amongst their own Kurdish population.[7]

Iran's Rearmament

These persistent concerns, however, must be evaluated against the growing assertiveness in Iran's foreign policy and its rearmament program, both of which indicate the beginnings of a search for a new role in the Gulf and beyond.

In 1989 Iran concluded an agreement with Moscow for modern weapons, including MiG-29s, T-72 tanks, missiles, air deterrent radar systems, and submarines. Much of this equipment was designed to replenish losses incurred in the Iran-Iraq War and to modernize Iranian forces. By 1991 Iran had only 40 percent of the tank force it had possessed in 1980; its navy had acquired no new ships, and its air force was a shambles, with only 70 to 80 planes.[8] In 1992 the troop strength of its regular army was about 500,000; its elite Revolutionary Guard force numbered about 170,000.

Iran's first modest rearmament program was accelerated early in 1991 when Iran requested more advanced Soviet equipment along with Russian training to use it. When this agreement is fulfilled, Iran may have 100 MiG-29 fighters, help in constructing a MiG assembly plant, SU-24 long-range fighter bombers, MiG-27 fighter bombers, MiG-311 long-range intercepts, SU-27 fighters, and two air reconnaissance and early warning aircraft. By the middle of the decade, the Iranian air force is likely once again to be the largest and strongest in the Gulf, with about 400 front- and second-line planes.[9] It may even get a Russian supersonic bomber with a radius covering all of the Middle East, the Indian subcontinent, and southeast and central Europe.[10] The newly acquired submarines, which began reaching Iran in 1992, would not be a match for U.S. nuclear-powered subs in deep water, but in the shallow waters of the Persian Gulf they could threaten shipping. In addition, Iran has Chinese Silkworm antiship missiles, which it can launch from ships or from the ground.

More disturbing than the growth of these conventional forces have been developments in the nuclear field. In 1987 Pakistan sent over 30 nuclear scientists to train Iranians, and in the same year Iran signed an agreement with Argentina for enriched uranium for a research reactor. China is also training Iranians in nuclear technology and Iran has purchased a small calutron from China (used for isotope separation), although it is not expected to be used in weapons research. These developments do not yet constitute a nuclear weapons program, but a number of scholars do not rule out the possibility that Iran could join the nuclear club by the end of the decade.[11] Iran is also engaged in a chemical weapons program and has announced that it will start mass production of long-range missiles.

The acquisition of advanced military technology by Iran raises contradictions for Iran and for U.S. regional policy. Some rebuilding of Iran's depleted military establishment is necessary for its defense. In 1992 its major Gulf adversary, Iraq, still had a military force of approximately 400,000, roughly comparable to that of Iran, as well as a larger supply of tanks and ground equipment. To achieve equilibrium, the United States has increased arms sales to GCC clients and has augmented its military presence in the Gulf. But the breadth of Iran's military buildup, its direction (high-technology weapons, long-range missiles, chemicals, and submarines), and indications that Iran may pursue a nuclear weapons program are worrisome and suggest that Iran is seeking to enhance its power projection capabilities. The implications of such power enhancement for the U.S. presence in the Gulf are addressed elsewhere.

Iran's Foreign Policy

Iran's foreign policy is likely to focus on four areas: the Persian Gulf, Iran's new northern frontier, events in Russia, and the U.S. military posture in the region.

Iran's Policy in the Gulf. Iran, under any foreseeable regime, will continue to regard the Gulf as the primary theater for its foreign policy. There is no doubt that Iran hopes to play the predominant role in the region, predicated on such factors as its size, extensive shoreline, and lengthy history of paramountcy. Although such a role may be regarded as "primacy" in Iran, it will be seen as "hegemonic" on the Arab side of the Gulf.

Under Rafsanjani, Iran has moved to accommodate the GCC countries, easing tensions that reached a peak during the Iran-Iraq War, when most GCC states supported Iraq. Iran restored diplomatic relations with Kuwait; signed commercial agreements with Bahrain, Oman, Qatar, and the UAE; and began a rapprochement with Saudi Arabia.

Whether Iran's rapprochement will be fully reciprocated by the Gulf Arabs is problematic. The GCC states harbor lingering anxieties about Iran's power aspirations in the Gulf, the possible resurgence of its messianic ambitions, and Iran's hostility toward the GCC's Western allies. In the past, Iran has frequently overstepped the bounds of behavior acceptable to the GCC, causing serious setbacks in attempts at détente. Though tensions with Saudi Arabia have diminished, cooperation between Iran and the strongest of the GCC countries will be hampered by a number of factors: doctrinal divergence between Sunni and Shiite Islam, opposing views regarding the Islamic revival, sharp competition for dominance in the Gulf, and above all, divergence over oil policy—Iran is likely to seek higher prices and a greater share of the market than Saudi Arabia is willing to concede.

For much of the coming decade, however, Iran's Gulf policy is likely to focus on Iraq. None of the issues that led to the Iran-Iraq War have been resolved, and the two have yet to sign a peace treaty. Despite Saddam Husayn's verbal commitment to recognize the 1975 boundary on the Shatt al-Arab, by 1993 no action had as yet been taken by Baghdad to formalize this agreement.

Although Iran does not want a revived Baath regime in Iraq, neither does it seek a collapse of Iraq, leading to ethnic or sectarian fragmentation. The latter would set a bad example for Iran's own ethnic communities. Thus, though Iran extended limited support to the Shiite insurgents in the south of Iraq after the 1991 Gulf War, such assistance was not sufficient to enable the insurgents to win. Tehran is likewise working against the establishment of an independent Kurdish state in the north of Iraq.

Iran's Northern Frontier. Iran's second security policy concern is its northern frontier, where it now faces an entirely unsettled situation. Though Tehran wishes to extend its influence into the newly created republics through commercial ties, subventions for Islamic movements, and development of infrastructure links such as roads and pipelines, Iran must also ponder the possible spread of political instability from these republics. Local civil and interstate wars could embroil Iran. Hence, Iran will have to calibrate its wish to extend its influence into the new republics with a felt need for secure borders and stability.

Iran and Russia. Moscow will be a third focus of foreign policy interest for Iran. A certain confluence of interests is already emerging between Moscow and Tehran, as evidenced in a series of economic and military agreements concluded after the Iran-Iraq War.[12] Both share a fear of instability in the new Islamic buffer zone between their two countries. Russia, anxious to curb the spread of Islamic revivalism, may find it useful to strengthen ties with Iran as a potential insurance policy. Iran, unable to obtain arms and technology from the West, may find ties to Russia promising and may have to moderate its policies in the Islamic republics to acquire them. Both countries also share a desire to constrict Western influence, especially that of the United States, within the region.

Beyond these shared interests, however, embryonic frictions are likely to set limits to the relationship. Russia, with its long-standing military, economic, and political ties to the new republics, expects to be the dominant player in Central Asia and the Caucasus. This expectation is bound to vie with Iran's desire to replace the secular Slavic culture with one closer to Iran's Islamic model. Iran can be expected to play on the local population's fears of a perpetuation of Russian imperialism, while Russia has every reason to fear the spread of Islam from Tehran.

Iran's Relations with the United States. Iranian-U.S. relations are likely to remain strained for much of the coming decade. Iran's Islamic regime will probably adopt strategies inimical to Western influence in the region, in particular to a continuing U.S. military presence in the Gulf. An easing of tensions could reduce but would not eliminate the U.S. presence. However, on the one hand, Iran's arms buildup and revived Western fears that Iran is contemplating a nuclear weapons program have already raised alarm signals. The United States may become the main target of Iran's weapons acquisition program. On the other hand, Iran may find its military buildup running counter to its desire to seek improved relations with Western Europe and Japan to meet its need for Western credit and technology. If such ties with the West are not forthcoming, Iran's economy may not escape stagnation as the decade progresses. Western, and especially U.S., attempts to counter nuclear weapons proliferation, most likely through economic restrictions, will militate against a commercial climate that relaxes restrictions on loans and technology.

Finally, Iran, like China, may well find itself the object of criticism by human rights groups. Rafsanjani has already indicated that Iran views human rights criticism as unwarranted intervention in Iran's domestic affairs. Yet, without improved performance, constraints on closer relations with the West will prevail.

Policy Dilemmas

In the new post–cold war environment, both Iran and the United States face significant policy dilemmas. On the one hand, Iran must resolve its conflicting policy objectives of gaining respectability abroad to acquire inflows of investment and technology for domestic development, while not diminishing its ambition to expand its influence both in the Gulf and in the new republics to the north. Clearly, Tehran cannot realize both objectives concurrently.

On the other hand, the United States and the West—and Russia—confront a basic dilemma. Their lending encouragement to Iran's economic development would strengthen those supporting the pragmatic policies of Rafsanjani and his colleagues; but it would also encourage Iran to use its new-found strength to challenge the U.S. position in the Gulf and to acquire weapons that could drastically alter the balance of power in the same region. Should the West continue to constrain Iran's economic development by denying credits, technology, and recognition and should it challenge Iran's position in the Gulf by increasing its military presence there and by continuing arms flows to the GCC, it runs the risk of encouraging conflicts it seeks to avoid. Given these considerations, the United States will probably attempt to tread a fine line between positive and negative incentives: encouraging Iranian pragmatism where possible; using economic incentives to achieve improved behavior; strengthening ties with Moscow to curb Iran's military buildup in nondefensive weaponry; and making its military presence in the Gulf less intrusive and threatening, but nonetheless, potent.

Iraq's Uncertain Future

Among the Persian Gulf countries, Iraq confronts the most uncertain future. Two wars, a widespread and destructive rebellion in 1991, and sanctions on oil sales for several years following the war have resulted in a dramatic decline in Iraq's fortunes. As a result Iraq may face continued economic stagnation. But the 1991 Gulf War has left a legacy of far-reaching problems that a regime hostile to the West cannot readily overcome. Because of Iraq's geostrategic position and the uncertainty of its future, U.S. decision makers will face a challenge in crafting a viable policy toward Iraq.

Iraq in the Power Equation

The events of the past decade have significantly weakened Iraq militarily and economically, but Iraq's regime has shown resilience in rebuilding its economic infrastructure since the end of the 1991 Persian Gulf War. That war inflicted substantial, but selective damage to the country's economy. The most extensive disruptions were directed at the national telecommunications system (with almost half of Iraq's original telephone lines destroyed), the electricity grid (with 17 out of 20 electrical power plants damaged), the country's ground transportation system (particularly roads and bridges), and the petroleum sector (with destruction concentrated on refining, storage, and pipeline facilities). Oil wells suffered little damage, in contrast to those in Kuwait.[13] Damage to Iraq's other primary productive sectors—agriculture, light industry, and construction—was also relatively light. To revive agriculture, the country must replenish depleted stocks of seed and livestock, repair irrigation pumps, and find replacement parts for machinery. Light industry and construction also require spare parts and electrical power to start up.

Despite extensive damage in some sectors, Iraq's ability for reconstruction—without far-reaching external aid—was impressive. Within two years after the termination of hostilities, much of the communications system, the electricity grid, and the road and bridge system had been repaired. As for the petroleum industry, production, refining, and distribution networks were brought up to 70 percent to 80 percent capacity by the end of 1992.[14] In the geographic center of the country, Baghdad and its environs, little war damage was still visible; in the Basra region, which bore the brunt of the war, reconstruction was slower.[15]

The primary difficulty Iraq faces in efforts to rehabilitate its economy lies in the financial realm. The continuation of the international sanctions against the regime depleted Iraq's reserves and the resources of its well-to-do upper classes; no new oil revenue was available to replenish capital. Iraq also faces the need to meet its previously accumulated debt (at least $80 billion owed to Europe, Japan, and the United States), a hangover from the Iran-Iraq War, which gives Iraq a poor international credit position. Because of this debt burden and reparations owed to Kuwait from the 1990 invasion, available revenues are likely to fall well short of reconstruction requirements, even when sanctions are lifted.

The war weakened but did not neutralize Iraq's military capabilities. The Iraqi army preserved an estimated 50 percent of a huge military inventory of approximately 2,400 tanks, 4,400 armored personnel carriers, 1,000–2,000 artillery pieces, and 250 multiple-rocket launchers.[16] The air force suffered more extensive losses. Of an inventory of 700 combat planes at the beginning of the war, Iraq saved not more than 350 to 400; most of these were of poor quality. Over 115 of its best warplanes were flown to Iran, where they were incorporated into that nation's inventory. Nevertheless, Iraq retained almost all of a substantial helicopter gunship fleet.[17]

In the wake of the war, Iraq's army has been restructured. Out of a million-man force at the start of the 1991 Gulf War, the Iraqi armed forces have now been reduced to about 350,000 to 400,000 men. Poorer performing militia and infantry units have been demobilized, leaving the tougher and presumably more loyal Republican Guards as the core of the army. In addition, selected special forces and the regular army's mechanized and mobile forces have been retained. This standing army is still the second largest in the Middle East after that of Israel, and, as of 1992, it was roughly equal to that of Iran in manpower and combat potential.[18] Iraq's power projection capacity has been considerably reduced, but it does retain the ability to maintain control over refractory ethnic and sectarian groups and to defend its frontiers.

Social Consequences of the War

The human and social costs of Iraq's two wars and the 1991 rebellion may have been higher than the economic and military damage. Estimates of the number of Iraqis killed in the eight-year Iran-Iraq War range from 135,000 to 150,000, roughly 4 percent to 5 percent of the country's military-age population.[19] There are no authoritative figures on the 1991 Gulf War losses. The U.S. military originally offered an estimate of 100,000, but more recent calculations have significantly lowered that figure. Some military analysts put war casualities between 10,000 and 30,000. One authoritative study claims that war casualities—dead and wounded—were well below 10,000.[20] To these must be added Iraqis who died in the rebellion, during the Kurdish exodus to the hills, and as a result of malnutrition from war and sanctions. These tentative estimates could add up to a total of 5 to 7 percent of the military-age population over the past decade. In addition to the obvious trauma inflicted on the population by this loss, the reduction of such a high percentage of Iraq's work force, including some of its most skilled professionals, can only impact adversely on Iraq's capacity to produce goods and services. However, one should not overemphasize Iraq's military losses. During the Iran-Iraq War, the government sought to preserve and replenish its skilled manpower pool, allowing students to finish high school and college before being drafted for military service. Iraq retains a substantial educated middle class compared to other developing countries. Much of its human skill level has apparently been preserved, and with it the capacity to organize and to reconstruct war damaged systems. Indeed, the repairs of its infrastructure undertaken in the two years since the Gulf War are ample testimony to the vigor and skills of its productive population.

A further social consequence of the war and the rebellion, brutally repressed by the regime, has been the exacerbation of ethnic and sectarian tensions in Iraq, a factor that does not bode well for national cohesion. The uprising in the south, almost wholly confined to Shiite areas, resulted in such fierce fighting—particularly in the holy cities of Najaf and Karbala—that a legacy of bitterness is bound to remain in the Shiite community. Shiite atrocities against Baathist leaders (often Shiites themselves) and the damage and destruction visited by government forces on holy shrines, including the venerable tomb of Husayn, have left deep and lasting scars. The rebellion and government actions reinforced Shiite alienation from the regime and awakened a distinct Shiite political consciousness.

Even more profound alienation has materialized in the north, where some two million Kurds, at least half the Kurdish population, fled to the mountains or into neighboring Turkey and Iran to escape Iraqi army retribution and the restoration of draconian Iraqi government controls. By early 1992 the majority of Kurds had returned under the protection of UN forces, led by the United States, Britain, France, and the Netherlands. Located in an internationally protected zone north of the 36th degree parallel, the Kurds established a separate government under the leadership of several political parties, notably the Kurdish Democratic Party under Masuud Barzani and the Patriotic Union of Kurdistan under Jalal Talabani. By 1992 they had organized an elected parliament and an executive committee similar to a Western-style cabinet. As this autonomous administration took shape, with support from the international community, it became clear that it would be increasingly difficult to contain the aspirations of Kurds for self-determination within the bounds of Iraqi sovereignty.

The Survival of Saddam Husayn

Although the war, the rebellion, and the international oil sanctions weakened Saddam Husayn and his regime, Husayn managed to survive. In the two years after the war, the military, the secret police, and the party apparatus were partially rebuilt. These, together with the apparent unwillingness of the military or the population to endure further hardships, permitted the regime to perpetuate itself in power. Nonetheless, it still confronts serious liabilities, among the most damaging the loss of control over large portions of Iraqi territory.

In addition to protecting Kurdish territory in the north, the United States, with the support of some of its allies, established a "no-fly" zone over territory south of the 32nd degree parallel, including the holy city of Najaf. This was done to protect the Shiite population from ongoing Iraqi government repression, particularly in marsh areas where a virulent insurgency was underway. In addition, Iraq's southern borders with Kuwait were adjusted—in Kuwait's favor—and a demilitarized zone 10-kilometers (6-miles) wide was monitored by a UN observer force.

Above all, Saddam Husayn lost control over revenues from oil. Despite these difficulties, the government managed the economic crisis shrewdly, allowing the Iraqi currency to float, establishing a free market for goods, and instituting an effective rationing system that provided the population with an estimated 50 percent of its normal intake of food. By selling about 50,000 barrels of oil a day to Jordan; by smuggling essential goods through Jordan, Turkey, and Iran; and by producing at home some of its own commodities Iraq managed to survive with a lowered but still acceptable standard of living.

Nevertheless, questions about Husayn's staying power and Iraq's future abound. Can Saddam Husayn and his regime survive the decade? Or will the regime succumb to domestic and international pressures? Should the regime collapse, what might take its place? And perhaps most important, can the Iraqi state survive the challenges of ethnic and sectarian separatism, most advanced in the Kurdish area? No answer can as yet be given to these questions, but they indicate the uncertainty that surrounds Iraq's future. Only the most tentative estimate of Iraq's future can be sketched, based on several alternatives scenarios.

Iraq's Future Under the Baath

If the Baath regime should remain in power, particularly under Saddam Husayn, there is little to suggest that it will alter its modi operandi or its goals and objectives. If Saddam Husayn survives, he is likely to continue to rely on his extended family, the secret police, and key military units—carefully screened for their loyalty—to perpetuate himself in power. The Sunni-dominated center of the country would continue to dominate the south, while the status of the northern Kurdish area would probably remain in limbo or become increasingly independent of Baghdad.

There would not likely be a basic change in the direction of Iraq's foreign policy. The emphasis on making Iraq a powerful state in the region, despite evidence of its shrinking capacity, has continued into the postwar period, along with aspirations for Iraq to lead the Arab world as well as to serve as guardian of the Arab world's eastern front against an increasingly aggressive Iran.

Even after defeat, the Baath regime has refused to relinquish its claim to Kuwait or to accept the newly demarcated boundaries with that country. Compliance with UN cease-fire resolutions was gained only grudgingly, after persistent diplomatic pressure and threats of recourse to military force.

Iraq's intransigence poses several dilemmas for the United States and the West. By early 1993 full compliance had still not been obtained, leaving sanctions intact. Sanctions, the main instrument to achieve compliance were inflicting hardships on the population, while marginally affecting Saddam Husayn and his security structure. A serious attempt by the United States to unseat the regime, even in cooperation with Iraqi opposition elements, would probably entail far more U.S. involvement in Iraq's domestic affairs, including the application of military force and possibly a civil war, unlikely to meet with international acceptance. Even if compliance were obtained, the West would face challenges in Iraq. If sanctions were removed, Iraq would have the financial resources to rebuild its war-torn infrastructure, and it might, in time, be able to resuscitate its chemical, biological, and even its nuclear programs. Preventing or containing a nuclear weapons program would depend on the vigilance of the international community in preventing imports of critical nuclear technology to Iraq and on the degree of intrusive inspection established in Iraq to detect an indigenous nuclear weapons program. International Atomic Energy Agency (IAEA) inspections of Iraq's nuclear facilities prior to the 1991 Gulf War had not detected the progress made in nuclear weapons later discovered after the war. Without this vigilance, Iraq, under Saddam Husayn or a similar Baath regime, could once again constitute a threat to its neighbors, possibly by the end of the decade.

Alternative Futures

Iraq's future might be brighter if the regime were to be replaced by one with more acceptable behavior, but its forcible removal raises more questions than can be answered. How is a regime as tenacious as that of Saddam Husayn to be removed? What type of successor can be envisioned? Would any new political leadership be able to stabilize its rule, or would a collapse of law and order ensue? If overthrow of the Baathists is fostered by dissident members of the regime or by the military, would their action be greeted with enthusiasm by all of Iraq's diverse communities? A more benign although authoritarian regime would probably secure international recognition and speed Iraq's economic rehabilitation, but such a regime would still face severe policy challenges and economic dilemmas. Would a Sunni-dominated authoritarian regime be able to satisfy newly liberated aspirations for democracy and power sharing espoused by the Shiites and by educated Sunnis? Would the regime be disposed to reach accommodation with the Kurdish government established in the north? And would a militarily based regime be willing to abide by the arms controls imposed by the international community? Inability to respond effectively to these policy questions could spell failure, collapse, and widening instability.

Still another future could confront Iraq, one in which the state as it is presently constituted undergoes far-reaching change, either through a gradual erosion of central government authority or through the emergence of a separate Kurdish state in the north. Separatism is far advanced among the Kurds, who, as indicated, are today gradually establishing the foundation for a self-governing state. In the south, an episodic Shiite insurgency against the central government persists in the marsh areas north of Basra bordering Iran. Meanwhile, an exiled Iraqi opposition group composed of all three communities—Kurds, Shiites, and Sunnis—has taken shape, claiming to represent a viable democratic alternative to the authoritarian regime in Baghdad. In 1992 the opposition convened a meeting in "liberated" territory in the north and elected a parliament and executive committee that was pledged to the establishment of a democratic Iraq. However, this opposition faces two major difficulties: how to remove the Baath regime, given Baghdad's repressive system, and, once that has been accomplished, how to avoid national fragmentation.

A Weakened Iraq

A collapse of central government authority under any circumstances could mean increased influence, if not control, by neighboring powers. Turkey has increasingly extended its influence over northern Iraq through agreements with the Kurds, through armed incursions over the border to control its own Kurdish insurgents, and through cooperation with the UN in protecting the northern zone from Baghdad. Iran likewise retains the potential to increase its influence over the Shiite population in the south and over some of the Kurds in the north. Saudis and Syrians are also likely to exert influence over what happens in Baghdad, and Jordan already plays an important role in providing the regime and the population in Baghdad a lifeline.

Any scenario in which Iraq grows weaker, particularly in peripheral geographic areas, could be destabilizing for the entire region. Rather than Iraqi aggression against its neighbors, the reverse might well occur. Ethnic and sectarian consciousness among the Kurds and the Shiites would spill over into surrounding states. This prospect is more readily anticipated in the case of the Kurds. The growth of a separate, democratic entity in the north of Iraq, even one that espouses federation with the central government in Baghdad, would become a model for Kurds in Turkey and Iran, upsetting the political status quo in these countries. Less evident but potentially potent would be the impact that rising Shiite political consciousness in Iraq might have on Gulf states to the south. Any accretions of Shiite power in Baghdad would challenge the supremacy of the Sunni ruling families in Kuwait, Bahrain, and even Saudi Arabia.

These forces and potential developments pose dilemmas for U.S. policy. As the leader of the coalition that fought the war against Saddam Husayn, the United States bears considerable responsibility for the denouement of that conflict. It continues, with several of its allies, to be deeply involved in Iraq's domestic affairs, notably through protection of the Kurds in the north and the Shiites in the south and through U.S. commissions working to achieve compliance with UN arms control and reparations resolutions.

One set of policy dilemmas arises from the U.S. commitment to encourage democracy, pluralism, and political reform. Saddam Husayn's ability to disturb regional peace and stability was widely ascribed to the authoritarian nature of the regime, so repressive that it had cowed its domestic opposition and was therefore able to launch its military ventures. Under such conditions, postwar intervention in Iraq's domestic affairs in support of humanitarian causes was deemed by the United Nations Security Council to be wholly justified. Unanswered is the question whether intervention should extend to removal of a regime, even one as unsavory as that in Iraq. Removal has proved extremely difficult to accomplish. On the one hand, intrusive interference in Iraq's domestic politics, particularly outside the framework of UN resolutions, is likely to be viewed by many in the developing world as a recrudescence of neocolonialism or as an effort to establish U.S. hegemony in the region in violation of the principle of state sovereignty. On the other hand, if the United States accepts Saddam Husayn's continued rule in Iraq, however grudgingly, it will appear to be condoning Husayn's human rights abuses and undermining calls for self-government on the part of minorities. Moreover, it could ultimately contribute to the emergence of a stronger, rearmed Saddam Husayn, anxious to renew his ambitions in the Arab world. A delicate balance must be maintained between support for creation of democratic institutions and encouragement of ethnic and sectarian separatism, which could engender widespread regional instability.

Saudi Arabia and the GCC States

The third essential element in any regional equation is the Gulf Cooperation Council, which embraces six conservative Arab states (Kuwait, Saudi Arabia, Bahrain, Qatar, the UAE, and Oman) ruled by traditional tribal monarchies. Formed in 1981, the GCC gives these member states more defensive depth and greater weight in the regional balance of power than they would have individually. Nevertheless, they are no match for their stronger and more militarily powerful neighbors, Iran and Iraq.

The small population base of the GCC states makes it impossible for them to mobilize and sustain a military force capable of defending against their more populous northern neighbors, although both Saudi Arabia and Oman have sufficient populations to field larger ground forces than they now do. The same constraints do not apply to air power, however. Saudi Arabia's considerable oil wealth has allowed it to make strides in developing a respectable air defense network. Nonetheless, the GCC states are compelled to remain dependent on outside powers for their defense, a dependency that will not change in the near future.

The importance of the GCC lies in its oil reserves and production facilities—especially those of Saudi Arabia, whose ability to produce 10 million barrels of oil per day dwarfs that of any of its local rivals, allowing it to help set production quotas and pricing of oil exports on world markets. These assets give the GCC economic, if not political, leverage, but it is leverage that can come at a high political and economic cost. In the wake of two costly Gulf wars, Saudi Arabia's financial reserves have been drawn down and it has incurred a debt burden. Under these circumstances, its economic flexibility and its willingness to sacrifice its own interests to gain economic leverage over its adversaries have been significantly reduced.

GCC Characteristics

Over the past decade, GCC states have exhibited several characteristics that have set them apart from their larger Gulf neighbors and that have enabled them to avoid domestic instability. First, the GCC states are under the control of conservative, pro-Western monarchies that, despite the traditional nature of their societies, have shown sufficient flexibility to adjust to dramatic changes brought on by economic modernization and an increasingly volatile security environment. Though Saddam Husayn's invasion of Kuwait severely frayed that country's political fabric, the return of the ruling Sabah family and the election of a new parliament have restored a modicum of normalcy, although the system may undergo serious alteration in the future. Elsewhere, the GCC regimes remain in place. Within Saudi Arabia, the royal family has managed to maintain continuity by successfully balancing pressures from a liberal, Westernized elite, demanding more political participation, and from a conservative

Islamic front, opposed to liberalization and maintenance of close ties with the West. This policy of balance is likely to continue.

A second encouraging development has been the ability of GCC governments to coalesce and cooperate in regional structures. The creation of the UAE from seven small shaykhdoms in 1971 and the formation of the GCC itself are examples. GCC cooperation in spite of intramural disagreements over border delineation and other issues has been significant in a region known for its factionalism and conflict. Within the GCC, this cooperation has now been institutionalized in annual meetings of heads of state; in a permanent secretariat; in defense and intelligence cooperation, including the creation of a defense force—the Peninsula Shield—(largely Saudi in structure); and in the establishment of a joint trade policy to coordinate agreements with the European Community. Such cooperation has not eliminated all outstanding disagreements among the Gulf states, but these have not been sufficiently virulent to cause serious fissures in the coalition.

A third characteristic of the GCC states has been their considerable wealth, which has cushioned GCC regimes against the kind of popular discontent now afflicting poorer Arab regimes. Although oil wealth is not evenly distributed among GCC states—Oman and Bahrain have fewer resources than the rest—all, except Oman, have welfare programs that assure cradle to grave security for the disadvantaged. Thus far, the most disaffected elements in these states have been foreign workers, who can be displaced at the first signs of disruption.

A fourth distinguishing characteristic has been the de facto integration of the Arab Gulf states into the Western security system. Twice in the decade from 1980 to 1990, GCC security needs have been fully met, first during the Iran-Iraq War, when the United States reflagged Kuwaiti tankers and Western naval assets protected shipping in the Gulf, and second in 1990–1991, when a coalition of over 30 states, under UN auspices, liberated Kuwaiti territory from Iraqi occupation. The individual Gulf states have since developed manifold arrangements for hosting a foreign military "presence," ranging from providing port facilities for U.S. ships (Bahrain) to prepositioning military equipment and providing military training missions (Oman and Saudi Arabia). They have done so thus far without compromising their sovereignty or overly offending the nationalist sensibilities of important segments of their populations.

The issue for U.S. defense planners over the coming decade is whether Desert Storm and actions taken in its aftermath have set in motion forces that could upset the domestic stability of these countries and threaten GCC relations with their Western protectors.

Lessening Cohesion

In the Persian Gulf, as elsewhere, the collapse of the Soviet Union and the end of the cold war have removed the threat that lent impetus to regional cohesion, thus allowing local squabbles and tensions to come to the fore. Among these are traditional border problems, previously mentioned, and the threat felt by smaller states of Saudi aspirations for hegemony. The fact that the GCC is faced by two strong and potentially hostile powers—Iran and Iraq—will help keep GCC countries focused on the need for cooperation, but local differences could unhinge this cooperation. Both Iran and Iraq encourage actions designed to split the GCC by inducing them to take one side or another in regional disputes. If agreements are not resolved, the divisions could weaken the ability of the GCC to serve as a balancing force in the Gulf, in the process making a less valuable instrument through which the United States and the West can mount a credible defense of Gulf oil flows.

GCC Isolation

The second force at work in the aftermath of the Gulf War is a sharply altered relationship between the GCC and the remainder of the Arab world, a trend that, if it persists, will increase GCC isolation and possibly degrade its security environment. The tacit support given to Iraq by a number of Arab countries, notably Jordan, Algeria, Tunisia, and Yemen, and also by the Palestinians, during the 1990-1991 Gulf crisis, deeply offended GCC governments, especially those in Kuwait and Saudi Arabia, and this support has created a rift between the GCC and some of their northern Arab neighbors. The rift, particularly noticeable between Saudi Arabia and Jordan, has not healed in the two years since the war.

Also contributing to this division with the rest of the Arab world is the perennial problem of maldistribution of wealth between the oil rich states of the Gulf and the more disadvantaged Arab countries of the Mediterranean rim. A decline in financial resources in the Gulf states as a result of a decade of contributions to two war efforts will make it more difficult for GCC states to proffer financial assistance to their less well-off northern neighbors. This new reality is likely to widen, rather than narrow, the existing division. In addition, the gradual collapse, in the year following the 1991 war, of a security initiative that would have linked the six GCC states with Egypt and Syria in a mutual defense agreement further served to isolate the GCC. The demise of the "six plus two" concept may have been due to pressure from Iran, which rejects Egypt's involvement in Gulf security, and to the preference of the GCC for a security relationship with the West rather than with weak Arab states. Whatever the reason, the GCC is now tied more closely than ever to its Western allies for defense arrangements. If alienation between the wealthier Gulf states and the rest of the Arab world is not gradually reduced, the GCC could be increasingly isolated in an era in which anti-Western sentiments show every sign of increasing. Such isolation would complicate political-military relations between the United States and its most important pillar in the Gulf, Saudi Arabia.

Oil Struggles

An additional trend likely to impact adversely on GCC stability in the coming decade is the potential for conflict among the Gulf powers for control over oil production, pricing, and markets. In recent years, such struggles have become sources of serious tension. During the Iran-Iraq War, Saudi Arabia's production policy, which served to keep prices low, was perceived as a tilt in favor of Iraq. In 1990 Kuwait's perceived manipulation of oil prices through overproduction of its OPEC quota was cited by Iraq as one major cause for its invasion. Oil production and pricing will continue to be a very divisive issue among Gulf oil-producing states, with attention focused on Saudi Arabia as the "swing" producer. In an era when oil prices may fall—also at a time of unrelenting revenue needs in Iran and Iraq—this issue could place the GCC on a collision course with both of these northern powers, as well as with each other. Moreover, Saudi Arabia, as well as Kuwait, needs increased oil revenue. The 1991 Gulf War was expensive; it not only devastated Kuwait's economy but also drained Saudi Arabia's financial reserves and compelled the government to borrow abroad. If Saudi reserves are not replenished and funds remain tight, Riyadh will face serious domestic problems. A shortage of money to alleviate domestic and regional discontent is likely to make the monarchy less willing to pursue oil-pricing policies that erode public support at home.

Destabilizing Domestic Forces

Finally, the GCC states will almost certainly be subject to destabilizing domestic forces arising from a myriad of pressures generated by modernization. These pressures will include middle-class demands for more open, accountable governments, from emerging Islamic political movements opposed to close ties with the West, and from the need to make room at the top of the political and social ladder for a new generation of educated Arabs. In its mildest form, change will come to most regimes through a carefully orchestrated process of succession accompanied by the emergence of a new political class. In all GCC states, a new generation of Western-educated technocrats and intellectuals are demanding a greater say in policy.

More fundamental changes in attitudes toward ties with the United States could come with the emergence of viable Islamic political movements, which are even more conservative than existing Gulf regimes. Such movements are already exercising social pressures for stricter observance of Islamic precepts, an end to corruption, and reduction of secular influences in their countries, most notably the foreign military presence.

More secular democratic forces are also emerging in the Gulf region and are challenging existing political systems. Demands for constitutional reform, including attenuating the monopoly of power held by the ruling families; for full-franchise elections; and for participation in public policy-making are increasingly heard within the Arab Gulf states. Emerging reform groups have already changed the shape of politics in Kuwait, where a free election, though with a limited franchise, has produced a Parliament dominated by a "loyal opposition."

Ethnic and sectarian consciousness is a particularly vibrant force that could destabilize the peninsula. Rising Shiite consciousness in Iraq could have an impact on the Shiite population in Kuwait (where Shiites constitute a third of the population), in Bahrain (where they are a majority), and in Saudi Arabia (where Shiites are an overwhelming majority in the oil-producing regions of the Eastern Province). Shiite-Sunni relations could worsen dramatically if economic, cultural, and political accommodation is not made between Sunni ruling groups and their dispossessed and restive Shiite populations in Kuwait and Bahrain, and possibly in Saudi Arabia as well.

If domestic discontent continues to grow while financial resources remain at a low ebb, Gulf-state leading families could experience a period of painful upheaval, or, at a minimum, pressures for reapportionment of political power. Though the past performance of governments in these small states indicates a remarkable ability to accommodate change while preserving control over the essential core of their societies, their ability to do so in the future will be sorely tested. Over the coming decade, this may be the most serious threat to U.S. interests in the Gulf.

Implications for U.S. Policy

These prospective alterations in the Gulf balance of power and the potentially destabilizing political forces at work in the GCC may compel the United States to play a more vigorous role in the Gulf; indeed, if the United States is forced to assume the unwanted burden of "policeman" anywhere in the world, it might be in the Persian Gulf. Yet this prospect arises at a time when the United States, under economic pressures at home, may feel compelled to draw down some of its forces in the Gulf and in Europe. Such a reduction will make future rapid deployment to the Gulf in a timely fashion more difficult than it was during Desert Storm, when substantial numbers of troops were deployed from Europe.

If Iran decides to embark on a nuclear weapons program or if it attempts, again, to destabilize neighboring governments, it is the United States that will have to counter Iran. Should Saddam Husayn and his regime remain in power, it is the U.S. force that will have to contain them; if he is removed and Iraq goes through a period of instability or, worse, disintegration, the United States would have to prevent Iraq's neighbors, most particularly Iran, from taking advantage. Indeed, a balance of power between Iran and Iraq, however precarious, may become increasingly difficult to sustain or to use as a guiding principle of U.S. policy in the Gulf. Even under the most benign circumstances, the United States and its Western allies will likely be required to deal with these two countries whose regimes and systems are hostile to U.S. and allied interests and inimical to our professed values of democracy and support for human rights. In attempting to preserve U.S. interests in the Gulf, the United States, on occasion, may be required to have recourse to military instruments to deter aggression. Alternatively, to ensure the domestic stability and continued close ties with the GCC states, the United States will have to be increasingly sensitive to expressions of anti-American sentiment and charges of U.S. neo-colonialist ambitions. Hence, less rather than more military visibility may once again be the best posture. Balancing divergent interests and goals will pose the real challenge to U.S. conflict management capabilities in the coming decade.

To deal with the looming challenge, the United States will have to develop a mix of both *coercive diplomacy*, backed by a credible military presence in the Gulf—to be used sparingly and preferably under UN authority—and of *constructive engagement*, based, at a minimum, on dialogue with all parties. With respect to potential adversaries, the United States will need to develop with them some clearly understood guidelines for acceptable international behavior and to identify the limits of U.S. tolerance if these guidelines are breached. Acceptable actions should include nonaggression against neighbors, verifiable adherence to international arms control agreements, and abjuring terrorism. Failure to abide by such norms would involve costs to those violating them. Coercion need not depend on application of military force but might involve such measures as denial of economic and technological support and international condemnation (including isolation). Effective policy cannot consist solely of coercion, however. It should also provide positive incentives to encourage reduction of regional tensions, improvement of human rights performance, and movement toward more democratic and broadly based government. These incentives might include most-favored-nation trade benefits, greater political dialogue and cultural interaction, technology transfers for economic growth, and widening opportunities for training and education in a world in which revolutionary changes in technology are taking place. Above all, the United States must maintain consistency in policy and the political will to remain involved in creating a nonviolent security environment in the Gulf. This will necessitate patience in dealing with Gulf problems. Demands will be taxing, but in few places in the world are the stakes higher.

Notes

1. Eliyahu Kanovsky, *The Economy of Iran: Past, Present, and Future*. Paper prepared for the director, Office of Net Assessment, Office of the Secretary of Defense. (Arlington, Va.: Systems Planning Corporation, April 1992).

2. Ibid., p. 37.

3. Nikola Schahgaldian, "The Current Political and Economic Environment in Iran," in *Balance of Power in Central and Southwest Asia*, Steven R. Dorr and Neysa M. Slater, eds. (Washington, D.C.: Defense Academic Research Support Program, 1992), p. 114.

4. Patrick Clawson, *Iran's Challenge to the West: When, How, and Why* (Washington, D.C.: Washington Institute for Near East Policy, 1993), p. 30.

5. Eric Hooglund, "Iran's Security Policies: 'New Thinking' or New Means to Pursue Old Objectives," in *Balance of Power*, Dorr and Slater, eds., p. 58.

6. Ibid., p. 58.

7. Ibid., pp. 58–60.

8. Ahmad Hashim, "Resurgent Iran: New Defense Thinking and Growing Military Capabilities." Unpublished paper delivered to the Middle East Institute, Washington, D.C., November 18, 1992, p. 21.

9. Kenneth Timmerman, "Iran Poised to Become Regional Superpower," *Mednews* (Paris) 5, no. 8 (January 20, 1992), pp. 1–2.

10. Glen Howard and Robert Kramer, "Backfires to Iran: Increased Combat Potential or Headache," *Notes on Russia and Central Eurasia* (Greenwood Village, Colo.: SAIC, The Foreign Systems Research Center, August 20, 1992), p. 3.

11. Richard MacKenzie, "Iran Resurgent," *Airforce Magazine*, July 1992, p. 78; "A Bomb for the Ayatallahs," *The Middle East* (London), October 1992, p. 23.

12. In 1989 Iran concluded a $15 billion trade agreement with Moscow, of

which $6 billion was for modern weapons. In 1991 an additional agreement for more weapons was concluded. (Anoushiravan Ehteshami, "Iranian Rearmament Strategy Under President Rafsanjani," *Janes Intelligence Review*, July 1992, p. 313.)

13. There have been numerous UN reports assessing Iraq's war damage. This account has been drawn from Sadruddin Aga Khan, "Report to the Secretary General on Humanitarian Needs in Iraq" (New York: United Nations, July 15, 1991), pp. 6–7.

14. Anne-Marie Johnson, "Iraq's Refineries Largely Back Up and Running," *Petroleum Intelligence Weekly*, July 20, 1992, p. 8.

15. Mariam Shahin, "Iraq's Rebuilding Success Fosters Pride," *Christian Science Monitor*, January 29, 1993, p. 7.

16. Ahmed S. Hashim, "Threat or Threatened: Security in Iraq and Impact on Its Neighbors," in *Balance of Power*, Dorr and Slater, eds., p. 24.

17. Ibid., p. 26.

18. Ibid., pp. 25–26.

19. Phebe Marr, "The Iran-Iraq War: The View from Iraq," in *The Persian Gulf War: Lessons for Strategy, Law and Diplomacy*, Christopher C. Joyner, ed. (New York: Greenwood Press, 1990), pp. 40ff, 70.

20. The 10,000 to 30,000 figure was cited by Air Force Lieutenant General Charles Horner based on revised Defense Department estimates. Patrick Sloyan, "Iraqi Loss Estimates Reduced," *Philadelphia Inquirer*, January 25, 1992, p. 3. For the 10,000 figure, see John Heidenrich, "The Gulf War: How Many Iraqis Died?" *Foreign Policy* 90 (Spring 1993), pp. 123–124.

Suggested Reading

Chubin, Shahram, and Tripp, Charles, *Iran and Iraq at War*, Boulder, Colo.: Westview Press, 1988.

Clawson, Patrick, *Iran's Challenge to the West: When, How, and Why*, Washington, D.C.: Washington Institute for Near East Policy, 1993.

Cordesman, Anthony, *After the Storm: The Changing Military Balance in the Middle East*, Boulder, Colo.: Westview Press, 1993.

Crystal, Jill, *Kuwait: The Transformation of an Oil State*, Boulder, Colo.: Westview Press, 1992.

Doran, Charles, and Buck, Stephen, eds., *The Gulf, Energy, and Global Security: Political and Economic Issues*, Boulder, Colo.: Lynne Rienner, 1991.

Freedman, Lawrence, and Karsh, Efrian, *The Gulf Conflict 1990–1991: Diplomacy and War in the New World Order*, Princeton, N.J.: Princeton University Press, 1993.

Hunter, Shireen, *Iran and the World: Continuity in a Revolutionary Decade*, Bloomington: Indiana University Press, 1990.

Marr, Phebe, *The Modern History of Iraq*, Boulder, Colo.: Westview Press, 1990.

Sandwick, John, ed., *The Gulf Cooperation Council: Modernization and Stability in an Interdependent World*, Boulder, Colo.: Westview Press, and Washington, D.C.: American Arab Affairs Council, 1987.

6

Hazards to Middle East Stability in the 1990s: Economics, Population, and Water

Thomas Naff

The most serious hazard to the stability of the Middle East in the coming decade will arise from the region's indigenous socioeconomic problems, particularly those caused by population growth, in conjunction with an increasing scarcity and maldistribution of water resources. The fundamental determinants of stability—adequate food, health, housing, education, employment, and other quality-of-life factors—can no longer endure the perennial neglect and deferral for the sake of ideology and security that has characterized past governmental policies in the area. Failure to make significant progress in ameliorating these problems has brought several key countries in the Middle East to the threshold of crisis. Although all of these problems will not necessarily be shared by every nation of the Middle East, they will almost certainly affect, in varying degrees, five key regional actors who are crucial to U.S. strategic and political interests in the area: Egypt, Israel, Jordan, Syria, and Turkey.

This strategic quintet has historically engaged U.S. security interests and will continue to do so in the decade of the 1990s for several reasons: They are all strategically located in the eastern Mediterranean along the southern flank of NATO; they encompass two of the most important international waterways of the region, the Suez Canal and the straits of Turkey; except for Syria, they all are friendly toward the United States and, for the most part, represent the forces of moderation; they all play a critical role in the balance of power and stability of the entire region; and they are all centrally involved in the issue of peace in the Middle East. They all suffer critical water problems that could destabilize the region if these problems are not mitigated.

The loss of any of these friends in the region would adversely affect U.S. security and political interests. For example, if Egypt or Jordan were to succumb to radical regime changes, the United States would lose their moderate leadership in promoting U.S. peace initiatives and in mediating U.S. policies among other Arab states. The radicalization of these two pivotal Arab actors could (1) alter the Middle East's balance of power, (2) make the basic U.S. policy of protecting Israel more complicated and difficult, (3) reduce the corps of moderate governments, (4) add to the forces of extremism, (5) possibly lead to attacks on U.S. facilities and citizens, (6) cause normally friendly countries to distance themselves from the United States, and (7) in general significantly increase the processes of destabilization in the entire region.

There are three key variables, each integral to the others, that will determine the extent to which the Middle East will become destabilized in the 1990s: economic conditions, demographic trends, and the availability and distribution of vital water resources. The nations of Egypt, Israel, Jordan, Syria, and Turkey provide a good representation of how the variables of economics, population, and water may operate in the changing circumstances of the region.

Economic Factors

The contours of the economic landscape encompassing this regional quintet are discouraging. Collectively, unemployment averages 16 percent: Egypt and Jordan have the highest, about 20 percent; Syria and Turkey follow at 15 percent each; and Israel has the lowest rate, about 9 percent, but this is rising. Annual inflation rates average a collective 32 percent and are climbing: Turkey and Syria head the list with 90 percent and 50 percent, respectively, followed by Egypt with 45 percent and by Jordan and Israel each with 25 percent. Combined, the foreign debt among the five countries is $125 billion: Egypt leads the way, owing $55 billion; followed by Turkey, which owes $40 billion; Syria, $20 billion; Jordan, $8 billion; and Israel, $2 billion.[1] The prognosis for the first half of the decade is for the rate of inflation to hold steady or to decline by a few percentage points and for debts to increase at current rates.

This small but indicative compilation of statistics hardly reveals the seriousness of the situation. When one looks more closely, the picture becomes even darker. For example, in Jordan, the ranks of the unemployed are filled mainly by persons under thirty years of age who are married, have children, and have a secondary or college education. Even before the 1991 Gulf War, they were no longer able to find relief through employment in the Gulf countries, and there was already a reverse flow of Jordanians (including Palestinian citizens of Jordan) from the Gulf states who were made redundant by the economic slowdown in the Gulf. The war worsened these trends exponentially and decimated Jordan's economy, which is barely able to cope with the more than 300,000 Jordanian/Palestinian repatriots. Jordan has lost its international credit rating and is unable to borrow significant amounts of urgently needed funds in the international financial market. It is these educated younger members of Jordan's middle class who have been at the forefront of the newly revived opposition to government policies. They are demanding radical political and economic changes; particularly, they want a greater share of power for themselves.[2] It is among this segment of the population, which has its counterparts throughout the Middle East, that anti-American feelings are growing most rapidly.

Israel would appear to be insulated from drastic economic hardship by its special relationship with the United States. The bulk of its foreign debt is owed to U.S. government institutions and to members of the American Jewish community. Nevertheless, Israel is vulnerable to economic deterioration and to serious economic erosion in vital sectors of the economy. If the Russian Jewish immigration becomes too great a strain, there could be repercussions throughout the economy, leading to rapid degeneration. The agricultural sector, for example, is in a downward spiral, with the kibbutzim and moshavim in deep trouble.[3] (A kibbutz is a collective farm or settlement, and a moshav is a cooperative settlement consisting of small individual farms.) Only 3 percent of Israel's population live on kibbutzim, but among them they have accumulated a debt of $4 billion. On a per capita basis, this debt is thirty times that of Mexico. Israel is experiencing an 11 percent unemployment rate (it is 14 percent to 15 percent among Israeli Arabs), which is predicted to rise to 14 percent by 1994. Israeli economists foresee the need for a 10 percent annual growth rate, necessary for employing 140,000 new immigrants a year, but growth is currently averaging 6 percent and is expected to average, at best, only 7 percent for the next five years. Moreover, the movement of Israeli capital out of the country is estimated to be about $50 billion, and these funds come mainly from the middle class. Foreign aid is required to avoid a destabilizing economic crisis.

The most serious impact on Israel's economy, and the factor that has the greatest potential for political and social dislocation, comes from the *intifada*, which drains 2 percent of the gross domestic product

(GDP) per year, or from $700–900 million.[4] Until the beginning of the 1990s the *intifada* was clearly the most destablizing challenge facing Israel and was probably the prime determinant of the nature and shape of Israel's future. The *intifada* will continue in some form until the issue of a Palestinian state is resolved; until then, the uprising will persist in draining the Israeli economy and traumatizing the national psyche and will have a molding influence on the country's future.

Of potentially equal significance, however, will be the socioeconomic and demographic impact of an expected one million Jews from the former Soviet Union who must be sheltered and given employment within the next two or three years.

The contrasts between Turkey and Egypt help to illustrate the socioeconomic uncertainties and dangers that may face the entire region in the 1990s. Turkey is in better economic order than Egypt but faces potential economic problems. Egypt, however, is already in the midst of a very real crisis. Both nations are vital to U.S. strategic planning in the Middle East: Turkey is a member of NATO and the only Middle Eastern country with U.S. military bases that shares a border with the former Soviet Union, and Egypt is a key Arab player in the U.S. peace-seeking process.

Despite the collapse of communism and central authority in the USSR, Turkey's geopolitical importance in relation to Iran, Iraq, and Syria helps to sustain its strategic importance to the United States. Turkey enjoys many advantages denied its neighbors. It is a landmass of rich resources, with extensive areas of fertile soil and surplus water stocks. It has the potential to become a significant actor in the Middle East. Nevertheless, for all its advantages, Turkey's direction is not clear, nor is a successful future assured.

The Turkish economy suffers from serious internal regional disparities in prosperity. The current 90 percent inflation rate, most of which spiraled upward within the last two years, has been accompanied by aggregate government and commercial interest rates of over 100 percent.[5] If the foreign debt, which trebled in the last decade, continues to grow at its present rate, within a few years Turkey will have great difficulty in servicing it, with commensurate consequences for the government's international credit rating. The prognosis is for a continued rise in the foreign debt.

The Southeast Anatolia Project (GAP) is a vast hydrological undertaking involving the Euphrates and Tigris rivers that, as planned, will encompass about 10 percent of Turkey's landmass. GAP aims to bring under irrigation 1.6 million hectares of land and to generate 7,561 megawatts of hydroelectric power. If successful, GAP would transform the economy and society of Turkey. But because Turkey has placed most of its economic eggs in the GAP basket, the difficulties and risks are proportionate to the size and ambitions of the project. For example, GAP involves massive spending; upward of $25 billion is the projected cost of the completed project for both the Euphrates and the Tigris basins. In some important respects GAP is a "crash" program requiring the acquisition of millions of dollars per day to keep it going. Such large amounts of foreign exchange funds are not readily available to Turkey; this has forced the government into large-scale international borrowing which has been difficult and has been often delayed. Turkish authorities have already been forced to request a rescheduling of the cost of foreign borrowing from short-term to midterm obligations.[6]

GAP will require major social rearrangements in the southeast region of Turkey where considerable tensions already exist, principally because Turkey's rebellious Kurdish minority is clustered in southeast Anatolia. GAP requires large-scale resettlement of the population (mainly through internal migration), land redistribution, alteration of traditional life-styles, development of social infrastructures, and regional planning. By allowing the Kurds to share in the economic benefits of GAP and by the social restructuring of southeast Anatolia, government authorities apparently intend to use the GAP project as a means of settling their Kurdish problem. However, it should be noted that the social-science research necessary for effective planning and policy implementation, such as impact studies, has yet to be done.

It is clear that very soon after the turn of the millennium, Turkey must begin to realize some of the financial and social benefits from GAP that the public has been encouraged to expect, otherwise, the consequences of unrequited hardships and an economic crisis will be unavoidable. There is little evidence of serious contingency planning in the event that GAP does not meet its economic and social targets in a timely fashion. However, despite perils and problems, it is unlikely that GAP will fail completely, and there is a reasonable chance that it will succeed.

Turkey's natural, professional, and technical resources provide an economic safety net and options for recovery that its neighbors, notably Egypt, lack. This means that although Turkey will be susceptible to destabilization in this decade, it is generally believed that it is not likely to fail, and there is even a good chance that Turkey will remain relatively stable. Given Turkey's strategic position and its friendly disposition toward the United States, the latter circumstance will strengthen Ankara's putative claim to being the United States' most important Middle Eastern ally.

In comparison with Turkey, Egypt is struggling to avoid economic and demographic disaster. Fortunately for the Egyptian people and for the general stability of the Middle East, in the past Egypt has somehow muddled through its perennial economic crises. Underlying this has been an assumption that with some structural economic reforms and with massive amounts of foreign aid, the Egyptian economy would eventually right itself. However, circumstances in the 1980s changed so much for the worse as to cast serious doubt on whether the Egyptian economy is able now to recover sufficiently and quickly enough to avoid a major dislocating crisis.

The supporting statistics are somber: the foreign debt is $55 billion; debt service in 1989 was $6.6 billion, with a projected rise to $8 billion by 1992; but the government has never been able to service the debt at more than $3.3 billion per year. The inflation rate is averaging 35 percent to 45 percent. Unemployment is officially pegged at 15 percent but is certainly higher given the return flow of repatriated manpower from around the region, particularly in the wake of the 1991 Gulf War. There is a net increase of 1.2 million Egyptians every nine months, forcing Egypt to become a significant importer of grains, meats, fruits, and vegetables paid for with dwindling hard currency reserves, paradoxically earned in large part by the export of agricultural products.

The flight of Egyptian capital to offshore havens is about $25 billion and may be even more. A worrisome trend has emerged in the offshore capital flow: Heretofore, most of the capital came from wealthy entrepreneurs and politicians, but now a rapidly increasing number of middle-class Egyptians are sending their money out of the country, putting even greater stress on the Egyptian pound.[7]

Essential, deep structural reforms in the economy—that is, changes in the organization and units of production, in the agencies and institutions of the economy, in the allocation of resources, and in the processes of economic decision making—that may have been possible in the late 1970s or early 1980s, when there was a positive balance of payments, are all but impossible now. The political risks of such structural reforms are too high, especially in the face of the growing strength of the religious right. As in the past, those risks would probably materialize in the form of widespread violent demonstrations. Just about the only reform the government can safely undertake is of the nibbling-around-the-edges variety. Even if all the difficult and correct actions were taken immediately, the benefits would not be felt for at least five or six years, a time lag during which the Egyptian government would be hard-pressed to contain the potentially violent political and social consequences of such reforms.[8]

Arguments have been made that a stable Egypt is so critical to the interests of the United States and the Gulf states that together they would not allow the Egyptian economy to collapse. That is probably true. But two factors militate against this proposition: (1) Just keeping the Egyptian economy functioning at its present level will not suffice to avoid crises whose effects would be cumulative and would produce destructive political and social dislocations; and (2) current events in Europe are very likely to reorient U.S. foreign aid priorities toward Eastern Europe.

Given the limitations the U.S. deficit places on foreign aid, Congress may not be so willing to continue to pour money into Egypt (or other comparable recipients of U.S. assistance) at present levels if no tangible progress on economic reforms is made or if the need for massive aid appears unending.

The major implication to be drawn from the destabilizing economic trends just examined is that all five countries suffer significant structural economic weaknesses that are both products of and contributors to their social ills. All nonoil-based economies in the region are still handicapped by very low GDP and gross national product (GNP) levels. They urgently need to make improvements in their economies that, owing to their structural natures, will require fundamental reordering of key sectors and changes in established policies (such as dropping or substantially reducing subsidies on basic commodities).

Without some amelioration, however, destabilizing domestic strife will be inexorable rather than only probable. In such economically hard-hit countries as Egypt, Jordan, and Syria, the most likely outcome would be new regimes more radical, nationalistic, bellicose, and anti-American than their predecessors, which in turn would generate even more potential regional instability in the 1990s. If improvements are to be accomplished with any hope of success, strong, effective leadership, careful planning, and outside assistance specifically dedicated to cushioning the worst impact of change will be essential. But owing to the high levels of poverty endemic to the Middle East, there remains a strong probability of violent reactions even during the process of reform itself.

As so often happens, leaders could be powerfully tempted to create external crises to channel their people's frustrations and anger away from domestic problems.

These circumstances confront U.S. policymakers with complex and difficult challenges in the coming decade. Although in some respects the end of the cold war and the fragmentation of the Soviet Union may appear to have given the United States some advantages in the Middle East, these may well be counterbalanced by the uncertainties of having the former Soviet client states—the most bellicose and authoritarian regimes in the region—cut loose from the restraining influence that the Russians could exert. The old certitudes are gone, a new order has yet to be constructed. Competing religious and political factions are seeking new bases of authority and legitimacy, and the established regimes are trying to find a new footing to maintain their balance and power.

All actors in the Middle East have been propelled by events in Eastern Europe into a new, less stable world where their economic and political margins of safety have receded. They must, consequently, rethink economic development and security issues in the light of both old and new realities, which include the growing population problem and shrinking international financial markets together with sources of foreign aid. Moreover, competition for what aid is available has been made more intense by the demands of all the newly created states carved from the carcass of the former Eastern Communist bloc. Even more threatening is the possibility that as the United States changes its perception of the strategic and economic importance of the Middle East in relation to Eastern Europe and Russia, it may well shift the importance of the region downward in its order of international priorities. This prospect has injected an element of even greater uncertainty in the relationships between the United States and the five key actors named in this study.

The formulation of U.S. policies in response to such evolving conditions are limited by three factors: the inability of any outside power to control or direct the indigenous forces of change in the region; the expected ongoing budget deficits accompanied by a growing emphasis on domestic priorities in U.S. politics; and the burgeoning demand on diminished U.S. aid resources. Despite these limitations, there are still several things that policymakers could do. Obviously, the Arab-Israeli peace process must be pursued relentlessly and as evenhandedly as possible. Another approach is to build into U.S. aid policies encouragement for the five key nations to reduce expenditures on armaments. These expenditures inhibit the production of urgently needed investment capital, and the armaments will not purchase additional security commensurate with the economic and social costs involved. Instead, policymakers should provide incentives for these countries to improve and restructure their economies toward light industry, electronics, and service. This would not only free up enormous amounts of energy and water for more productive uses (light industry contributes about 30 times more to gross national product [GNP] per unit of water used than does agriculture) but would also generate greater indigenous capital for investments in economic productivity and debt reductions.

The anticipated limitations on the U.S. capacity to provide assistance practically dictate a collective approach to these problems. Although this will not be an easy task, policymakers, in the coming decade, may have to consider whether any given foreign policy problem might best be handled collectively or cooperatively with other interested parties. In the case of the Middle East, where the strategic stakes will remain high but the likely costs of maintaining U.S. interests may outstrip the U.S. government's capacity to pay (or the public's willingness to go on paying), the most effective policy approach may well be collective/cooperative efforts with the EC, Japan, Canada, the UN, World Bank, and the Gulf States (or any combination thereof). This would spread the cost, spread the risk of economic (or political) consequences, and make various forms and conditions of aid more ideologically and politically palatable and safe to local governments. It would also effectively strengthen the idea and institutions of collectivity and cooperation regionally and globally. Although one must not underestimate the potential difficulties of a collective approach, policymakers who remain wedded to the alternative of some form of the present policies could find the changed face of the Middle East to be hostile in the not too distant future.

Demographic Trends

Underpinning intrinsically all that happens in the economic life of the region are the demographic realities. The unchecked increase in the number of inhabitants across the Middle East has become the prime long-term determinant of prosperity or poverty, stability or conflict.

Viewed from almost any aspect, the statistics are alarming. Since World War II the region's population has doubled and is projected to double again within the next twenty years (Table 6.1 and Table 6.2). The combined average population growth rate for the five countries under examination is about 3.25 percent per annum. That is a rate estimated to be 2.5 times higher than the economic and natural resources of the area can sustain.[9] (Turkey might be a local exception.) If there is not a sharp downward swing in present trends, by about the year 2010 the combined population of this five-nation cluster will be 200 to 210 million (Figure 6.1 and Figure 6.2). None of the governments has as yet devised an effective and coherent policy to stabilize or reduce population growth or to manage the attendant problems.

In this context, it should be noted that, historically, Islamic religious doctrine and law do not prohibit the practice of birth control.

TABLE 6.1 Population Projections for Euphrates-Tigris Basin (population in millions)

	1985	1990	1995	2000	2005	2010	2015	2020	2025
Iraq	15.9	18.9	22.4	26.3	30.7	35.3	40.1	45.1	50.0
Syria	10.5	12.5	14.9	17.6	20.6	23.3	26.6	29.5	32.2
Turkey	50.4	55.6	61.2	66.7	71.8	76.6	81.2	85.4	89.6

Source: Projections based on *UN World Population Prospects 1989.*

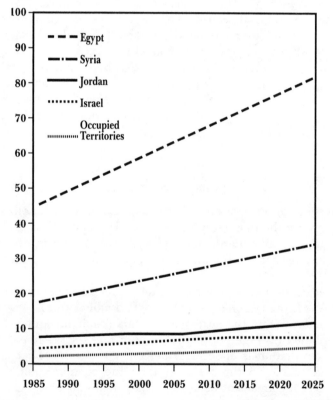

FIGURE 6.1 Population Projections for Jordan Basin and Egypt (population in millions). Projections on Israel based on *UN World Population Prospects 1989;* projections on the Occupied Territories and Jordan are based on in-country data by author. (Soviet immigration not included.)

TABLE 6.2 Population Projections for Jordan Basin and Egypt (population in millions)

	1985	*1990*	*1995*	*2000*	*2005*	*2010*	*2015*	*2020*	*2025*
Syria	10.5	12.5	14.9	17.6	20.6	23.3	26.6	29.5	32.2
Jordan	2.7	3.2	3.8	4.4	5.4	6.4	7.6	9.8	11.6
Israel[a]	4.2	4.6	5.0	5.3	5.6	6.0	6.3	6.7	7.0
Occupied Territories	1.5	1.8	2.1	2.5	2.9	3.4	4.0	4.7	5.5
Egypt	47.6	54.1	60.5	66.7	72.7	78.4	84.0	89.0	94.0

[a]Soviet immigration not included.
Sources: Projections on Syria and Israel based on *UN World Population Prospects 1989;* projections on the Occupied Territories and Jordan based on in-country data obtained by author.

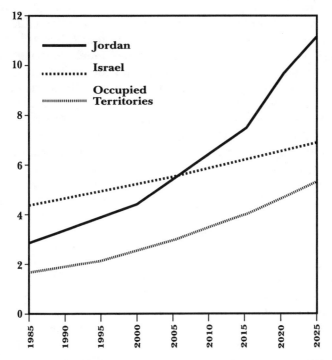

FIGURE 6.2 Population Projections for Jordan, Israel, and Occupied Territories (populations in millions). Projections on Israel based on *UN World Population Prospects 1989;* projections on the Occupied Territories and Jordan are based on in-country data by author. (Soviet immigration not included.)

Indeed, in the Middle Ages, Muslim Arabs, drawing on their experience in animal husbandry, were among the most knowledgeable, the most sophisticated, and some of the earliest scientific practitioners of human birth control methods, even in the aftermath of the great plagues.[10]

Although the demographic factor is evident in virtually every major issue challenging the region, its manifestations, like an endlessly variable mosaic, can be seen to overlap and to differ from country to country. Local values and attitudes, social and behavioral traditions, ideologies, national priorities, political and economic organization, and ecological systems account for the diverse situational and interrelated effects of demography.

For example, at 3.8 percent a year, Jordan's population is increasing annually at a faster pace than is Egypt's. From 1986 to 2015, Jordan's citizenry is projected to grow by 178 percent, from 2.7 million to 7 million.[11] This rate of growth in a country that receives a net average of 150 millimeters of poorly distributed rainfall per annum portends serious problems. Jordan, where much stress is placed on education by both native Jordanians and resident Palestinians, has traditionally produced a surplus of well-trained professionals and technocrats. Throughout the oil-boom years the demand for trained manpower in the Gulf states provided an outlet for this accumulated talent. But the oil price recession of the late 1980s produced a return flow of this educated labor force, with the resultant political and social consequences already cited. The probability is small that the symbiotic economic relationship between Jordan and the Gulf states, which was destroyed by Jordan's pro-Iraqi stance during the 1991 Gulf War, will ever be restored to what it was. Nor will the Gulf states be more inclined to share their wealth with their fellow Arabs at prewar levels, and the future largess will be spread with more ideological and political conditions.

It is not likely that another economic boom similar to that of the 1970s and early 1980s will ensue. But an anticipated increase in oil revenues during the coming decade and Kuwait's postwar recovery program should produce a modest employment market for select Arab states that supported Kuwait, such as Egypt and Syria; however, cash flow problems in Saudi Arabia and Kuwait will mean smaller foreign aid packages to other Arab states, at least in the short run. However, an economic upturn in the Gulf could not by itself offset all the negative socioeconomic consequences of overpopulation. Moreover, the oil-producing states over the last two decades have trained their own technical and managerial specialists, reducing the number of opportunities for labor from other Middle Eastern countries.

In Syria the demography-education link functions differently due mainly to a combination of ideology and national priorities. Syria, which has the same population growth rate as Jordan, is endowed with more abundant natural resources, but a less educated elite. Although Syrians value education as much as Jordanians, Syria's educational system has been deeply politicized and poorly administered, and the best talent has been co-opted by the military establishment at the expense of the civilian sector. Because Syria's population is so heterogeneous, much educational effort is devoted to producing Syrian males whose traditional loyalties to region, group, or sect are superseded by an overriding loyalty to state, party, and Arabism. A concomitant of this Baathist strategy has been to use the educational system for political socialization and to mobilize its youth for the achievement of its economic development targets. Hence there has been a "knowledge for the sake of work" approach to Syrian education since the advent of Baathist power.[12]

Although considerable improvements have been made in the system, the results, overall, have been disappointing. The attack on illiteracy has not succeeded, especially in rural areas. In 1960 rural illiteracy was 70 percent, but it is still over 50 percent and is an important factor in Syria's high birth rate. The educational system suffers from lack of attendance, shortages of qualified teachers, overcrowding, poorly equipped schools, maladministration, and inefficiency. These conditions are reflected in the government's budget priorities. In the last five-year plan, ending in 1985, 8 percent of the budget was allocated to culture and information—the category of expenditures under which education was lumped—30 percent to the military, and 12 percent to industry. Education received about half of the 8 percent allocated to culture and information.[13] Should this pattern continue into the 1990s, Syria will be unable to use education as an effective tool for birth control; President Hafiz al-Asad has already given up his goal of strategic parity with Israel.

The authorities' failure to institute an effective program to reduce the rate of population increase has contributed to Syria's failure to overcome illiteracy. This in turn continues to undermine the ability of the government to achieve its ambitious social and economic goals. Efforts to eradicate illiteracy and to raise the standards of education have been unable to keep pace with population growth. Much of this failure can be attributed to the authorities' primary efforts to control and indoctrinate rather than to educate. The upshot has been a largely undereducated population and a serious "brain drain" among those who are trained. Syrian students and other emigrants tend to stay abroad in larger proportions than those from many other Arab countries, owing to political discontent, poor job opportunities at home, and low standards of pay and working conditions.

For the future of Syria, whose population will approach 18 million in the year 2000 (a 71 percent increase), these conditions mean that unless improvements are made quickly, the human and financial resources required to maintain political and socioeconomic stability will simply not be available. There is solid evidence that current policies could permanently impair the long-term viability of the economy, as in Egypt, creating a potentially destabilized internal situation that could have unpredictable repercussions, not only for Syria but for its neighbors as well. Israel, Jordan, and Lebanon can never be indifferent to the possible consequences that events in Syria could have on their security.[14]

Should the consequences of present trends materialize in the course of the 1990s, the United States and Israel (and Syria's other neighbors) will face a Syria that has less capacity to generate an effective military machine even if it had the resources to do so. But they would also face a less stable country that has far greater economic and political problems; therefore, in some respects, a Syria that would be potentially more problematic as regards regional politics, conflicts, and any peace-seeking process.

The demographic factor operates in other ways in Israel. There, the disparity in birth rates between Arabs and Jews and the problems of immigration and settlement have made the demographic issue a politically volatile one. The Jewish population within Israel proper, that is, excluding the Occupied Territories, is growing at a rate of 1.9 percent per annum, while the Palestinian population is increasing at slightly more than 3 percent per annum. Put another way, the Jewish birth rate is 22 per 1,000 as compared to 34 per 1,000 for Israeli Palestinians. In the Occupied Territories, the Jewish settlers' annual birth rate is 2 percent and the Palestinians' is about 3.4 percent, or 23 births per 1,000 for the settlers and 44 births per 1,000 for the Palestinians.[15] In the course of the *intifada* the growth rate in Gaza has ballooned incredibly to 5.9 percent, a doubling time of only a dozen years in an area that is already the most densely populated in the world. This has been a problem that has concerned Israeli leaders for decades.

The demographics of Israel cut across the vital questions of the future Jewishness of Israel, the status of Israeli Arabs, the disposition of the Occupied Territories, the peace-seeking process, and Israeli democracy. Unless Israel chooses to create a society that is permanently segregated both politically and socially—perforce at the expense of democracy—it is conceivable that Palestinians could in the future control one-quarter of the Knesset seats.

The projected immigration of one million Jews from the former Soviet Union to Israel in the next few years is bound to have an immediate impact on the demographic pattern, but the long-term effects are indiscernible at this juncture. There is an informal consensus among specialists that in the short run the influx would alter the Jewish-Palestinian ratio in absolute numbers, but would not significantly alter the birth ratios. Since the new emigrants will be mostly educated middle-class Russians who are ambitious to improve their economic status, it is assumed that they will not reproduce at a rate greater than that of Israel's Jewish population; thus, the current disproportionate Jewish-Palestinian birth ratio will be maintained.

However, settling the new immigrants will place a great burden on Israel's fragile economy and the regional tensions already generated by the Russian Jewish ingathering will certainly complicate the peace-seeking process and Israel's relations with its neighbors. If the government settles large numbers of the immigrants in the Occupied Territories, then the level of violence can be expected to rise, and Israel's relations with the United States will also be made more difficult.

However emotionally and ideologically satisfying immigration of Russian Jews may be to the Israelis and whatever future national benefits they are expected to bring, among their baggage they also carry problems of major proportions for Israel. They must somehow be absorbed without dislocating Israeli Jews and Arabs, without pauperizing the country, and without displacing Palestinians in the Occupied Territories. The new Jewish influx is perceived by the Arab camp not only as a serious threat to the Palestinians in the form of creeping annexation of the Occupied Territories but also as a disruption of the present uneasy balance of power in the region, making peace more difficult and war more likely.[16]

The imminent presence of a million additional Jews in Israel confronts U.S. and Israeli policy strategists with several critical questions: What will be the effect on Israel's domestic political balance? Will the new citizens give Likud a decisive electoral majority with a concomitant influence on U.S. peace initiatives? Will they touch off violence among Israeli Arabs who already consider themselves second-class citizens and fear that the Russian Jews will rob them of the limited number of jobs open to them? How will disadvantaged Israelis react to the perceived loss of housing and economic opportunities to the emigrants? Will social relations between Ashkenazic and Sephardic Jews be worsened? Will Israel become a more Zionistic nation? Can Israel avoid a significant reorganization of its economy? What would be the implications of an Israel in turmoil for several years?

Beyond individual national patterns, there are certain general demographic characteristics that apply to the region as a whole. The population of the Middle East is quite young. About 40 percent are less than sixteen years old, the world average is twenty. Over 50 percent are thirty years or less.[17] Because of their numbers, the younger generation constitutes the greater part of the poor and underclasses of the region. At the same time, from the ranks of the young there is emerging an educated elite in larger numbers, politically sophisticated and aware of world events, more receptive to new ideas, with higher political and social expectations, and with a growing demand for the introduction of democratic systems of government. They want a greater share of power, appear to be committed to nationalistic and Islamic causes, and are critical of regimes that ignore public sentiments—especially their own. Their loyalties are more oriented toward the nation as opposed to a particular government or to subnational groups.[18] When this generation assumes power, because its attitudes toward the United States would probably be more negative than the current leadership, it could consequently be more difficult to deal with.

The principal implications of the region's population growth rates and the other general demographic features are obvious: Enormous strains are placed on all major economic sectors—housing, education, health services, labor, agriculture, and so on—not to mention vital natural resources such as water. Development needs consistently outrun the capacity to satisfy them, and development targets must grow ever more ambitious just to keep pace with the expanding populations.

The results in economic terms are unmanageable chronic debts, poor performance, low per capita incomes, corruption, and maldistribution of wealth, manifested in extreme poverty often accompanied by extreme wealth among a small elite, a highly visible discrepancy that intensifies social tensions.

In human terms, these conditions produce a low quality of life, if not oppressive misery; a sense of powerlessness and frustration accompanied by rising anger, and by dashed hopes and expectations; and a receptivity to radical or violent solutions, whether inspired by ideologies of the right or left, religious or secular, especially among the younger generation.

U.S. policymakers will be confronted by the consequences of the region's demographic growth trajectory. For example, the water resources of the Jordan basin will support a population of 13 to 14 million people. Using medium projections, sometime between 2015 to 2020, the basin's inhabitants, excluding Syria and Lebanon, are expected to number between 16 to 18 million. Since this issue goes to the heart of the Israeli-Palestinian problem (not to mention Jordan), it becomes an acute policy issue for Washington, which will have to engage it not only within the parameters of less control and less money but also with the additional strictures of cultural and ideological attitudes toward birth control in the United States and the Middle East. There is general agreement among demographers that the most effective proven birth control is the education of women to at least an eighth-grade level. In the circumstances, a coordinated policy with other interested parties, one that encourages and assists universal education and economic restructuring on a regional basis, would probably be the least risk-laden course.

Water and the Prospects for Conflict

All of the foregoing socioeconomic issues relate integrally to the question of the region's vital natural resources. The most patently reciprocal problems are those of scarce water supplies and rising demographic trends. In the Middle East the water issue is a chief determinant of all other socioeconomic factors. There is virtually no human artifact or commodity that is produced in the absence of water. Agriculture is impossible without it and so are most manufacturing processes.

As a contemporary issue of security and international relations, water displays certain distinguishing characteristics:

- Water is pervasive, a highly complex issue, and is utterly vital.
- Water is always a terrain security issue, especially when scarce, since all concerned parties feel compelled to control the ground on or under which water flows.
- The relationship between water dependency and security is perceived as absolute, that is to say, as zero-sum, especially where two or more mutually antagonistic actors compete for the same water source.
- As a zero-sum security issue, water carries a constant potential for conflict.
- Because of its complexity, water tends to be dealt with piecemeal—problem by problem rather than comprehensively, both domestically and internationally—thus tending to be fragmented as a strategic and foreign affairs issue.
- International law as a means of settling and regulating fresh water issues remains rudimentary and relatively ineffectual without prior treaty arrangements in place.

The five countries that share the Jordan and Euphrates river basins constitute excellent case studies of the complex nature of water problems and the role of water in future prospects for stability or conflict in the Middle East.

The Jordan River Basin

Very serious problems of water scarcity and water quality exist in the Jordan River basin (Table 6.3). The basin's principal riparian countries, Jordan and Israel, have been consuming about 108 percent of their total usable water stocks, in other words, overusing their renewable water stocks by 15 percent per year. The prognosis is for continuing water shortages and for overexploitation of water supplies in both the short term and the long term through 2015, unless essential and politically difficult remedial action in the interrelated areas of conservation, distribution, consumption, and efficiency are taken—ideally basinwide.

Another complicating dimension is the issue of energy, water, and oil. Significant amounts of energy are needed to extract and move water in the Jordan basin. For example, Israel uses about 18 percent of its total national energy supply to pump water, and Jordan's water-energy ratio is not far behind. In both countries oil is the principal source of energy, thus linking water issues with petroleum.

The effects of ongoing water deficits, already an exigent factor in the Jordan basin, are cumulative and can quickly become irreversible. Neither known natural sources nor water technologies, now or in the

TABLE 6.3   Water Supply and Demand in Jordan Basin (in million cubic meters/yr)

	1987–1991 Average Supply Nondrought Conditions	Average Supply Pre-1992 Drought Conditions	1987–1991 Average Total Demand	1987–1991 Average Deficits Nondrought Conditions	Average Deficits Pre-1992 Drought Conditions	Projected Demand 2015–2020
Israel	1,950	1,600	2,100[a]	150–200	200	2,500–2,800
Jordan	900	700–750	800	100–125	100	1,600–1,800
Occupied Territories	650	450–550	600–650	75–100	100	—[b]

[a]Includes settlements in Occupied Territories and Golan Heights
[b]Future status indeterminate
Source: Author's figures.

near future, have the capacity to generate new usable water in needed quantities at an affordable cost. Failing a solution to the scarcity, both Israel and Jordan will have to curtail their social and economic development. The result will be heightened competition among these riparian countries and among domestic sectors within each country for the decreasing amounts of water, with concomitant destabilizing internal and regional repercussions. According to Israeli and Jordanian sources, Israel and Jordan already suffer an annual deficit of 220 million cubic meters (Mcm) and 100 Mcm a year, respectively; their cumulative deficits are equal to about one full year's supply.

Because of the current disparity in power among the Jordan basin's riparian countries—Jordan, Israel, and Syria—there appears to be no immediate prospect of a water war; although, despite Israel's overwhelming power, water-based hostilities are possible. However, water issues are central to the strategic planning of all the basin's riparian countries and water problems contribute importantly to the basin's interriparian tensions.

If current policies and patterns of consumption in Jordan and Israel persist, a mounting series of water crises will be touched off before the end of the decade, particularly if economic conditions deteriorate further or if there is a sustained drought. (This is highly probable, given the drought history of the basin.) The severity of the crisis could break present restraints on the conflict. If that occurs, water will combine with other underlying forces of instability and hostility among the basin's riparian countries, and water-driven warfare would almost certainly ensue, spilling out into the region beyond the basin. Jordan's King Husayn has stated privately that although he could conceive of few reasons to go to war with Israel, he could be compelled to fight over water despite the prospect of defeat.

Unless Israel and Jordan are able very quickly to devise effective policies for the reduction of water consumption, they will be unable to meet the developmental needs of their societies by the end of the decade. Whatever combination of actions might be taken, some degree of economic restructuring and a reduction in population growth must be a part of the process. Such alterations always result in social dislocation and hardship. Consequently, rather than warfare among the riparian countries (which is certainly possible), what is more likely to ensue from water-related crises in the coming decade is internal civil disorders, regime changes, political radicalization, and instability, particularly in countries where there is a combination of water and economic problems such as Jordan, Syria, Egypt, and under certain conditions, Israel.

The waters of the Occupied Territories have become so integral to

Israel that the delicate balance of Israel's water system has become dependent on the water system of the Territories. Typically, 70 percent of the groundwater on which Israel is dependent and between 35 percent and 40 percent of its sustainable annual water supply originates in the Occupied Territories. Israel is able to consume such a large portion of the Territories' waters because of its total control of their sources and a disproportionally small allocation to the two million Palestinian inhabitants of the West Bank and Gaza, who are allowed only 17 percent of the total water supply. West Bank farmers are still allocated the same amount of water they used in 1967; permits to dig new wells or improve existing ones are rarely granted, and they must pay higher costs for water than Israeli settlers whose water is subsidized. Israelis consume for domestic purposes alone about 300 liters per capita each day (l/c/d) while Palestinians use about 69 l/c/d, and in a few villages in Gaza, which is rapidly becoming a water wasteland, the consumption is less than 45 l/c/d, the minimum set by the World Health Organization for the maintenance of public health.

Given the extent to which Israel depends on the waters of the West Bank, it is inconceivable that an Israeli government would ever give up any part of the West Bank without an effective plan, replete with a full array of guarantees and inducements, that gives Israel secure, permanent access to sufficient quantities of the Territories' waters or guaranteed access to other comparable sources in the area, probably the Litani and Awali rivers in Lebanon. Since Israel already consumes 83 percent of the Territories' waters on both sides of the Green Line, there would be too little remaining to share in a meaningful way under any "Jordan-is-Palestine" arrangement.[19]

It might eventually be possible to overcome Israel's security justifications for retention of the Occupied Territories, but not the hydrological arguments, which will persist unless the water issue is settled. Water is a prime constituent of the security, political, and demographic factors that concern the region. It is water, in the final analysis, that will determine the future of the Occupied Territories, and by extension, the issue of conflict or peace.

In the meantime, unless patterns of consumption change, sometime between 1995 and 2005 Israel, Jordan, and the Occupied Territories will begin to experience such acute and progressively worsening recurrent water shortages and degradation of water quality that the effect can be likened to a situation in which the three areas were to run out of all renewable sources of fresh water. However, owing to insufficient financial resources, shortage of technical and managerial expertise, domestic and political constraints, and deep-seated, even implacable, feelings of mistrust and hostility among the basin's actors, the leaders of

Israel and Jordan will be unable to solve their water-related problems without outside assistance, preferably from a combination of sources: the United States, the EC, and the UN, and such international funding agencies as the International Monetary Fund (IMF) and the World Bank. Should water-driven hostilities break out in the Jordan basin, the conflict would almost certainly spill out to other parts of the region, with potential major damage to U.S. security and political interests.

The Euphrates Basin

The Euphrates basin does not suffer from water scarcity, except in a few highly localized situations. Rather, its problems lie in the hydropolitics of Turkey, Syria, and Iraq, the riparian countries that must share the river. The principal issues revolve around the reduction and diversion of flow to the lower riparian users (Syria and Iraq) and the degeneration of water quality. These problems stem from the large hydrological projects being undertaken in the upper reaches of the basin (chiefly, Turkey's GAP project) without sufficient prior consideration of their political, economic, and strategic implications. Moreover, water quality has been deteriorating because of indiscriminate polluting and too few purification facilities. Turkey and Syria are engaged in massive hydrological development schemes that if fully carried out will use up much of the available water in the Euphrates River.

Without an apportionment agreement among the riparian nations— and if Turkey utilizes all the water its plans call for—the flow to Syria would be reduced by 40 percent. And when both Turkey and Syria have taken what they need, the flow to Iraq would be reduced to "a briny trickle sufficient only to flush the river bed," that is, only one-eighth to one-fourth of what it currently receives.[20]

If the present situation is not resolved soon, several consequences could ensue: Turkey, as the upper riparian nation controlling the headwaters of the Euphrates, could alter the balance of power in the basin and enhance its role in the hydropolitics of the region; the probability of a water-driven conflict between Syria and Iraq could intensify; basic changes in the social, economic, and political structures of the basin's riparian countries could occur—for example, a shift away from agriculture; and current indebtedness, already serious, could increase. Any combination of these eventualities could seriously destabilize the basin's users and heighten the prospects for conflict.

Most of these consequences are real, although the likelihood of a Syrian-Iraqi conflict has been reduced in the aftermath of Iraq's defeat in the 1991 Gulf War. At present, a brief opportunity for urgently needed negotiations is available since neither the Turkish nor the Syrian projects are proceeding on schedule, due mostly to a shortage of funding.

If the issues are to be effectively resolved, they must be negotiated on a basinwide basis and ideally must produce a basinwide authority. So far, owing chiefly to Syrian-Iraqi antagonism, two decades of effort have only been sporadic, largely bilateral, and unsuccessful. Because of the gravity of the situation, the pace of the talks among the three riparian nations is picking up a little, but the discussions remain preliminary.

Turkey and Syria need hard-currency financing and expert help in water management, technology, and social planning. Neither is yet treating seriously the social impacts of their projects. Iraq has the same needs plus the need of a foreign work force to supplement Iraqi manpower reduced by the casualties of war. All three riparian nations need a basinwide agreement, the two lower riparian countries, Syria and Iraq, profoundly so.[21]

Generally speaking, the most plausible expectation for the Euphrates basin is that little international progress over the Euphrates' waters will be made for some time. The situation will fester in a minor way until sharp shortages are experienced downstream, at which time the tensions may erupt dramatically. Effecting a resolution before a dangerous flash point is reached is plainly an important interest for all the concerned actors, including the United States.

U.S. Role in the Region's Hydropolitics

If the hydraulic problems of the region are to be mitigated in time to avoid conflict, the United States must play an immediate, sustained, central, and genuinely evenhanded role, acting mainly as a facilitator/mediator, providing necessary inducements and guarantees for agreements as well as mobilizing and working with other outside parties to assist in the effort. Also, the United States must be prepared to provide—preferably in conjunction with other powers—sufficient, strictly dedicated financial resources to make possible the economic restructuring essential to solving the region's water problems without destabilizing political and socioeconomic hardships.

Clearly, the ideal solution to the hydropolitical problems of both basins would be the creation of basinwide authorities with enough independence, power, funding, and expertise to determine and regulate water usage among the riparian nations.

U.S. influence among the principal users of the Jordan basin's waters is sufficiently strong that the United States could play a positive role. However, U.S. influence (or that of any other single outside party) in the Euphrates basin is in most respects very limited. Nevertheless, there is a circumscribed but effective role for the United States. Its largest stake is in Turkey, which is where its endeavors should be focused. In addition to using its limited leverage, the United States can mobilize international diplomatic efforts to encourage a basinwide agreement with inducements of economic aid and political support in the international arena when possible, for instance, for various initiatives in the UN or the World Bank. Such actions, together with judiciously proffered water technology and expertise could advance U.S. interests in the basins and in the region simultaneously.

In this regard, there is something significant that the United States can do to serve its own interests and simultaneously those of riparian nations globally; that is to form a special interagency group, encompassing both the executive and legislative branches, to coordinate U.S. policy formulation in the realm of international freshwater issues. This group should serve functions of coordination, data collection, policy and project assessment, education, and review. Its purview should include the technological, political, socioeconomic, strategic, and legal dimensions of international water-use issues.

Additionally, the United States could lead a cooperative initiative in encouraging the creation of Middle East regional water institutes that would be composed of staff, fellows, trainees, and other personnel from the world's major basins and would perform several functions. They would operate as technical and policy clearinghouses and would provide data, expertise, research, and educational opportunities necessary to develop the entrepreneurial, human, and technical resources that are currently lacking. They would supply hydrological, economic, and other social-scientific analytic tools and could foster interaction among basin and regional specialists. Eventually, those scientists and technocrats working at such institutes could communicate sufficiently to develop a shared understanding of the water situation, available technologies, and potential solutions. They could become a strong force for cooperation and a community of informed officials and experts throughout the region to press for and guide effective cooperative water policies.

A Final Observation: Interconnections

The very factors that entwine people, water, and economics also internationalize them. Water flows and people migrate, carrying issues and problems intrinsic to both across borders. In today's interdependent world, national economic determinants are powerfully influenced by larger regional and global forces, beyond the boundaries of individual countries. In the Middle East these linkages yield the following proposition: All major events in one area of the region will ultimately have an impact on events in all other areas. If the promotion and protection of U.S. interests in the region are to be successful, this axiom of Middle Eastern politics must be taken into account by policymakers.

Because of the basic, pervasive nature of water, demographics, and economics, negotiations focused on one of these variables must perforce involve consideration of the others as well; moreover, each of them is plaited with a host of political and ideological issues that also must be reckoned with. These are clearly very recalcitrant and complex issues that are conflict-prone. In particular, all parties, including the United States, should give more intense and comprehensive attention to the region's hydropolitics, a vital issue heretofore undervalued. In seeking to advance and maintain its interests in the Middle East, even with the end of superpower rivalry, the United States must devise policies and strategies that are broadly gauged, flexible, and fully commensurate with the region's complexities.

Notes

1. Delwin Roy, "The Egyptian Debt: Forgive or Forget?" *The Political Economy of Contemporary Egypt*, Ibrahim Oweiss, ed. (Washington, D.C.: Georgetown University Center for Contemporary Arab Studies, 1990), and "The Hidden Economy of Egypt and its Relationship to Current and Future Economic and Political Stability," unpublished paper, January 1989; I am grateful to Delwin Roy for permission to use this paper; "Turkey," *The Economist*, January 27, 1990, p. 109; *Jerusalem Post* (International Edition), March 10 & 17, 1990; Ruth Matson, *The Euphrates River Basin. Political, Socio-Economic, and Strategic Issues: Syria* (Carbondale, Ill.: Southern Illinois University Press, 1993), pp. 49–54; T. Naff, *The Jordan River Basin. Political, Socio-Economic, and Strategic Issues: Jordan and Israel* (Carbondale, Ill.: Southern Illinois University Press, forthcoming), pp. 23–24.

2. Naff, *Jordan River Basin*, pp. 22–23; *New York Times*, October 6, November 9 & 11, December 20, 1989; *The Economist*, June 2-12, 1990, pp. 39–40.

3. Geraldine Brooks, "The Israeli Kibbutz Takes a Capitalist Tack to Keep Socialist Ideal," *Wall Street Journal*, September 21, 1989; see also Alison M. Bowes, "The Experiment That Did Not Fail: Image and Reality in the Israeli Kibbutz," *International Journal of Middle Eastern Studies* 22, no. 1 (February 1990), pp. 85–101.

4. Naff, *Jordan River Basin: Israel*, pp. 84–85; Joel Brinkley, "Hard Facts Defeat Israeli Researcher," *New York Times*, October 22, 1989; Simcha Bahiri,

Construction and Housing in the West Bank and Gaza (Jerusalem: West Bank Data Project [WBDP], 1989), pp. 96–97.

5. Frederick Frey, *The Euphrates River Basin. Political, Socio-Economic, and Strategic Issues: Turkey* (Carbondale, Ill.: Southern Illinois University Press, forthcoming), pp. 8-12, 58–65; for a complete treatment of the GAP project, see John Kolars and William Mitchell, *The Euphrates River and the Southeast Anatolian Development Project* (Carbondale, Ill.: Southern Illinois University Press, 1991).

6. Frey, *Euphrates*, pp. 59–61.

7. Roy, "The Egyptian Debt" and "The Hidden Economy of Egypt."

8. Ibid.

9. United Nations, *World Population Prospects 1988* (New York: United Nations, 1989), pp. 74–77, 212–213, 236–237, 358–359, 414–415, 422–423, 540–541, 550–551; Israel, Central Bureau of Statistics, *Statistical Abstract of Israel* (Jerusalem, 1988), pp. 30–70; Hashemite Kingdom of Jordan, Ministry of Planning, *Five-Year Plan for Economic and Social Development, 1986–1990* (Amman, n.d.), pp. 61–65; Naff, *Jordan River Basin: Jordan*, pp. 22–24.

10. See Basim Musallam, *Sex and Society in Islam* (New York: Cambridge University Press, 1983).

11. UN, *World Population*, pp. 422–423; Jordan, *Five Year Plan*, pp. 61–65; Naff, *Jordan River Basin: Jordan*, pp. 22–24.

12. Delwin Roy and Thomas Naff, "Ba'thist Ideology, Economic Development, and Educational Strategy," *Middle Eastern Studies* 25, no. 4 (October 1989), pp. 456 and 461; Nidhal Taqi Addine and Abd al-Aziz al-Masri, "Water Policy in Syria and its Strategic Implications," (in Arabic), unpublished paper delivered at a conference in Amman on Middle Eastern water resources and their importance to the Arab world, April 2–4, 1989.

13. Roy and Naff, "Ba'thist Ideology," p. 454; Taqi Addine and al-Masri, "Water Policy in Syria."

14. Roy and Naff, "Ba'thist Ideology," pp. 472-477; UN *World Population*, pp. 540–541.

15. Naff, *Jordan River Basin: Israel*, pp. 8-12; Israel, *Statistical Abstract*, pp. 30–70; Meron Benvenisti, *The West Bank Handbook* (Jerusalem: WBDP, 1986), pp. 49–54.

16. Alan Cowell, *New York Times*, June 21, 1990, p. A9; Joel Brinkley, *New York Times*, July 18, 1990, p. A11.

17. UN, *World Population*, pp. 74–551.

18. Dale Eickelman, commentary in *Southwest Asia and the Middle East: Proceedings*, Strategy Development Seminar, Dec. 12–13, 1989, R. A. Cossa and Phebe Marr, eds. (Washington, D.C.: INSS, National Defense University, 1990), pp. 56–57; on the issue of population and conflict, see Nazli Choucri, ed., *Multi-disciplinary Perspectives on Population and Conflict* (Syracuse: Syracuse University Press, 1984).

19. Naff, *Jordan River Basin: Israel*, pp. 35–47; Brinkley, "Hard Facts," *New York Times*, October 1989; Benvenisti, *Handbook*, pp. 223–225.

20. John Kolars, *The Euphrates River and the Southwest Anatolian Project:*

Cornucopia or Pandora's Box? (Carbondale, Ill.: Southern Illinois University Press, 1992); Angus Hindley, "Battle Lines Drawn for the Euphrates," *MEED* October 13, 1989, pp. 4–5; *Financial Times* (London), "Shrinking Euphrates Raises Turkish-Syrian Tension," October 28, 1989, p. 20.

21. In papers delivered at the April 1989 water conference in Amman, experts from Syria and Iraq called for international, that is, basinwide, cooperation on the Euphrates River. See Taqi Addine and al-Masri, "Water Policy in Syria," and a paper submitted by the Ministry of Agriculture and Irrigation in Iraq entitled "The Water Resources of Iraq and the Evolution of Their Use" (in Arabic), unpublished. Thus far, there have been no moves in this direction by policy makers in either Syria or Iraq.

Suggested Reading

Ibrahim, Ibrahim, ed., *Arab Resources*, London: Croom Helm, 1983.

Ibrahim, Saad Eddin, *The New Arab Social Order*, London: Croom Helm, 1982.

Naff, Thomas, "Water: An Emerging Issue in the Middle East?" *Annals, Journal of the American Academy of Political and Social Science*, no. 482 (November 1985).

Naff, Thomas, and Matson, Ruth, *Water in the Middle East: Conflict or Cooperation?* Boulder, Colo.: Westview Press, 1984.

Richards, Alan, and Waterbury, John, *A Political Economy of the Middle East: State, Class, and Economic Development*, Boulder, Colo.: Westview Press, 1990.

United Nations, Department of International Economic and Social Affairs, *World Population Prospects 1988*, New York: United Nations, 1989.

7

Beyond Geopolitics: Ethnic and Sectarian Conflict Elimination in the Middle East and North Africa

Abdul Aziz Said

Ethnicity and sectarianism are major political and human fault lines in the Middle East. For centuries before the arrival of European colonialism, ethnic and religious allegiances determined the boundaries of communal loyalties and the framework in which political dynamics transpired. The Europeans helped to create new frameworks for interaction beyond the ethnic group and religious community in the Middle East, but they failed in many instances to fully integrate diverse people with a distinctive tradition and history of separateness into the newly created nation-states. As a result, throughout the Middle East, Southwest Asia, and the northern third of Africa, ethnicity and sectarianism have become forces for political instability that threaten the fragmentation of the nation-state in several regions. It is not clear whether, during the coming decade, nation-states will persist or whether fissiparous forces will be able to reconstitute themselves as viable new entities.

The nation-state is the arena in which ethnic and sectarian conflicts normally occur. Within its ambit, governments often try to ignore or, where necessary, suppress the aspirations of domestic ethnic and religious groups or to impose values of a dominant ruling class. Under such circumstances, ethnic and sectarian groups feel impelled to mobilize and to place demands upon the state ranging from political representation and participation in decision making to protection of human rights, autonomy, and even separation. Ethnic and sectarian activism takes a variety of forms, from formation of political parties to adoption of violent strategies.

163

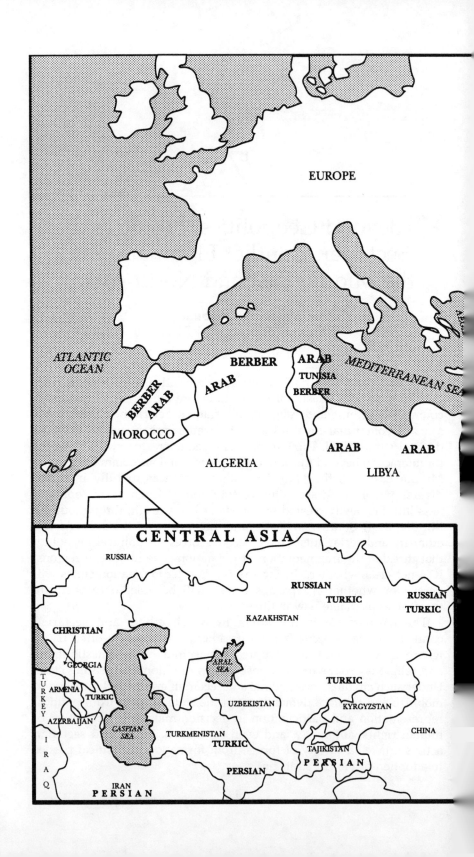

ATLANTIC
OCEAN

EUROPE

MEDITERRANEAN SEA

BERBER   ARAB
TUNISIA

BERBER
ARAB   ARAB
BERBER

MOROCCO

ARAB   ARAB

ALGERIA   LIBYA

CENTRAL ASIA

RUSSIA

RUSSIAN
TURKIC

RUSSIAN
TURKIC

KAZAKHSTAN

CHRISTIAN

GEORGIA

ARAL
SEA

T
U
R
K
E
Y

ARMENIA

TURKIC

TURKIC

AZERBAIJAN

UZBEKISTAN

KYRGYZSTAN

I
R
A
Q

CASPIAN
SEA

TURKMENISTAN

CHINA

TURKIC

TAJIKISTAN

PERSIAN

PERSIAN

IRAN
PERSIAN

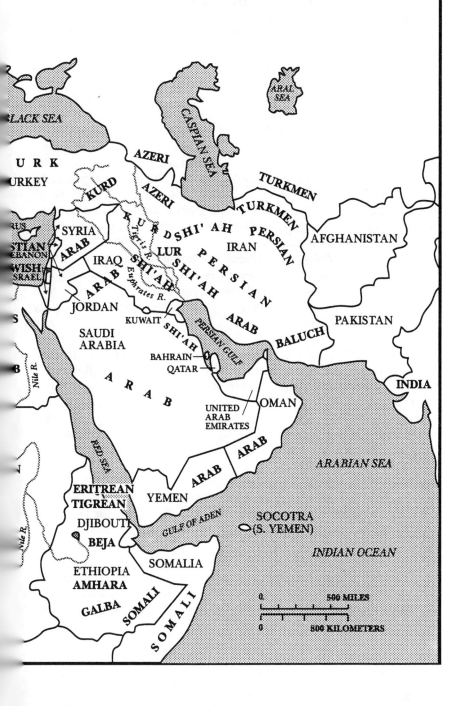

THE MIDDLE EAST
LINGUISTIC & RELIGIOUS
COMMUNITIES

ARAL SEA

BLACK SEA

CASPIAN SEA

TURK

URKEY

AZERI

KURD

AZERI

TURKMEN

TURKMEN

SYRIA

ARAB

KURD

SHI'AH

PERSIAN

AFGHANISTAN

RUS

STIAN
EBANON

WISH
SRAEL

IRAQ

ARAB

Tigris R.

LUR

SHI'AH

IRAN

PERSIAN

JORDAN

Euphrates R.

KUWAIT

SHI'AH

PERSIAN GULF

ARAB

PAKISTAN

SAUDI
ARABIA

BAHRAIN
QATAR

BALUCH

Nile R.

ARAB

INDIA

B

UNITED
ARAB
EMIRATES

OMAN

RED SEA

ARAB

ARABIAN SEA

ERITREAN
TIGREAN

YEMEN

ARAB

DJIBOUTI

GULF OF ADEN

SOCOTRA
(S. YEMEN)

Nile R.

BEJA

INDIAN OCEAN

ETHIOPIA
AMHARA

SOMALIA

GALBA

SOMALI

SOMALI

SOMALI

0   500 MILES

0   800 KILOMETERS

The context of international relations may be changing from the historic focus on nation-states as the predominant actors toward a more complex order in which ethnic and sectarian groups compete, as actors, for influence. The present global system is simultaneously more parochial and more cosmopolitan than the international system of nation-states we are leaving behind. On the one hand, Western Europe is moving toward economic unity and close political association; on the other hand, Eastern Europe is undergoing several processes of decomposition—most notably in Yugoslavia and the former Soviet Union. The Baltic Republics of Latvia, Estonia, and Lithuania have already become members in good standing in the United Nations. Fragmentation of the former Soviet Union is potentially destabilizing for neighboring states in the Middle East. Bonds of culture, language, and religion affect people in the Iran-Transcaucasus and Central Asian regions, as well as in Turkey and Afghanistan. As a counterpoint, the Kurds cross the borders of Syria, Turkey, Iraq, and Iran. Alawis are found in Turkey and Syria, and Shiites inhabit a region separated by the borders of Iraq and Iran. The latter are also located in Lebanon and in several Persian Gulf emirates.

Ethnicity, geography, and religion are not always unifying factors, however. Geography actually separates the Berbers of northern and southern Morocco, as well as Berber communities in Algeria, thus precluding effective political coordination. Even where propinquity exists, a common people can fall into rivalry of such depth and dimension as to destroy both the nation and the state—as in the tragic instance of the Republic of Somalia. Even where separatist impulses exist—as among the Nilo-Hamitic people of the southern Sudan or the Kurds in northern Iraq—local rivalries erode effective political action (see map).

Throughout the region, sectarian and ethnic challenges to the nation-state concept pose particularly serious issues for the international community. The legal foundations of international order rest on the principle of sovereignty and full recognition of territorial integrity; ethnic separatists argue in favor of the common "folk" principle and their inherent right of self-determination. At issue is the need for integration, on the one hand, and the desire for local self-determination, on the other. For U.S. policymakers the choices are Hobbesian:

- Turkey, a traditional NATO ally, has confronted a Kurdish separatist movement for more than a decade. Does the United States support Turkey's territorial integrity, or self-determination for the Kurds?

- Iraq, where Saddam Husayn has proved a regional trouble-maker, would fragment if his overthrow resulted in Shiite-Kurdish independence, thus upsetting the strategic balance in the Persian Gulf. Does the United States seek overthrow at the risk of fragmentation?
- Lebanon's Balkanization would have comparable consequences in the Near East—the only apparent alternative being subordination of Lebanon to Syrian hegemony. Does the United States support the sovereignty of Lebanon or does it sacrifice sovereignty for stability?

There has been some reconciliation between the competing interests of state and ethnic groups in the Middle East, but strong identification with one's ethnic group and disdain for others remain. Dispute resolution techniques among competing groups occasionally fail, and governments, charged with internal order, are inclined to turn to coercive instruments to stifle dissent. As a result, stability and order merge into issues of legitimacy and self-determination. For the U.S. policymaker, human and political rights frequently have to be weighed in the balance against U.S. national interests. As a result, policy choices inevitably displease constituencies at home and in the Middle East.

Explanations of Ethnic and Sectarian Politics

Analyses of ethnicity and sectarianism have favored ethnic over religious explanations and have placed sectarianism within the context of ethnicity. The boundaries of ethnicity are both broad and fluid. Jack Stack defines ethnicity as a "group identity that is essentially fluid depending upon how the boundaries of an ethnic group are drawn in a specific context, and hence the precise context of ethnic identity is defined in relation to distinct external stimuli.[1] Nation-states thus use ethnicity to legitimize their existence. Iraq, for example, emphasizes its Arab character to distinguish itself from non-Arab Iran and thus mobilize Arab support on behalf of its foreign policy.

Other scholars have their own unique perspective. Some see ethnicity and sectarianism as interwoven; others see ethnicity as mythic in character; still others contend that religion is the most cohesive element of ethnicity because it is associated with community and diminishes political and ethnic boundaries. Common among all these perspectives is the raising of people-consciousness—a sense of communalism, a shared identity, and a feeling of common aspiration.[2] Ascriptively, the ties may involve blood, language, religion, and custom.

The processes of state-building and modernization can play a moderating role among domestic groups if they are conducted without penalty to any particular people; alternatively, they can exacerbate endemic rivalries and tensions. All too frequently, governing institutions are viewed by ethnic minorities as the preserve of elite groups, concerned with the preservation and protection of special interest groups, clans, and others loyal to the leadership. Such arrangements of power and influence are patrimonial and rarely provide a solid foundation for processes of political development and modernization, as experienced and understood by the West in general and the United States in particular.

Indeed, awareness of one's ethnicity may be, to a great degree, a function of coercive assimilation that is fostered by modernization. When social groups are involved in the processes, cooperation does not necessarily occur. Increased contact, exposure, and communication may well exaggerate one's self-image, magnify cultural differences, produce conflict, and induce political disassociation. Expatriate Palestinians, Lebanese, and Syrians in the Arab Gulf states feel alienated from the tribal setting there. Economic development—an increase in material goods and services—does not immunize a society from ethnic conflict. Oil revenues in the Arab states of the Gulf have created a class of wealthy Arabs and a new class consciousness on the part of the less privileged population. The concomitants of economic growth—urbanization, secularization, industrialization—may lead to competition over limited opportunities and resources. Previous inter-ethnic differences may have fit stable patterns of comparative advantage or coexistence, although industrial-technical society tends to standardize economic behavior and produces competitive channels of achievement.

Policymakers, if they are to fashion a coherent approach to the problem, must evaluate the nexus between government strategies and the distribution of resources and rewards in Middle Eastern societies. Involved are majority and minority rights and the building of broad-based loyalties in pluralistic nation-states. What appears to be parochialism in American eyes, has far more dramatic meaning within the Middle Eastern context. Debates over the official language of government, religious foundations of the state, educational curricula, or the directorship of a state-run enterprise all too often mask deeper issues of culture, religious rights, or opportunities for group access to the ladder of social mobility or economic advantage. How the processes unfold determines whether modernization generates crosscutting, coinciding, or conflictual identities within the nation-state.[3]

Conceptually at the opposite extreme, ethnic consciousness may produce a broadened sense of common identity. This form of exclusivity may be expressed in a way that flattens out narrow geographic boundaries—as in a feeling of Egyptian or even Iraqi "Arabness." Indeed, an ethnic group is a culture. The Turkish inhabitants of the former Soviet Union also identify with the larger Turkic culture.

Psychology plays an important role in the configuration and matrices of ethnic interaction. It focuses on the roots of ethnic conflict and the fundamental differences between ethnic groups, and it requires an exploration of human beings, their levels of interaction, and cross-currents such as social change and economic development.[4] Predictability of ethnic conflict is determined by a wide-range of factors. "Competition" is critical among them. Although competition is inevitable and, in some instances, constructive, how it is managed and the issues and outcomes that are involved frequently determine whether competition achieves fruitful interaction or merges into outright conflict. Coptic Christian and Islamic reformist interaction in Egypt, for example, is of the constructive variety on most occasions. In neighboring Sudan, by comparison, competition between Muslim northerners and Christian southerners after independence from colonial rule has led to widespread armed conflict of the state-threatening variety. Conflict is almost inevitable where political representation is denied or when a particular community is economically disadvantaged. In such circumstances, the state most often is found to have recourse to instruments of repression, which in turn generates deeper conflict.

Whether we are dealing with the suppression of the Kurds in Iran, Iraq, or Turkey, the present ethnic conflicts in Lebanon, or the Israeli-Palestinian conflict, we are naturally attracted to an anomaly of the twentieth century—the impulse for Western modernization and the accelerating drive for self-determination among various linguistic, religious, and geographical ethnic groups. These conflicts underscore the tension between state-building, modernization, and human rights. When a state must assimilate ethnic groups within its borders in order to provide the modern economic, health, and social resources that citizens of the twenty-first century deserve, the same ethnic groups resist the devaluation of their ethnic identity. Middle Eastern governments have responded by forcing secessionist ethnic groups to adapt to the political economy of the state. Middle Eastern states wracked by ethnic conflicts, such as Lebanon, the Sudan, Iraq, and Israel, are less inclined to view the claims of self-determination and secession as expressions of some transcendent human struggle than are most other states that experience an acceptable level of ethnic conflict that does not approach disassociation. The extent to which human rights of most minority groups are compromised is almost uniformly beyond reasonable levels.

Regional Ethnic and Sectarian Conflicts

The likelihood of widening ethnic and sectarian conflicts in the Middle East is closely related to resources—financial and economic—and to their distribution, to processes of modernization, to development, and to prospects for political pluralism. Increasingly, issues of economic equity, political participation, and retention of traditional cultural values arise. Where governments are found wanting, either through misunderstanding, arrogance, or misapplication of resources, alienation between central authority and ethnic and sectarian forces crystallizes.

The result, almost ineluctably, is conflict, violent expression of opposition, or the emergence of separatist movements that not only threaten national cohesion but also spill across borders, destabilizing neighboring states. In such circumstances, ethnicity and sectarianism are transformed into security issues, and military establishments are called upon to suppress dissident sentiments. The Iraqi government suppresses the Kurds and the Shiites in the name of national security and the Syrian government suppresses the Sunni Muslim Brotherhood in the name of national cohesion.

Islam, Arabs, and the West

Some states in the Middle East, including Kuwait, Bahrain, and Jordan, are successors to European-administered colonial territories. Others, including Syria, Iran, and Iraq, are reconstructions of traditional entities. Communities in these states had status according to lineage and a role commensurate with work. When these states were consolidated following World War I and World War II, territorial arrangements were imposed by European powers, in many cases dividing ethnic groups indiscriminately.

The establishment of modern nation-states in the Middle East accompanied discontinuity both with traditional organization and with basic precepts and practices of Islam. Islamic institutions lost much of their effectiveness as organizing principles and as safeguards for social justice and political participation. The Sharia (Islamic law), which had served as a protective code for individual Muslims since the seventh century, suffers near total neglect. The universalism of Islam has not found expression in the new nation-states.

The West expected the newly emerging Middle Eastern countries to become imitations of the West; so did Middle Eastern leaders. Muhammad Ali Jinna's Islamic Pakistan, the first country to so declare itself, was Islamic only in name. In essence it was an adaptation of a Western nation-state system that became increasingly authoritarian. Iran moved from the Westernized Shah, through Bazirgan and Bani Sadr to Khomeini and to Rafsanjani. Perhaps a less Western Shah could have kept Khomeini in his Western exile in Paris.

The resulting dilemma for Middle Eastern leaders is that when they reject Western political, economic, and social values as inappropriate to their needs, the West views them as xenophobic and reactionary. They become isolated internationally—Khomeini and Qadhafi are two glaring examples. However, when Middle Easterners compromise their own values and traditions and adopt those of the West, they suffer internal displacement. They are rejected domestically. The Shah of Iran and Sadat of Egypt were two tragic victims.

The present nation-states in the Middle East were created where previously there were no nation-states based on territorial sovereignty. Today, many states are artificial entities, territorially defined but internally divided, trying to develop into a cohesive unit. In most cases, a given concept of nationality is incongruent with the political boundaries of a given state.

In the Arab world (Turkey and Iran are analyzed later), no state is free of major ethnic divisions except Egypt and Tunisia. Even in Egypt, sectarian conflict persists between the dominant majority of Sunni Muslims and the Christian Copts who constitute a significant minority.

In Iraq, more than 50 percent of the population belongs to the Shiite sect of Islam, yet the Arab Sunni Muslims occupy dominant government positions. Approximately 20 percent of the population is Kurdish. The Iraqi Kurds are organized into a number of political parties including the Kurdish Democratic party of Iraq (KDP) and the Patriotic Union of Kurdistan (PUK). The Kurdish struggle for self-determination continues to disrupt the national life of Iraq.

In some Arab Gulf states, there is a large minority of Shiites and non-Arabs, ruled by Sunnis and Arabs. Here ethnic and sectarian conflicts intersect. In Bahrain, for example, the majority of the population is Shiite, ruled by the Sunni Khalifa family. Additionally, a large number of third-country expatriates, including Iranians, Baluchis, Syrians, Lebanese, and Palestinians, live throughout the states of the Gulf. Even in Saudi Arabia, until recently an ethnically homogeneous country, the principal cities of Jidda and Riyadh comprise large numbers of nonindigenous inhabitants. Most of the non-Saudis are Muslim Arabs and non-Arab Muslims from Asia and Africa.

A large number of Shiites live in the Eastern province of Saudi Arabia. Calls by Shiites and expatriates for participation in the political systems of the Gulf Arab states continue to fall upon deaf ears.

Ethnicity and sectarianism have also played an important role in the formation and evolution of political parties and movements in the Fertile Crescent, that is, Syria, Lebanon, Jordan, and Iraq. Ethnic groups have been successful in altering party agendas. For example, in Iraq and Syria, the Baath party was originally secular with a pan-Arab platform. When the Baathists consolidated their power in the early 1970s, in Syria the party became involved in a sectarian struggle with the Sunnis and in an ethnic struggle with the Kurds. In Iraq, the Baath party became involved in a sectarian struggle with the Shiites and in an ethnic struggle with the Kurds. Furthermore, ethnic and sectarian groups have affected the way parties pursue their programs. The Muslim Brotherhood of Syria began as a political movement seeking Sunni domination of the government. Following the Alawi dominance of the Baath party and the erosion of political pluralism, the Muslim Brotherhood resorted to terrorism and violence.[5] In Lebanon, ethnic and sectarian conflict have combined and have evolved into a regional conflict involving Syria, Iraq, Iran, Israel, Libya, and the PLO. The Lebanese civil war reflected the inability of the Arab states, Iran, Israel, and the United States to forge a workable settlement. The war ended in 1989, and elections were held in September 1992. Jordan experiences increasing challenges from the Palestinian population.

Ethnic and sectarian conflict remains constant in contemporary Arab politics. Future developments in Lebanon, the course of the Palestinian-Israeli peace process, and the direction of democratization will be determined by the strength of ethnic and sectarian bonds. The decade of the 1990s could witness intensified struggles for power in the region. Secular ideology, such as state-centered nationalism, may also be under attack. The Baathist regime of Syria is becoming increasingly unpopular domestically, incapable of responding to emerging desires for privatization and democratization. In Iraq, the situation is far more serious. Here the Baath regime faced threats to its survival in 1991 from rebellions initiated by its Kurdish and Shiite populations in the wake of the 1991 Gulf War. Similarly, the small Arab states of the Gulf find themselves increasingly pressured by local demands for democratization as well as Islamization and are caught in the rivalries between Saudi Arabia, Iraq, and Iran. It is possible that the small Arab Gulf states could lose their independence in the process. The persistence of discrimination against Shiites in the eastern province of Saudi Arabia could lead to continued violence. The civil war continues to devastate the Sudan. Morocco and Algeria could experience increasing ethnic conflicts, as well as secular versus religious conflicts, as governments seek to resolve demographic, economic, and crosscutting class problems.

Turkey

Turkey's population is a mosaic of ethnic and sectarian groups with distinct cultural boundaries, including Greeks, Armenians, Chaldians, Jews, Kurds, and Alevis (known as Alawis in Syria). The most important ethnic groups are the Kurds and the Alevis. The Kurds live in southeastern Turkey and number about ten million, and the Alevis live in south-central Turkey and number about five million. (The total population of Turkey is approximately fifty-five million and is predominantly Sunni Muslim.)

The Alevis, an offshoot of Shiite Islam, are a rural people who have made important strides in the last twenty years. Their social mobility has been accompanied by economic clashes, since the suspicion by Sunni Turks of Shiite Alevis dates back to Ottoman history. Traditionally, Alevis are comfortable with secularism. Consequently, recent Islamic revival in Turkey has intensified Sunni-Alevi tensions.

The Kurds have resisted assimilation into Mustafa Kemal's ideal of Turkish nationhood. The language spoken in rural eastern Turkey is Kurdish, not Turkish. Since the early nineteenth century, the populations of the Kurdish regions have been the most fractious. Although the Kurdish region was secured by the Ottomans in 1849, rebellions in this area have persisted. In the 1890s the Kurds and Armenians were at war, and in 1925 there was a Kurdish rebellion led by the Shaykh of Palu. In 1930, 1936, and 1937 there were more Kurdish rebellions. In fact, Kurdish rebellions have been endemic in Ottoman and in recent Turkish history. Currently there is a movement, led by a leftist Kurdish revolutionary party, the PKK (Turkish Workers' party), supported by Syrian authorities and, recently, by the Iraqi government. The PKK is an offshoot of DISC, an acronym for the Revolutionary Workers Union, which was organized during the late 1960s and early 1970s. Some Kurdish fighters are trained in the Biqaa Valley in Lebanon, which is under Syrian control. Recently, terrorism has risen in villages in eastern Turkey. The Turkish government is pursuing a purely military response, with little allowance for peaceful settlement. The response has included cross-border raids into northern Iraq, areas considered refuge zones for Kurds fleeing Saddam Husayn's repression in the wake of the 1991 Gulf War.

Iran

Iran is a nation of ethnic groups, although Persian speakers predominate. The Azerbaijanis in the northwestern part of Iran, numbering approximately ten million, have been influenced by their geographical proximity to the former Soviet Union. In 1908 oil was discovered in Baku in Soviet Azerbaijan. Many from Tabriz went to work there and brought back ideas from the Mensheviks and the Bolsheviks. Historically, Tabriz has been a fertile ground for radicalism and progressive secularism. That tradition persists through the present.

In the Caspian Sea region, in Gilan, and in Mazandaran, interactions with Russia and then the former Soviet Union have produced a more liberal secular culture. For example, women used to work in the fields without veils. The region continues to resist Islamic revival through the present time.

In the northeast, the Turkomans, descendants of the Mongols, have been historically ignored, with the exception of the city of Mashhad, due to its religious significance. Historically, the Turkomans have been subdued and have not resisted the central government in Tehran. They did, however, organize a resistance movement between 1980 and 1981 over the issue of land reform. Aided by the leftist *Fidayiin* (guerrillas), they took over much of the land and created peasant *shuras* (councils). Because of this leftist orientation, Khomeini crushed this revolt and many of the Turkomen leaders were killed.

In the southeast, the Baluchis have been the most underprivileged, and in fact a minority have been almost totally ignored. Because of the easy Baluchi access to Pakistan and Afghanistan, the Iranian government has not been willing to allocate resources to this southeast region. Baluchis have traditionally relied on the drug trade for survival because there is no industrial base in their region. There has been, however, no real outcry or public rebellion over this trade.

In the south-central part of Iran, bordering the Gulf, there is a significant Arab population. The Arabs in this region have been economically well off. The Shah of Iran, Mohammad Reza Pahlavi, built huge naval ports there, as well as high-tech oil facilities to export oil.

Khuzistan in the southwest has been perhaps the most important region for the Iranian government, because 90 percent of the Iranian oil reserves are there. It used to be highly populated with Arabs, but with the discovery of oil many Persian technocrats came from all over the country. Thus the ethnic population has dramatically changed. Arabs have since been deprived of political rights. They are denied the right to organize politically. The control of the Iranian government remains intact. During the Iran-Iraq War of 1980–1988, Iraq tried to appeal to the Arabs of Khuzistan to revolt against the Iranian government and establish a Republic of Arabistan. This attempt failed, as did Iranian appeals to Iraqi Shiites to revolt. These failures indicate that the nation-state, though fragile, is not extinct.

The region of Kurdistan in north-central Iran has always presented the central government of Iran with serious challenges to its authority. Kurdistan is a mountainous region with approximately five million Kurds living mainly under a peasant rural economy. They have had close interaction with the Kurds of Iraq and somewhat more distant relations with the Kurds of Turkey and Syria.

There have been two dominant Kurdish political parties in Iran, the KDP and the KOMALA. The KDP, the strongest Kurdish political party in Iran, is nationalist. Its motto has been, "Autonomy for Kurdistan, Independence for Iran." The central government continues to ignore and resist its first demand.

KOMALA, which has been Marxist and leftist in orientation, joined with other small groups and founded the communist party. It has fought with the KDP because of that group's negotiations with the central government. KOMALA is committed to self-determination.

After the revolution of 1979, the Kurds raised the issue of autonomy almost immediately. They explained to the Khomeinists, "We have been suppressed by the Shah and so have you; you want an Islamic Republic and we want autonomy." The Khomeini regime felt threatened because much of the left supported the Kurds. In addition, because of the region was known for its opposition to the central government, other opposition groups became headquartered in the Kurdish region. Khomeini's response to this challenge was bloody and brutal. The KDP had to move back into the mountains. Since the revolution, Kurdistan has not seen much peace. At the same time, the KDP has sought the support of the Iraqi government, thus antagonizing the Iraqi Kurds. Traditionally, both Iran and Iraq manipulated the Kurds to their respective advantages.

Finally, in the central plateau of Iran is a group called the Lurs, who have not had as strong an impact on Iran as the Turks or the Kurds. The geography of the central plateau makes it difficult for them to carry out operations against the central government.

Ethnicity intensified in Iran in the twentieth century when Reza Shah began the process of national integration in the mid-1920s. Reza Shah patterned himself after Mustafa Kemal in Turkey. When the opportunities for resistance arose, however, tribes rebelled. Regardless of the regime in power. Iranian governments almost always crush these uprisings ruthlessly. A source of concern to the government has been the rise of separatist pressures from the independent republics emerging from the former Soviet Union. The existence of an independent Azerbaijani Republic could fuel comparable sentiment in northwestern Iran or, at minimum, calls for special political accommodation. Similarly, disjunction with Moscow by one or several of the Central Asian republics—Tajikistan—could have a destabilizing influence on Afghanistan—where Mujahidin insurgency persists—and on neighboring Turkmenistan populations.

Although it is hard to imagine dismemberment or secession in Iran, calls for autonomy will continue and ethnic conflicts will persist. There is no evidence of change in the Iranian response to ethnic conflicts.

The Caucasus and Central Asia: Emerging Problems

The collapse of the Soviet Union at the end of 1991 and the creation of a string of independent republics in the Caucasus and Central Asia (two Christian and six Muslim) are likely to have a profound although as yet unpredictable impact on ethnic and even sectarian politics in the region. For Moscow, fragmentation has spelled a loss of empire, and for Russians generally a loss of identity. The march of Russian imperialism to the south has finally been reversed after more than a century and a half of struggle by Muslims against Slavic domination.

This struggle has deep roots in the Muslim territory to the south. Resistance to the Russians by the Turkic Muslim population of Soviet Central Asia and the Caucasus began in the 1830s in the Caucasus and continued until the 1860s. During the latter part of the nineteenth century, another movement of resistance to Russian penetration took place in the Kazan area in the Crimean region. In the twentieth century, the Basmagi in Soviet Turkistan took arms against the Soviets from 1917 until 1925. The Soviet response was brutal. The Basmagi movement was repressed, and the Soviets changed the Arabic alphabet of South Turkistan to the Cyrillic alphabet. Since 1960, however, Moscow has allowed Muslims to perform the pilgrimage to Mecca.

Despite their cultural alienation from Moscow, the Muslim peoples residing in Azerbaijan and the five Central Asian republics were profoundly shocked by the collapse of the Soviet Union. There had been no advanced preparation for independence. Local institutions of government had been dominated by Moscow; discredited local leadership had to be replaced or transformed along nationalist lines. As Moscow's subventions and budgetary support evaporated, the leadership of the republics needed to look elsewhere for economic ties and for assistance in creating new economic structures and systems.

Critical are boundary issues directly bearing on ethnic politics. The former provincial borders inherited from the divide-and-rule politics of the Soviet Union were created to prevent solidarity among the Muslim population. As a result, the new states encompass multiple ethnic and religious communities, with diverse loyalties. Many seek separate political status themselves. The geographic borders of the new states, therefore, are exceedingly malleable. So, too, are the boundaries of military interdependence with Moscow, which must avoid the appearance, if not the substance, of subordination. These problems are certain to absorb much of the attention and resources of the new republics.

Even more critical are the ethnic, religious, and cultural overlappings that relate to Iran, Turkey, and Afghanistan. (See Northern Middle East map). They raise several questions for strategists and policy makers. Will the example of newly independent, ethnically based states stir separatist longings among related communities in Iran and Afghanistan? Will quarrels among ethnic and religious communities within these new states spill across borders into Turkey, Iran, and Afghanistan, creating a zone of instability along the northern rim of Southwest Asia? And will "secular" Turkey and "Islamic" Iran be drawn into the political dynamics of these states as they search for models of development and sources of identity?

The potential explosiveness of these problems is indicated by the size of the Muslim population of Central Asia. The five large republics on the eastern side of the Caspian Sea—Kazakhstan, Kyrgyzstan, Tajikistan, Turkmenistan, and Uzbekistan—embrace approximately 70 million people *and an area as large as all of European Russia.* Nuclear weapons and associated research and development centers are located in several of these republics. Even more worrisome, the know-how used in the construction of advanced nuclear weapons might be made available to interested parties in the Middle East and elsewhere. In addition, energy resources in some of these republics and their desire for outlets to the sea could tie them economically to Iran, or, in the case of Azerbaijan, to Turkey and the Black Sea community that Turkey is trying to create. Turkey and Iran are seeking to influence the orientation of government policies in the republics, as are Saudi Arabia, Pakistan, and others. The stakes are high in terms of access to oil and local markets, potential availability of military equipment, and a larger role on the world stage.

Both Turkey and Iran have long-standing ethnic and cultural ties to the people of the republics. In the late nineteenth century, the Turkic

Muslim intellectuals viewed themselves as Turks and reemphasized their Turkish culture. Turkic Muslims responded to the Young Turk Revolution of 1908 by identifying themselves with Turkish nationalism. In the mid-1920s the reaction to the Soviets took the form of violent resistance against them in south Turkistan. During the interwar period, Turkic Muslims identified themselves with cultural pan-Turkism, until the 1950s when pan-Turkism declined. Currently, Muslims in the former Soviet Union are reminding Turkey of their close relations and, especially in Azerbaijan, are seeking Turkish support for ethnic squabbles with their neighbors. Although the government in Ankara has reacted with caution to these requests, pressures inside and outside Turkey could draw it further into ethnic politics.

Initially, like other countries that have had revolutions, Iran tried to export its Islamic ideas. Now there are greater problems at home that command the attention of the revolutionary government. Moreover, the Iranians now share with Moscow a desire to keep the current borders intact lest their own society be unfavorably impacted. They have tried to mediate the dispute between Armenia and Azerbaijan in an attempt to keep on good terms with both. Nevertheless, Iran is already extending its influence north, especially into Azerbaijan (which is Shiite), Turkmenistan (where it shares a Turkic population), and Tajikistan (where Persian is spoken).

Whatever the outcome of this competition for influence in Central Asia and the Caucasus, the larger consequence of the dismantling of the USSR could be fragmentation of local loyalties and a transferal of instability into adjacent regions of the Middle East.

Implications for U.S. Security Policies

The 1991 Gulf War resulted in victory for governments and defeat for people in the Middle East. The political contours of the Middle East will undergo major change in the wake of the Persian Gulf War. Global as well as regional forces will have a growing impact in the region. The wave of democratization sweeping Europe and Asia seemed to pass the Middle East by during the late 1980s. Now, broader public support will be demanded of all governments in the Middle East. There will be no more security in obscurity for the princes of the Arab states of the Gulf or for the military dictators around them. The Middle East will be in the limelight for many years to come.

The 1991 Gulf War created new political realities for ethnic groups in the region. It may give a new sense of purpose and opportunity to the region's ethnic minorities and inspire them to rise up and resume their quest for autonomy and freedom. From the Israeli-Arab Palestinian conflict to the plight of Kurdish people, the possibility of reshaping the regional agenda on political reforms and the question of ethnicity and sectarianism has arisen. However, the Gulf War has created no real solution for these conflicts.

Ethnicity and sectarianism have become a potentially destabilizing ingredient in North Africa, particularly in Algeria and Morocco, where Berber minorities dissatisfied with the performance of national governments have begun to agitate for the preservation of their language and cultural traditions vis-à-vis Arabic and Arabism. In Tunisia and Algeria, Islamic movements are mobilizing, seeking to gain power from what they see as secular governments. In the Sudan, where southern Nilo-Hamitics have sternly resisted efforts by the Arab regime in Khartoum to impose Islamic law (*Sharia*) and Arab customs, ethnic strife is causing state disintegration. A new Islamic government in Khartoum has all but defeated separatists in southern Sudan, but the rebellion has not ended and peace is not at hand. Much depends on the tolerance extended by the Islamic government of General Ali Bashir to the non-Muslim population of the south. In the Horn region, the Ethiopian empire is fragmenting in the wake of the collapse of the Mengistou regime.

The dissidence found in ethnic and sectarian violence has produced large numbers of refugee communities. The UN High Commissioner for Refugees estimates that for the three regions of North Africa, the Middle East, and Southwest Asia approximately five million people were to be found in refugee camps in 1991. As past experience has demonstrated, the raw recruits for insurgent movements and terrorist organizations are often to be found in these camps, thus adding to security problems.

Several governments in these regions are themselves minority regimes. The Alawis, a religious minority, rule Syria; the Iraqi leadership is drawn primarily from the region of Tikrit; the Saudi ruling family belongs to the minority Wahhabi sect; and the Omani ruling family belongs to the minority Ibadi sect. The governments in the Gulf Arab states rule either religious or expatriate majorities. The governments of Egypt, Tunisia, and Algeria are secular military elites, ruling societies whose majorities are practicing Muslims.

Various governments in the three regions have responded forcefully to ethnic dissidence. Iraq used chemical weapons and a resettlement program to constrain its Kurdish population. Syria surrounds its Kurds with Arab tribesmen. The efforts of successive Sudanese governments have been less successful in the suppression of Nilo-Hamitic insurgency. The Sudan as well as Lebanon face a lengthy period of uncertainty regarding their capacities to create unified nation-states. The outlook for both is problematic at best.

Should these governments fail in their efforts to quell unrest or resolve ethnic and sectarian conflicts, we will continue to see multiplier effects in adjacent areas. The temptation for neighbors to intervene will increase, as with Syria's "peacekeeping" and Israel's "pacification" roles in Lebanon, Iran's support of the Shiites in Iraq in the aftermath of the Gulf War in 1991, and Turkey's military attacks on Kurds in Iraq during the same period.

Ethnic conflicts in the Middle East promise to complicate the implementation of national security policy for the United States. The declining utility of military power, alliances, and spheres of influence will compel the search for new instruments of power. These may include international, regional, and transnational institutions and coalitions to resolve these conflicts. Nowhere is this better illustrated than in Iraq, where the United States and its allies are faced with a classic foreign policy dilemma that pits security interests against widely supported democratic values.

The Iraqi Crisis

The defeat of Iraqi forces in the second Gulf war and their disorderly retreat from Kuwait was accompanied by popular uprisings in the Kurdish-inhabited region in the north of Iraq and by revolts by Shiite insurgents in the south. Initially, both groups were rejecting an unpopular and repressive government rather than expressing ethnic and sectarian separatism. The Shiites represent about 55 percent of the population; the Kurds about 23 percent. The government in Baghdad, dominated by an Arab Sunni minority, responded by employing draconian measures that reestablished government control over both regions. In the process, hundreds of thousands of Kurdish refugees fled to Turkey and Iran, and a smaller number of Shiites went to Iran. Roughly half of the Kurdish population of Iraq was left in mountain territory in harsh winter conditions that threatened their survival.

Faced with a serious breach of human rights of a kind defined in UN Security Council (UNSC) Resolution 688, which requires Iraq to treat its population in accordance with internationally accepted standards of conduct, the UN, under impetus from Britain, France, and the United States, acted to protect the Kurdish minority. In this it was supported by Turkey, which feared the intrusion of large numbers of Iraqi Kurds into an area in which Turkey's own Kurds were engaged in a long-simmering revolt. Under the UN umbrella, armed forces of the United States, Britain, France, and the Netherlands established a "safe haven" in northern Iraq, and under their supervision most Kurdish refugees gradually returned to their homes. At the same time, the Iraqi air force was also forbidden to fly north of the 36th degree parallel, and Iraqi troops were excluded from large parts of Kurdish-inhabited territory in the north.

Under these favorable circumstances, various Kurdish political groups held an election early in 1992 in territory under their control and launched an experiment in genuine Kurdish self-government. Although this satisfied human rights requirements, the new circumstances in northern Iraq nevertheless weakened Iraqi sovereignty. The democratic experiment also gave impetus to rising demands for Kurdish self-determination, not only in Iraq, but across the border in Turkey. The government, facing erosion of its control over eastern Turkey, found itself under increasing domestic pressure to terminate its cooperation with allied (UN) forces in northern Iraq, despite the international opprobrium this would bring.

While the Kurds were establishing a de facto administration in the north of Iraq, Shiite dissidents in the inaccessible marsh areas of southern Iraq, bordering on Iran, undertook military insurgency against Iraqi forces. By mid-1992, counterattacks by Iraqi government forces against the Shiites drew international attention, and the United States, Britain, and France established an air reconnaissance mission over southern Iraq, forbidding Iraqi flights south of the 32d degree parallel. Again they used the authority of UNSC Resolution 688 to justify their actions. This new exclusionary zone intensified fears in the Arab world and elsewhere of a diminution of Iraqi sovereignty and a further impetus to ethnic and sectarian separatism, this time on the part of the Shiites. In the Gulf, there was apprehension that singling out a part of Iraq's Shiite population for protection would inspire calls for Shiite rights in such states as Bahrain, where Shiites are a majority, and Kuwait, where they are a significant minority.

These protective actions carry with them unforeseen and unpredictable consequences. Although they are directed at a government grossly delinquent in human rights, if carried to extremes, they could result in a continued weakening—perhaps even in a collapse—of the Iraqi state. This, in turn, would endanger the stability and security of the Gulf region and the Middle East, leaving Iran, by default, the major power in the Gulf. Turkey, a country that plays a stabilizing role in the Mediterranean and might play a similar role in the new Muslim republics of Central Asia, could be threatened. A weakened Iraq would also invite interference by Syria, Turkey, and Iran in its domestic affairs, further undermining the fragile state system in the Middle East.

The Iraqi crisis is thus a test case for U.S. and Western policy, one involving two principles likely to be of critical importance in the coming decade. One involves the geostrategic imperative of national sovereignty and a recognition of territorial integrity—and the boundaries that go with it—as the basis of the international system. This may be difficult to maintain in a region where ethnic and sectarian groups, struggling for self-identification, cross these boundaries. The other is centered on a deepening commitment to universal standards of human rights and the values associated with more open, democratic systems. Although, in the Iraqi case, the UN has gone well beyond previous limits in approving human rights resolutions that limit Iraq's sovereignty, it is by no means apparent that it will countenance the permanent weakening or the collapse of a member state.

U.S. foreign policy will be further complicated by the "paradox of interdependence," that is, although interdependence provides increased points of leverage to a superpower, in a superpower-small power relationship it also raises the costs of exercising the influence and reduces the freedom of action of each actor.

There is a particular irony here for the United States in that interdependence also circumscribes the exercise of global power. The uninformed or careless use of power—particularly military power—in such circumstances can easily be self-defeating. The conduct of national security policy will require impressive sophistication, data, and skill if power is to be exercised effectively in what is an increasingly complex and challenging environment.

The United Nations Charter may be instructive in this regard, when a country or nation is attempting to secure recognition of its right of self-determination. In a declaration stipulating how that right should be exercised (adopted by the General Assembly in 1970), the UN specifically stated that it should not be applied so as to jeopardize the territorial integrity of composite states: (1) if those states are based on democratic principles and respect for human rights; (2) provided that they allow for the development and assertion of those rights for their citizens and peoples. As previously indicated, the aftermath of the 1991 Gulf War has raised new, humanitarian issues unwelcome to some governments in the United Nations. The intervention by the Western powers to create "safe havens" for protection of Iraq's Kurds and other minority groups may have set a precedent with far-reaching consequences for traditional notions of state sovereignty.

The policy implications of this type of situation for U.S. security interests will vary from region to region and country to country. Quite obviously, the ethnic conflicts in the Sudan and in Ethiopia have less immediate impact on U.S. interests than do rivalries in Southwest Asia. In some instances, Washington will wish to adopt an abstemious position as local forces sort themselves out. Elsewhere, the United States might wish to encourage regional organizations or the UN to serve as mediator or to play a peacekeeping role. Rarely should Washington intervene when ethnic problems have acquired a religious overlay. This cautionary note applies with special force where Islamic revivalist movements have been intertwined with ethnic groups and organizations.

Increasingly, forces of change will place burdens on governments in the Middle East to maintain national cohesion and stability. Where Middle Eastern governments fail to provide opportunities for ethnic groups to align themselves with national institutions and policies, the region will experience fragmentation of political life, growing recourse of governments to draconian security measures, and a challenge to the nation-state system. Friends and allies of the United States will be tempted to fill the growing vacuum, adding to rivalries and tensions in some instances. These prospects for the decade of the 1990s and beyond will pose painful policy choices for the U.S. government. As stated earlier, the application of military force (particularly by an outside power, that is, the United States) is of declining utility in addressing the challenges.

The United States has traditionally cited regional stability as one of its primary objectives. The Middle East is a political seismic zone in which a degree of instability is probably inevitable. This situation is further exacerbated by Middle Easterners' perceptions of actual or imaginary U.S. intentions in the region. The challenge facing the United States is that of encouraging the process of change to proceed with minimal violence. In the past, the United States has often found itself supporting the forces of the status quo.

Other policy prescriptions need to be borne in mind for strategic planning purposes. Salient among them are the following:

- *When social class and religious affiliation crosscut with ethnic loyalty* they tend to mute or soften conflict and build elasticity and staying power. This is the case in the Arab Gulf states where Shiites, though not in power, include a range of economic classes. When social class and religious affiliation coincide, however, the system becomes fragile and brittle and intense violence is often the result. Lebanon, where most Christians are in the higher economic strata while Shiites are in the lower strata, is a good example.
- *Modernization and economic development,* laudable as overall

goals, can be uneven processes of evolution that can add to friction and rivalry among competing groups.

- *Development as an economic goal may assume political dimensions.* Questions about development of the GNP and the increase of per capita income may be supplanted on national agendas by questions revolving around dependency on external sources of assistance and derogation of national sovereignty. This is an increasing form of "scapegoating" in the region.
- *Questions of national survival* could overshadow humanitarian considerations. For U.S. policymakers this could pose painful dilemmas involving diplomatic condemnation and sanctions, on the one hand, and the provision of humanitarian assistance, on the other.
- *Questions of arms transfers and crowd-control equipment sales* could arise in the same context. Here, once again, the United States will have to weigh with care the ties with traditional friends and allies, the costs of national collapse and fragmentation, and the implications of such collapse on the overall stability of the region.
- *The future formulation and pursuit of U.S. interests in the Middle East should include the legitimate aspirations of the people of the region.* The United States should play a positive role in regional affairs. In an effort to facilitate the articulation of social and political goals, the United States could assist Middle Easterners in the redefinition of democratic forms appropriate to their respective conditions; the rediscovery of the life-affirming side of Islamic precepts; and the development of economic and technological models that serve human needs and foster a social and cultural future.

With the demise of the cold war, U.S. foreign policy is badly in need of new orientations and objectives; ideology alone cannot dictate it. Indeed, realism makes clear that a cardinal sin of U.S. policy in the past has been a proclivity for universalism. There may be circumstances in which the United States will wish to support international sanctions against genocide regimes or to provide material aid to grievously treated ethnic groups on humanitarian grounds. But some caution should be taken against full cries for democracy or self-determination when the ultimate consequence is regional instability or local disorder. This is not to gainsay a foreign policy that, on a selective basis, emphasizes "democratization" as a criterion for U.S. aid. This coincides with the World Bank emphasis on improved "governance," although the latter is more modest in goal and prescription.

The United States will have to make diplomatically sensitive judgments in human rights and political performance evaluations—much as occurred in the shaping of U.S. policy in the wake of the Tiananmen Square massacres of mid-1989. On the one hand, assistance calibrated to democratization may be viewed as punitive, may diminish U.S. freedom of action, or may curtail dialogues with other governments. On the other hand, reluctance to cut aid or to terminate most-favored-nation status will undermine U.S. credibility. Although moral judgments have a "feel good" effect, they could prove counterproductive to ultimate foreign policy goals.

Notes

1. The theoretical part of this chapter is adapted from Abdul Aziz Said and Luis R. Simmons, "The Ethnic Factor in World Politics," in Abdul Aziz Said and Luis R. Simmons, eds., *Ethnicity in an International Context* (New Brunswick, N.J.: Rutgers Press, 1976), pp. 15–17. The discussion on Turkey was augmented through an interview with Serif Mardin, Professor of Islamic Studies at the American University. Mehrzad Boroujerdi, a Ph.D. candidate completing his dissertation at the American University, provided many valuable insights on the politics of ethnicity and sectarianism in Iran.

2. Milton Esman and Itamar Rabinovich, "Ethnic Politics in the Middle East," in Milton J. Esman and Itamar Rabinovich, eds., *Ethnicity and the State in the Middle East* (Ithaca: Cornell University Press, 1988), pp. 12–23.

3. Clifford Geertz, "The Integrative Revolution: Primordial Sentiments," in Clifford Geertz, ed., *Old Societies and New States* (New York: Free Press, 1963).

4. Francis Hsu, "Psychosocial Homeostases and Jen," *American Anthropologist* 18, no. 2 (Fall 1971), p. 24.

5. Anthony D. Smith, *The Ethnic Origins of Nations* (New York: Blackwell, 1987), p. 35.

Suggested Reading

Esman, Milton, and Rabinovich, Itamar, eds., *Ethnicity and State in the Middle East*, Ithaca: Cornell University Press, 1988.

Geertz, Clifford, ed., "The Integrative Revolution: Primordial Sentiments," in *Old Societies and New States*, New York: Free Press, 1963.

Goble, Paul A., "Coping with the Nagorno-Karabakh Crisis," *The Fletcher Forum of World Affairs*, 16, no. 2 (Summer 1992), pp. 19–26.

Gunter, Michael, *The Kurds in Turkey: A Political Dilemma*, Boulder, Colo.: Westview Press, 1990.

Gurr, Ted Robert, "Ethnic and Religious Minorities," in *Conflict Resolution in the Post-Cold War Third World*, Washington, D.C.: U.S. Institute of Peace Conference, October 3-5, 1990.

Held, Colbert C., *Middle East Patterns: Places, People and Politics*, Boulder, Colo.: Westview Press, 1989.

Lewis, Bernard, *Race and Slavery in the Middle East*, New York: Oxford University Press, 1991.

Montville, Joseph V., ed., *Conflict and Peacemaking in Multiethnic Societies*, Lexington, Mass.: Lexington Books, 1990.

Norton, Augustus R., *Amal and the Shia of Lebanon*, Ithaca: Cornell University Press, 1987.

Pinto-Dobering, R., *North-South Migration: The Challenge of the 1990s.* Occasional Paper no. 2/1991, Geneva: Graduate Institute of International Studies, 1991.

Said, Abdul Aziz, and Simmons, Luis R., eds., *Ethnicity in an International Context*, New Brunswick, N.J.: Rutgers Press, 1976.

Tapper, Richard, *The Conflict of Tribe and State in Iran and Afghanistan*, New York: St. Martin's Press, 1983.

8

Islamic Movements, Democratization, and U.S. Foreign Policy

John L. Esposito

For more than a decade the specter of Islamic fundamentalism has often been regarded as a threat to the regional stability of the Middle East and to U.S. interests in the region. In the 1990s Islam continues to be a factor in world politics and international relations. From North Africa to Southeast Asia, people associated with Islamic movements have participated in parliamentary elections, filled cabinet positions, and challenged and confronted governments. Moreover, in the Gulf War of 1991 Saddam Husayn combined an appeal to Islam and Arab nationalism to mobilize popular support within the Muslim world. Measuring the significance of Islamic movements, like understanding their natures and their activities, has often required walking a fine line between myth and reality.[1] The need for careful discernment remains, for Islam will continue to be an important ideological political force for the remainder of the decade.

The scope of the Islamic resurgence in recent years has been worldwide, embracing much of the Muslim world from the Sudan to Indonesia.[2] Events in the Muslim republics of the former Soviet Union, in Kosovo, Bosnia-Herzegovina, Kashmir, Jordan, Algeria, Tunisia, and in the Gulf War of 1991 have reinforced images of an expansive reassertion of religion in Muslim politics. The impact of Islam has been substantial and, at times, particularly dramatic in the Middle East. If the 1950s and 1960s were dominated by Arab nationalism and socialism, since the 1970s the rise of Islamic revivalism has challenged secular ideologies and Muslim governments by appeals to religious ideology, symbols, and rhetoric: "Formulated in moral and corresponding political categories, Islamic fundamentalism expresses mass sentiment and belief as no nationalist or socialist ideology has been able to do up until [sic] now."[3]

Islam reemerged as a dominant force in the politics of the region during the 1970s and 1980s. Heads of Muslim governments as well as opposition groups increasingly appealed to Islam for legitimacy and to mobilize popular support. Islamically oriented governments (Saudi Arabia and Pakistan) have been counted among the United States' staunchest allies and among its most vitriolic enemies (Libya and Iran). However, like the media, some U.S. policymakers have viewed the Muslim world and Islamic movements through the prism of extremism and terrorism. Although this is perhaps understandable in light of events in Iran and Lebanon, it fails to do justice to the complex reality of Islamic revivalism and it can undermine U.S. policy in the region. In the 1990s it is important that the vacuum created by a receding threat in the region from the former Soviet Union not be filled by exaggerated fears of Islam as the new major ideological menace to Middle East stability and U.S. interests. Headlines such as "The New Crescent in Crisis: The Global Intifada" and "Rising Islam May Overwhelm the West" capture attention but amplify and distort the political reality.[4] Islamic movements may constitute an ideological challenge and potential threat to regional stability; however, they are not all automatically a threat to U.S. interests. The United States will need to distinguish between those movements that are irreconcilably anti-American and those that are not.

This chapter will review the worldview and organization of contemporary Islamic movements, assess their current strengths and agendas, evaluate their ideological challenges, their attitudes toward political liberalization and democratization, and their impact on U.S. foreign policy.

The Diversity of Political Islam

Far from a monolithic reality, the ideological challenge of Islam has been as diverse as the countries in which it has occurred. It has spanned the political and ideological spectrum, influenced as much by local socioeconomic and political conditions as by religious faith. The diversity of Islamic politics continues today in such countries and areas as Algeria, Lebanon, Tunisia, Egypt, the Sudan, Jordan, the West Bank and Gaza, Iran, Iraq, the Persian Gulf, Afghanistan, Kashmir, and Pakistan. In many of these nations and regions, Islamic actors and organizations constitute formidable mainstream oppositional political forces that are often capable of mobilizing popular support. However, in contrast to an earlier generation, many activists today press for change in the name of political liberalization and democratization.

An Islamic revolution has indeed occurred and has affected Muslim politics, but its causes and manifestations are pervasive and diverse. Recognition of this complex and multifaceted reality, ideologically and organizationally, is critical to U.S. policy in the coming decade.

Ideological Worldview

Common to the worldview of contemporary Islamic movements is the affirmation of an Islamic ideological alternative to secular nationalism, western capitalism, and Soviet Marxism. Despite vast differences in their methods and agendas, Islamic movements share some common ideological principles. First, Islam is a total way of life, a comprehensive blueprint for personal life as well as for state and society. Second, Westernization—the uncritical adoption of Western secular models of development (separation of church and state, unfettered capitalism or materialism, radical individualism)—is the cause of the political, military, economic, and social ills of Muslim societies.

Despite their liberal parliamentary forms of government, the growing disparity between rich and poor, the failure of many governments to stem the tide of illiteracy and poverty, the negative impact of modernization and urbanization on the family and on social values, and the military impotence of the Arabs in their confrontations with Israel, Muslim rulers have failed significantly to improve their societies. Although decades of independence, modernization, Westernization, and secularization have resulted in transformations, they have not ameliorated the problems nor have they changed the authoritarian natures of many of the Muslim rulers. Moreover, the Westernization of Muslim societies is condemned as a new form of colonialism that has often left them politically, economically, militarily, and culturally dependent on the West (as in Lebanon, Egypt, and Pakistan, and as in Iran under the Shah). Though Westernization and secularization are condemned, modernization, as such, is not. Science and technology are accepted, but the pace, direction, and extent of change are to be subordinated to Islamic belief and values.

Third in the beliefs of Islamic movements is the idea that restoration of power and success require a return to the straight path of Islam, the divinely mandated alternative to capitalism and Marxism. Fourth, the reintroduction of Islamic law (*Sharia*) as the sacred blueprint for society will produce a more moral and socially just society. Finally, they believe that it is the duty of all Muslims to sacrifice and struggle (*jihad*), if necessary to suffer and die as martyrs, against all odds in the way of God.

Radical movements (such as al-Jamaat al-Islamiyya, al-Jihad, Hizballa, and the Army of God) have gone beyond these principles. They see Islam and the West locked in an ongoing historic battle that includes the Crusades, European colonialism, U.S. and Russian neocolonialism, and Zionism. The West (Britain, France, and the United States in particular) is blamed for its support of unjust, un-Islamic regimes (the Shah's regime in Iran, Lebanon, Egypt, the Sudan under Numayri, Habib Bourguiba's regime in Tunisia) and for its unbalanced support of Israel. Violence against "un-Islamic" rulers and those governments that support them is regarded as a sacred duty. It is the legitimate defense of Islam, incumbent upon all true believers.

Membership and Organization

Islamic organizations, like Islamically oriented governments, vary widely in ideology and methods, from moderate to radical, from traditionalist to reformist. The leadership of both moderate and radical organizations comes from lower-middle and middle-class backgrounds and from cities and towns; these people are pious and highly motivated. Many are recruited from schools, universities, and mosques. The challenge of Islamic movements to the integrity and legitimacy of existing institutions calls for the moral transformation of society. Espousal of an agenda to mobilize popular support to save the very soul of their societies often finds a ready audience among the younger generation of students and professionals.

Many activists combine traditional backgrounds with modern educations at major centers of learning in the Muslim world and in the West. In contrast to popular expectations, most are laypersons rather than clericals and are graduates of faculties of law, science, medicine, education, engineering, agriculture, and economics rather than of religion. Unlike many of their more secular-oriented peers, however, Islamic activists are more critical of the Westernization of Muslim society and of the political, economic, religious, and cultural failures and excesses of Western-based modernization. They espouse a more indigenously rooted, Islamically oriented alternative to prevailing Western forms of modernization. Some are so alienated or marginalized that they resort to violence and to armed revolution.

Contemporary Politics: What of the 1990s?

Revivalism continues to grow as a broad-based religiosocial movement (*Daawa*, the call to Islam), functioning today transnationally and in virtually every Muslim country. It is a vibrant, multifaceted movement that will embody the major impact of Islamic revivalism for the near term. Its goal is the transformation of society through the transformation of individuals at the grass roots level. Islamic organizations and societies work in education (schools, child care centers, youth camps), in religious publishing and broadcasting, in economic projects (Islamic banks, investment houses, insurance companies), and in social services (hospitals, clinics, legal aid societies). Their common programs are aimed at young and old alike.

Youth movements represent the focus of Islamic organizations. Muslim student associations exist in every country. Active in schools and universities, they have produced a new generation of leaders in government, the bureaucracy, the professions, the military—a modern and educated generation that is Islamically oriented, not secularly oriented. That new generation may be found in Egypt, the Sudan, Tunisia, Jordan, Iran, Kuwait, Saudi Arabia, and Pakistan. As a result, Islamic ideology and movements have become part and parcel of mainstream Islam and society rather than a marginal phenomenon limited to small radical groups or organizations.

The political strength and durability of Islamic movements and their ideological impacts are reflected in a variety of ways. They have forced government changes and, where permitted, have successfully contested elections. Rulers from Morocco to Malaysia have become more Islamically sensitive and have sought to co-opt religion and to not suppress Islamic organizations. Many have employed Islamic rhetoric and symbols more often, expanded support for Islamic institutions (mosques and schools), increased religious programming in the media, and have been more attentive to public religious observances such as the fast of Ramadan or the restrictions on alcohol and gambling.

When free from government repression, Islamic candidates and organizations have worked within the political system and have participated in elections in Tunisia, Algeria, Turkey, Jordan, the Sudan, Egypt, Kuwait, and Pakistan. Activists have even held cabinet-level positions in Jordan, the Sudan, and Pakistan. In countries such as Algeria, Tunisia, Egypt, Jordan, and Pakistan, Islamic organizations have been some of the best organized leading opposition forces and have often been willing to form alliances or to cooperate with political parties, professional syndicates, and voluntary associations to achieve shared political and socioeconomic reforms. Islamic student organizations often have successfully competed in student elections in the universities.

In Egypt thousands of Islamic organizations and voluntary associations provide cheap, efficient clinics, hospitals, and social and educational centers. Local mosques serve as alternative places of learning, offering tutoring to students who struggle to get by in Egypt's over-crowded schools and universities. Voluntary Islamic organizations offer a nongovernment social infrastructure that parallels state insti-tutions, an alternative that can be seen as an implicit indictment and critique of government that has failed to meet the socioeconomic needs of its society.

At the same time, clandestine radical Islamic organizations that advocate violence to seize power and establish an Islamic state have been active. In Lebanon such pro-Iranian Shiite groups as Hizballa and al-Jihad figured prominently in Lebanon's civil war, battling other Shiites, such as Nabi Berri's Amal, as well as fighting Christian militias and taking foreign hostages. Egypt has fought Islamic funda-mentalist groups, in 1989–1990 arresting thousands of fundamentalists who demanded implementation of Islamic law.[5] Egyptian officials continue to crack down on those they deem "Islamic militants," in particular underground groups in Cairo and Asyut. They have raided and closed mosques that serve as headquarters for Islamic organizations and have fired on demonstrators, who often protest economic conditions and call for the implementation of Islamic standards of dress and behavior.[6]

Islam and the Gulf War of 1990–1991

The Gulf crisis of 1990–1991 divided the Arab and, indeed, the Muslim world.[7] Similarly, it evidenced multiple appeals to Islam by Muslim political and religious leaders to legitimate both sides in the conflict and the crisis tested the ideology and allegiances of Islamic movements.[8] Perhaps nothing seemed more incongruous than that Saddam Husayn, the head of a secularist regime who had ruthlessly suppressed Islamic revivalism at home and abroad, would cloak himself in the mantle of Islam and call for a jihad.

Saddam Husayn stepped into a leadership vacuum in the Arab world. Although not a charismatic leader, he created a popular persona by appealing to Arab nationalism and Islam, shrewdly exploiting deep-seated populist issues: the failures of Arab govern-ments and societies (poverty, corruption, and the maldistribution of wealth), the plight of the Palestinians, and foreign intervention leading to Arab dependency. Like the Ayatollah Khomeini, Saddam Husayn appealed to Islam to enhance his image as the champion of the poor and oppressed and the liberator of the holy places, as well as to legitimate his call for a holy war against the United States and the overthrow of those Arab regimes that opposed him.

The deep divisions within the Muslim world were reflected in competing appeals to Islam and demands for a jihad. Saudi Arabia and Egypt's leading religious leaders legitimated the presence of foreign troops in Saudi Arabia, the home of Islam's holy sites and cities (Mecca and Medina), which are forbidden to non-Muslims. At the same time, Saddam Husayn, Iran's Ayatollah Khomeini, and the Jordanian ulama and Muslim Brotherhood called for a jihad against foreign intervention.[9]

Islamic movements, reflecting their societies, were initially pulled in several directions. At first, most condemned Saddam Husayn, the secular persecutor of Islamic movements, and denounced his invasion of Kuwait. Many had long enjoyed the financial support of Saudi Arabia. However, with the infusion of large numbers of foreign troops in the Gulf, their rejection gave way to a more populist Arab nationalist, anti-imperialist support for Saddam Husayn and to the condemnation of foreign intervention and occupation of Islam's homeland, Saudi Arabia. The key catalyst was the massive Western (especially U.S.) military buildup in the region and the threat of both military action and a permanent Western presence.

For many in the Muslim world, the buildup of foreign troops, announced after the U.S. elections in November 1990, transformed the nature of the conflict from a defensive operation to an offensive force. "Desert Storm" had been transformed into "Desert Sword"; the defense of Saudi Arabia and the liberation of Kuwait had become not just a war against Saddam Husayn but an all-out attempt to destroy Iraq politically and militarily. Who would benefit most from the resulting power vacuum? A common answer was the United States and its ally Israel.

Domestic politics, pressure not to run counter to popular sentiment, as much as religious conviction and ideology influenced Islamic activists' support for Husayn and his call for a jihad. Initially, thousands of Muslim activists in Algeria demonstrated against Iraq's invasion of Kuwait; subsequently, on a visit to Baghdad Ali Abbasi Madani, the leader of the Islamic Salvation Front (FIS), declared: "Any aggression against Iraq will be confronted by Muslims everywhere."[10] In Jordan, the Muslim Brotherhood initially condemned the Iraqi invasion. After the deployment of U.S. forces, it demanded a jihad against "the new crusaders in defense of Iraq and the Islamic world." As one American Muslim observer noted: "People forgot about Saddam's record and concentrated on America. . . . Saddam Hussein might be wrong, but it is not America who should correct him."[11] Even in countries that sent forces to support the anti-Husayn "international alliance," popular sentiment often differed from that of the government. In a poll taken by a Pakistani magazine, *Herald* (in Pakistan a majority had opposed the annexation of Kuwait), 86.6 percent of those polled responded negatively to the question: "Should U.S. troops be defending the Muslim holy places in Saudi Arabia?"[12]

The Gulf War had its military winners and losers. However, the credibility of the coalition partners and the righteousness of their cause remain to be proven by their actions and policies in the postwar period. Failure to move significantly toward resolution of the Palestinian issue, to bridge the growing gap between rich and poor, and to respond to increasing demands and expectations for greater political liberalization would reinforce the contention of cynics who see a West that has managed to tighten its oil security, to increase its military presence and access to the Gulf, to bolster Arab autocrats, and to create a Middle East stability that is dependent on external powers and their regional "partners" rather than on an internal, regional balance of power.

The 1991 Gulf crisis interrupted, and in some cases became, an excuse to curtail the movement toward greater liberalization in many Arab and Muslim countries in which Islamic activists have often played a prominent role. Algeria postponed scheduled national elections; Tunisia quietly stepped up its crackdown on its Islamic opposition; and Egypt limited the activities of opposition parties. With peace restored, many wondered whether the "new world order" would see governments such as those of Egypt, Saudi Arabia, and Kuwait or regimes such as those of Algeria, Tunisia, and Morocco that had felt the force of popular demonstrations, marches, and strikes, prove responsive to the winds of change or fall back on old authoritarian patterns.

Democratization

Democracy has been slow to come to the Middle East. Despite Western influence and a facade of parliamentary systems of government in some countries, the political reality has more often been one of authoritarianism. Political parties are banned or severely restricted; elections are often rigged. Of the more than seventeen states in the Middle East, six are monarchies and seven dictatorships; Algeria, Egypt, and Tunisia have historically been dominated by one party. As the Soviet Union and Eastern Europe were swept along by the wave of democratization in 1989–1990, the Middle East showed signs of modest change, from relatively open parliamentary elections in Egypt, Tunisia, and Jordan to Algeria's move to a multiparty system and open elections in June 1990. Yet these remain small gains in countries whose rulers continue to enjoy enormous powers. The example of Muslim nationalities in the former Soviet Union seizing on the new freedoms of *glasnost* to protest their socioeconomic grievances as well as to assert their demands for greater autonomy and the primacy of their Muslim national identities and languages with greater militancy, along with the Palestinian *intifada* and the Kashmiri demands for independence, captured the attention of many in the Muslim world. Both secular and Islamic organizations and political parties pressed for political reforms.

An escalation of popular calls for democracy brought nervous responses from governments, including greater liberalization and government repression. The rulers of Syria and Iraq, shaken by the example of democratization in Moscow and Eastern Europe, their long-time allies, sent clear warnings that they would not tolerate such movements in their countries, and they also countered calls for liberalization with new policy responses. Both regimes had experienced domestic Islamic opposition. In the late 1970s and 1980s Iraq's Saddam Husayn managed to control the threat of Shiite Islamic militancy through a policy of repression and co-option. On the one hand, he exiled or executed Shiite opposition leaders; on the other, he poured economic aid into Shiite areas and brought Shiites into top government positions. In the end, despite Iran's religious appeals in the Iraq-Iran War, the majority of Iraqi Shiites patriotically placed national self-interest ahead of sectarian affiliation.[13] However, rather than addressing issues of political pluralism, Saddam Husayn concentrated on building Iraq's military capabilities and asserting his role as a pan-Arab spokesman, calling for a militant Arab response to Israel and threatening to destroy half of Israel if the Israelis ever attacked Iraq.[14] These threats proved to be only the first steps that eventually culminated in Iraq's invasion and occupation of Kuwait in August 1990.

Syria's Hafiz al-Asad has had a history of the use of brute force, as demonstrated in the bloody suppression of the Muslim Brotherhood uprising in Hama in 1982. Yet the weakened Syrian leader struck a more accommodationist posture in Arab politics: mending fences with Egypt's Husni Mubarak, accepting the Saudi-brokered Taif Accords for Lebanon, and finally joining the coalition against Saddam Husayn. Reports circulated that Asad would permit new opposition political parties including a moderate Islamic revivalist party.[15]

Egypt and Jordan, long regarded as moderate, pro-Western governments, both introduced liberal political reforms to alleviate pent up pressure and growing political opposition due to deteriorating economic conditions and high unemployment, and to defuse the threat of "revivalism." Both tried to keep Islamic moderates separated from "militants" and to avoid their radicalization. Husni Mubarak pursued a path that distinguished between political dissent and direct challenges to the authority of the state more sharply than did his predecessor Anwar Sadat. Islamic groups such as the Muslim Brotherhood were allowed to participate in parliamentary elections (though not as a political party), publish newspapers, appear in the media, and run schools, clinics, and financial institutions. At the same time, Mubarak has moved firmly against militant antigovernment Islamic groups.

In Jordan King Husayn initiated a process of political liberalization in 1989, calling for parliamentary elections for the first time in twenty-two years in November 1989. Despite King Husayn's warning to voters prior to the elections not to mix religion and politics, Islamic candidates, campaigning with slogans such as "The Quran Is Our Constitution" and "Islam Is the Solution," scored an upset in Jordan's elections, taking 32 of 80 parliamentary seats. The Muslim Brotherhood took 20 seats and 12 went to other Islamic candidates. In January 1991 the Brotherhood gained 5 cabinet positions and subsequently a Muslim Brother was elected speaker of the parliament.[16] However, when King Hussein supported the Madrid (Arab-Israeli) conference, the Brotherhood ceased to participate in the Cabinet.

During the 1980s, Islamic organizations in Algeria and Tunisia joined with their fellow citizens in pressing their governments for reforms, including the establishment of a multiparty system and representative elections. Both Algeria and Tunisia had a record of rigorously controlling and suppressing Islamic movements. Algeria's one-party socialist state under President Chadli Bin Jadid brooked little opposition. Tunisia's leader, Habib Bourguiba, imprisoned and threatened to execute leaders of the Islamic Tendency Movement (MTI) in the 1980s.[17] Zina Abidin Bin Ali, after seizing power from Habib Bourguiba in 1987 and promising democratization, held parliamentary elections in April 1989. Though the government did not permit the MTI to participate as a legal political party, Islamic candidates won 14.5 percent of the vote nationwide and a stunning 30 percent in such cities as Tunis, Gabes, and Sousse, and they emerged as the leading political opposition. MTI renamed itself the Renaissance Party (an-Nahda) as a precondition for recognition as a legitimate political party. Contrary to previous indications and expectations, however, Bin Ali reneged on his earlier promises to recognize the Renaissance Party as a political party.

During the 1991 Gulf War, Bin Ali initiated a policy of harassment and arrests aimed at his Islamic opposition, a policy that was stepped up after the war in an attempt to crush the movement. Both Western governments and international human rights organizations expressed concerns over charges of mass arrests and torture as well as the deaths of a number of Renaissance Party members in prison.

The suppression of the Renaissance Party precipitated an attack against the ruling party's headquarters. This action was later tied to a government allegation of a plot by the Renaissance Party (which the ruling party charged included members of the Tunisian military) to overthrow Bin Ali in June 1991. In July and August 1992, the Tunisian government held mass trials of some 279 members of the Renaissance Party before military courts. Charges of faulty judicial procedures, forced confessions, torture, and lack of access by lawyers to their defendants led international human rights organizations and others to echo the conclusion of the Lawyers Committee for Human Rights, which found "grave irregularities" in the trial proceedings and the treatment of the defendants during the trial.[18]

The Tunisian government's shift to a more hard-line policy toward Islamic activists was influenced not only by the Tunisian elections but also by events in neighboring Algeria. In Algeria, which has long been regarded as one of the most monolithic single-party political systems in the Arab world (with the National Liberation Front, or NLF), Chadli Bin Jadid introduced greater political pluralism with recognition of a multiparty system that included the Islamic Salvation Front led by Shaykh Ali Abbasi Madani.[19] Islamic groups had flourished in recent years as Algeria's state socialism failed to resolve the social and economic problems that caused the riots of 1988. The FIS, the largest of the Islamic groups, emerged as the strongest opposition party in municipal elections in June 1990, with 54 percent of the vote.

In the face of pitched battles in the street and FIS calls for the establishment of an Islamic state, President Chadli Bin Jadid declared a "state of siege" on June 5, 1991. Public order continued to disintegrate amid pitched battles between government forces and the FIS, and fears of insurrection mounted. When Madani threatened to call for a holy war if the state of siege was not lifted, the military intervened and arrested many of the top leaders of the FIS on June 30 for plotting against the state, and they imprisoned nearly 5,000 of its members.[20]

Moreover, despite the imprisonment of the key leaders of the FIS, Ali Abbasi Madani and Ali Bin Hajj, and gerrymandering by the government, which redrew voting districts to favor the National Liberation Front, in the first round of parliamentary elections on December 26, 1992, the FIS overwhelmed the NLF and scored a landslide victory, garnering 188 of 202 parliamentary seats. Although President Bin Jadid seemed determined to strike a compromise and

work with the FIS, the Algerian military intervened, forcing Bin
Jadid to resign after dissolving the Parliament by a secret decree on
January 4 and appointing a committee, the High Security Council, to
replace him. In January, Muhammad Budiaf returned from twenty-
eight years in exile and was installed as Algeria's president, at the
head of an army-appointed Council of State. The government cracked
down on the FIS, arresting more than 500 FIS leaders, imprisoning from
7,000 to 15,000 of its members in desert camps, and bringing to trial FIS
leaders. Although FIS leaders initially "urged calm and avoided calls
for violence [and] vowed that `FIS will remain within the legal
framework without renouncing its plan for an Islamic state,' . . .
resistance to the operations of the security forces intensified."[21] The
army-led government move to suppress dissent was increasingly
accompanied by armed clashes between FIS and government forces.
Violence erupted in many quarters in the midst of a "seven month
campaign of repression, press censorship, mass arrests of Islamic
fundamentalists and stiff jail sentences."[22] As John Entelis and Lisa
Arone have observed, "The brutal fighting between the army and
Islamist supporters indicates that the conflict lies less in a partisan
rivalry between the FLN and the FIS than in the nature of the
authoritarian structure of the state and its legitimacy in the eyes of
the people."[23] Despite initial questions about the true character of the
FIS in its orientation to democracy, the response of Algeria's military
and government raised the question, "Who had hijacked democracy in
Algeria?"

For rulers in the Gulf, the response to the strength and threat of
Islamic political activism was complicated by the presence of significant Shiite minority communities as well as by the fact that in Iraq
and Bahrain Sunni rulers governed predominantly Shiite populations.
Despite initial eruptions by Shiite groups in the early 1980s and strong
opposition from Sunni activists, Gulf rulers had managed to stabilize
the situation by implementing policies that included greater sensitivity to Islamic sensibilities and by presenting a tough posture toward
militants.

In Kuwait a number of political groups including Muslim revivalists
demanded the reinstitution of the elected National Assembly, which
had been dissolved in 1986 by the Amir of Kuwait. The government
response was a crackdown on prodemocracy leaders in May 1990 and a
government-controlled election was denounced by many parties.[24] The
Saudis assiduously avoided the establishment of a Parliament,
although in times of crises, such as the seizure of the Grand Mosque in
1979, they set up committees to study the question. Sensitive to Islamic
critics outside the Kuwaiti kingdom who maintain that kingship is

antithetical to Islam and concerned about the growth of Islamic revivalism on its campuses and among those Saudi students who return from study abroad, the royal family remained nervous about suggestions that traditional Islamic concepts and institutions such as *shura* (consultation) should be equated with democracy and greater political participation. However, in the post–Gulf War period, both Kuwait and Saudi Arabia have been pushed to deal with increased popular pressure and demands for liberalization and democracy.

On March 1, 1992, Saudi Arabia's King Fahd, responding to a petition from leading intellectuals, businessmen, and public servants, as well as one from religious leaders, introduced reforms that included the creation of a consultative council, all of whose members are appointed by the king. He ruled out elections and reasserted that the Quran and Sharia (Islamic law) remain Saudi Arabia's creed and primary source of legislation, making it equally clear that he believed that Western democratic practices are not suited to the Persian Gulf's traditional Arab societies. Commenting on the relationship between Islam and Western-style democracies, he noted that although there is "no harm benefiting from what is good . . . the nature of our people is different. . . . The basic system prevailing in the world does not suit us in the region . . . Islam is our social and political law . . . it is a complete constitution of social and economic laws and a system of governance and justice."[25]

In October 1992 Kuwait held an election for its National Assembly, as promised by the Amir. Opposition candidates won 31 out of 50 seats. However, the franchise was extremely limited. Women were not allowed to vote; only males descended from families living in Kuwait in 1920 had that right. At the end of 1992 it remained unclear as to how much authority the National Assembly would be able to exercise in practice.

Islam and Democracy

The democratization movement in the Middle East and the electoral successes of Islamic movements raise the question of the compatibility of Islam and democracy.[26] Like other religions and ideologies, the Islamic tradition is capable of multiple interpretations; it has been used to support democracy and dictatorship, republicanism and monarchy. The twentieth century has witnessed both tendencies.

The Islamization of democracy has often been based on a modern process of interpretation of traditional Islamic concepts of political deliberation or consultation (*shura*), community consensus (*ijma*), and personal interpretation (*ijtihad*) or reinterpretation to support notions of parliamentary democracy, representative elections, and religious reform. Although some radical revolutionaries reject any form of parliamentary democracy as Westernizing and un-Islamic, most Islamic activists have Islamized parliamentary democracy and have appealed to democracy in their opposition to incumbent regimes. Islamic organizations such as the Muslim Brotherhoods in Egypt, the Sudan, and Jordan, the Jamaat-i-Islami in Pakistan, Kashmir, India, and Bangladesh, as well as Algeria's Islamic Salvation Front, Tunisia's Renaissance Party (formerly the Islamic Tendency Movement), Kuwait's Jamiyyat al-Islah (Reform Society), among others, have advocated the principle of democratic elections and, where permitted, have participated in parliamentary elections.

Electoral successes of Islamic candidates in Algeria, Egypt, Jordan, Tunisia, and the Sudan feed the fears of nervous rulers. During the post-1979 period, in a climate in which most governments have been traumatized by the specter of "Muslim revivalism," this fear, whether real or imagined, has provided an excuse for governments to limit democratization. At the same time, a major question and hurdle facing Islamic movements is their ability to tolerate diversity when in power. The record of Islamic experiments in Pakistan, Iran, and the Sudan raises serious questions about the rights of women and minorities in Islamically oriented governments. Without a reinterpretation of the classical Islamic legal doctrine regarding "protected people" (*dhimmi*), an Islamic ideologically oriented state would be, at best, a limited democratic state with a weak pluralistic profile whose ideological orientation would restrict the participation of non-Muslims in key government positions and the existence of political parties that represent a competing ideology or orientation: secular, communist, or socialist.

Multiple and conflicting attitudes toward democracy continue to exist. Though Ali Abbasi Madani, the leader of Algeria's Islamic Salvation Front, affirmed his acceptance of democracy in the face of accusations that he had opposed the democratic process in the past, some of the Front's younger voices such as the popular preacher Ali Bin Hajj, rejected democracy as an un-Islamic concept.[27] Only time will tell whether the espousal of democracy by many contemporary Islamic movements and their participation in the electoral process are simply a means to power or a truly embraced end or goal, a transformation of tradition that is the product of a process of religious reinterpretation informed by both faith and experience. Based on the record thus far, one can expect that where Islamic movements come into power, like many governments in the Middle East, secular as well as "Islamic," issues of political pluralism and human rights will remain a source of tension and conflict until time and experience have enabled the development of new political traditions.

The Islamic Revival and U.S. Foreign Policy

Islamic movements challenge the United States to reexamine U.S. foreign policy. The following are among the key issues raised by critics of U.S. foreign policy:

1. The subordination of Middle East policy to the United States' special relationship with Israel. Although some Islamic movements adamantly oppose any compromise or recognition of Israel, the issue for many in the Middle East is not support for the state of Israel but the need for a more balanced policy, one which judges all parties by the same standards and thus treats all parties fairly and equally. The issues often cited by U.S. critics (Islamic as well as secular) concern Israeli settlement policy, occupation in the West Bank and Gaza, and the reluctance in the past of the United States, where warranted, to publicly criticize and condemn Israeli policy as it does other countries in the United Nations.[28]
2. The uncritical past support for pro-Western governments in the Sudan, in Lebanon, Iran, and Tunisia, even when these governments became authoritarian and lost popular support. Egypt, Jordan, Tunisia, Algeria, and Morocco present similar problems for U.S. foreign policy in the 1990s.
3. The assumption that the mixing of religion and politics necessarily and inevitably leads to fanaticism and extremism. Failure to differentiate between Islamic movements, that is, between those that are moderate and those that are radical (violent) and extremist convinces many Muslims that the United States is simply anti-Islamic. Activists point out that the U.S. government does not equate the actions of Jewish or Christian extremist leaders or groups with Judaism and Christianity as a whole. Many charge that a comparable level of discrimination is absent when dealing with Islam.

President Reagan's linking of Qadhafi and Libyan terrorism with a worldwide Muslim fundamentalist movement in his announcement of the U.S. bombing of Libya confirmed what many saw as the United States' monolithic, anti-Islamic approach to the Muslim world. Similarly, Muslims were quick to note Vice President J. Danforth Quayle's comment in an address to the graduating class at the U.S. Military

Academy in May 1990, "The world is still a dangerous place. . . . We have been surprised this past century by the rise of Communism, the rise of Nazism, and the rise of Islamic fundamentalism," sentiments that he repeated in an address to the 31st Annual Policy Conference of the American Israel Public Affairs Committee (AIPAC) in June 1990.[29]

There continues to be a need to move beyond facile stereotypical language and judgments. Required is a political discourse and policy that distinguishes between moderate religious revivalism and violent extremism, between moderate political activists and radical revolutionaries. If Americans resented the generalized view of the United States as the "Great Satan," then it must avoid the pitfalls of a similar attitude toward Islam and Muslim movements in the recent past. A tendency to view Islamic movements through the prism of Qadhafi and Khomeini have obscured the majority Muslim experience which is not one of radical Islamic politics. Stereotyping distracts from addressing the more broad-based, substantive issue, the roots and causes of anti-Americanism.

Muslims who challenge U.S. policy and media coverage of Islamic movements can not simply be dismissed as "radical fundamentalists" or as irrational. Their criticisms represent competing viewpoints or interests and ask provocative questions: Why are Lebanese Shiites, fighting in southern Lebanon "to defend" their own country, described as guerrilla fighters or radical extremists while Israeli forces are regarded not as an army of occupation but as soldiers defending a security zone? Why did the Bush administration fail to acknowledge the linkage between its enforcement of UN resolutions against Iraq's invasion and annexation of Kuwait and UN resolutions against Israeli occupation of the West Bank and Gaza?

Contrary to what some have advised, the United States should not in principle object to the implementation of Islamic law or involvement of Islamic activists in government.[30] Islamically oriented political actors and groups should be evaluated by the same criteria as that of any other potential leaders, populist movements, or opposition parties. Though some are rejectionists, most Islamically oriented leaders or governments will be critical and selective in their relations with the United States. They will generally operate, however, on the basis of national interests and demonstrate a pragmatic flexibility that reflects acceptance of the realities of a globally interdependent world. The United States will be challenged to demonstrate, by word and action, its belief that the right of self-determination and representative government includes the acceptance of an Islamically oriented state and society if that reflects the popular will and does not threaten U.S. interests.

Although U.S. national interests may make a U.S. presence desirable and necessary, the government must avoid that which smacks of political or cultural domination or intervention. U.S. policy should, however, deemphasize massive military assistance and make more provision for agricultural and socioeconomic aid in such areas as housing, education, social services, and public works.

Without a perceptible shift in U.S. Middle East policy, pro-American regimes will continue to be vulnerable and will be condemned as client states, especially where the United States maintains a major diplomatic, military, or multinational presence and provides substantial assistance to governments. Criticism of U.S. policy is voiced by moderates as well as by radicals. However, even if a major shift in U.S. Middle East policy were to take place, problems for the United States would persist due to the widespread perception that this country constitutes the most important cultural threat to traditional Islamic life and values. Western ideas, literature, dress, music, and movies have proven a seductive alternative for modern Muslim youth and elites. This cultural threat is seen as implicit in modern legal, social, and educational reforms, and is symbolized by the presence of U.S. advisers, banks, and corporations.

It is not modernization through the application of modern technology and science that is being rejected, but rather a competing ideology of Western ideas and values. The problem is not radio and television, but the content of its programming. The gap or disagreement is ideological, not technological or economic. Many study the sciences and mass communications. The United States should ordinarily take care to avoid being seen as intervening in state-initiated Islamization programs or as opposing the activities of Islamic organizations where such programs or activities do not directly threaten U.S. interests. U.S. policy should, in short, be carried on in the context in which ideological differences between the West and Islam are recognized and, to the greatest extent possible, accepted or at least tolerated.

What of the Future?

The influence of Islam and activist organizations on sociopolitical development will increase rather than diminish in most Muslim societies. Islamic organizations in many Muslim countries can be expected to press their demands for political and social change by championing the calls for greater liberalization and political participation. As Islamic politics in recent years (in Egypt, Jordan, Tunisia, Algeria, the Sudan, Pakistan, and Malaysia) has shown, Islamic candidates have been quite successful in gaining political leverage and power through electoral politics. The moderate or pragmatic majority of Islamic organizations will continue to pursue a policy of gradualism, seeking to bring about change within the political system. Government suppression, directly or indirectly supported by Western powers, can radicalize moderates or pragmatists, transforming reformers into violent revolutionaries whose targets are both the government and its foreign allies. The extent to which governments prevent participation in elections, limit self-determination, and unjustly imprison political activists will contribute to a context in which violence and revolt are regarded as legitimate self-defense.

Algeria and Tunisia in 1991 demonstrated the precariousness and potential explosiveness of the Islamic politics in the 1990s. Despite the declaration of a new era of democracy, writers' observations in *The Economist* in May 1991 were to prove even truer in 1992 as President Bin Ali of Tunisia moved to decapitate the Renaissance Party,

> rigged the poll in the 1989 general elections and took every seat in parliament. Far from legalizing the leading opposition group, the Islamic party, Ennahda [Renaissance], the president has sought to crush it. Hundreds of members have been arrested, and some are blamed without good proof for terrorist incidents. The party's newspaper was shut down, and its editor jailed for printing an article calling for the abolition of the military court that passed his sentence. Its students' union was banned after police said they had found bomb-making equipment on its premises. . . . Ben Ali's Tunisia is a disappointment. There is no real democracy and no press freedom.[31]

Similarly, the Algerian government's arrest of FIS leaders; its change of electoral laws to limit the electoral success of the FIS in national elections; its subsequent military intervention, mass arrests, and detention of FIS members; its bloody confrontations between the government and FIS; the outlawing of FIS; and, finally, the assassination of President Muhammad Budiaf and government control of the press all continue to be signs of Algeria's continued deterioration.

Both the Tunisian and the Algerian governments used the challenge from their Islamic opposition and the alleged threat to violently overthrow the government and impose an Islamic state to ban the Renaissance Party and the FIS, respectively, and to rally support at home and abroad for their suppression. At the same time, both the Renaissance Party and the Islamic Salvation Front experienced defections and divisions in their ranks. Shaykh Abd al-Fatah Muru, a founding member and leader of the Renaissance Party, and several others denounced the violence and established a new political party.

In Algeria, a number of new Islamic groups such as HAMAS, the Arabic acronym for the Islamic Resistance Society, distanced themselves from Madani's actions. The leader of HAMAS placed the blame squarely on Madani's shoulders: "It is wrong to say the F.I.S. was decapitated by the army. . . . It has hurt itself with its own actions. Madani's insistence on ignoring the advice from other Islamic leaders and imposing his own views was suicidal."[32] However, in contrast to government actions, these defections have had little impact on the strength of the movements.

A minority of revolutionary Islamic organizations with such names as al-Jihad, Salvation from Hell, the Army of God, al-Jamaat al-Islamiyya, and the Islamic Liberation Front will continue to resort to violence and terrorism. They will remain small, marginal groups who disrupt rather than overthrow governments or substantially dominate their societies. As the experience of recent years has demonstrated, the threat of violence is lessened by the more flexible and discriminating tendencies of some Muslim governments such as Jordan and Egypt. Greater liberalization serves to drive a wedge between the moderate mainstream and the radical fringe.

Islamic revivalism is not a passing fancy. It has deep historical roots in the Islamic tradition; it was a dominant force in the 1970s and 1980s and lacking any substantial change in political and socioeconomic realities, it will continue to be a dynamic force in the Middle East during the 1990s. One can expect the continued growth of Islamic social and political movements. Yet these movements will continue to take many forms, since they are primarily conditioned by national and local conditions and are inner directed, that is, primarily concerned with domestic issues and secondarily with international affairs. Thus, for example, Islamic activists have consistently demonstrated a greater concern for obtaining cabinet posts in education, law, religious affairs, and information rather than in foreign affairs and defense.

Islamic movements face internal problems and challenges similar to those of their secular counterparts. Though they have often been able to identify and mobilize opposition against a common enemy or threat, once successful, internal power struggles and problems quickly emerge in the definition and implementation of an Islamic system of government. Islamic politics, like secular politics, is influenced by factionalism due to diverse ideological interpretations or visions of Islam; internal power struggles for leadership; and the influence of family, ethnic, and tribal or regional ties; and is constrained by the pragmatic demands and compromises of an interdependent global environment.

Given the popular push for political liberalization and democratic reforms in the 1990s, the United States will need to use persuasion and pressure with its Middle East allies for democracy. Although some will remain intransigent, Middle East rulers will try to balance some liberalization in the political process with the retention of the lion's share of power. Given the nature and power of most governments, a "limited democracy" will be the best that they are prepared to offer their people. Fear of Islamic movements "hijacking democracy," that is, simply using the political process to come to power, must be balanced by recognition that the vast majority of governments are at best open to "risk-free democracy." The record demonstrates that they will not tolerate political liberalization that jeopardizes their power. Neither a strong secular opposition nor an Islamic opposition will be permitted.

The United States will continue to be challenged by its ability to walk the fine line between support for old friends and an openness to and dialogue with new and contending populist forces and opposition groups, secular and Islamic. Continued credibility with some rulers or allies and the equation of stability with preservation of the status quo will need to be balanced by care not to undermine long-term interests and regional stability. The latter are both dependent on the relations with potential new leaders and authentic populist movements, including Islamic parties and candidates who have been democratically elected, as well as dependent on the containment of anti-Americanism.

A strong anti-Western, and especially anti-American, sentiment continues to exist among many moderates as well as among some radicals (secular as well as Islamically oriented). This is manifest in a tendency to regard the United States as anti-Muslim, anti-Arab, and uncritically pro-Israeli and in a tendency to blame the ills of Muslim societies on Western political, economic, and sociocultural influences. U.S. interests will best be served by policies that consist of selective and discreet cooperation with friendly Muslim governments, combined with a clear consistent public policy concerning the rights of citizens to determine their future democratically. *U.S. presence and U.S. policy, not a genetic hatred for Americans,* are often the primary motivating forces behind acts against U.S. government, business, and military interests. "Regrettably, the U.S. is no longer seen by most Middle Easterners, Muslims included, as the symbol of decolonization, self-determination, human rights, freedom, etc. Rather it is seen as the legatee of British and French imperialism, and as an interventionist element in local politics."[33]

The challenge for Islamic activists today is one of personnel and resources, ideology and pluralism. Islam has proven an effective rallying force to mobilize opposition to a government, as in Iran, Pakistan, and Afghanistan. However, for the future, the real test will be to produce effective representative governments and programs for sociopolitical change.

Islamic movements continue to be faced by the need to move beyond slogans and vague promises to concrete socioeconomic programs. They need to bridge the gap between traditional Islamic beliefs and institutions and the sociopolitical realities of the contemporary world, to demonstrate their ability to be effective problem solvers who can transform their ideological commitment into concrete policies and programs that respond to national and local concerns in diverse sociopolitical contexts. They must do this in a manner that is pluralistic enough in scope to enjoy the support of a broad constituency, and of fellow activists, secularists, and religious and ethnic minorities, and of that broad-based majority of Muslims who, although they want to be good Muslims, do not want to see the stability of their societies and their lives disrupted. The examples of Islamically legitimated authoritarianism in Iran, Libya, Pakistan, and the Sudan, as well as the extremist activities of radical groups in Egypt and Lebanon, constitute formidable hurdles. Similarly, the impact of Islamization on the status of women in Iran and Pakistan, the clashes between Muslims and Copts in Egypt, the discrimination against Bahai in Iran and against Ahmadiyya in Pakistan, and the imposition of Islamic laws on non-Muslims in the Sudan raise grave concerns about the rights of minorities in an Islamically oriented state. Serious questions remain about whether or not the members of Islamic movements, who insist on their democratic rights and self-determination as fundamental human rights, would, if in power, extend those same rights to all citizens.

Islam will continue to be a significant force in Muslim politics and thus will constitute an ideological alternative and a challenge to regimes in the Middle East and to Western governments. The extent to which governments in predominantly Muslim countries (1) fail to meet the socioeconomic needs of their societies, (2) block calls for liberalization by restricting political participation, (3) prove insensitive to the need to effectively incorporate Islam as a component in their national identity and ideology, or (4) appear exceedingly dependent on the West will contribute to the appeal of an Islamic political alternative. Events in the 1990s will test the ability of political analysts and policymakers to distinguish between Islamic movements that are a threat and those that represent legitimate indigenous attempts to reform and redirect their societies.

Notes

1. See John L. Esposito, *The Islamic Threat: Myth or Reality?* (New York: Oxford University Press, 1992) upon which I have drawn for part of this discussion.

2. See, for example, John L. Esposito, *Islam and Politics* 3d rev. ed. (Syracuse, N.Y.: Syracuse University Press, 1991); James P. Piscatori, ed., *Islam in the Political Process* (Cambridge: Cambridge University Press, 1983); John L. Esposito, ed., *Islam in Asia: Religion, Politics and Society* (New York: Oxford University Press, 1987); Shireen T. Hunter, ed., *The Politics of Islamic Revivalism* (Bloomington, Ind.: University of Indiana Press, 1988); "Islam and Politics," *Third World Quarterly* 10, no. 2 (April 1988).

3. Hisham Sharabi, *Neopatriarchy: A Theory of Distorted Change in Arab Society* (New York: Oxford University Press, 1988), p. 136.

4. Charles Krauthammer, "The New Crescent of Crisis: Global Intifada," *Washington Post*, February 16, 1990; and Patrick J. Buchanan, "Rising Islam May Overwhelm the West," *New Hampshire Sunday News*, August 20, 1989.

5. *New York Times*, August 21, 1989.

6. *New York Times*, January 25, 1990.

7. See John L. Esposito, "Jihad in a World of Shattered Dreams: Islam, Arab Politics, and the Gulf Crisis," *The World & I* (February 1991), pp. 68–74.

8. James Piscatori, ed., *Islamic Fundamentalism and the Gulf Crisis* (Chicago: American Academy of Arts and Sciences, 1991).

9. Those in North Africa (Algeria, Morocco, Tunisia, Mauritania, and the Sudan) witnessed large demonstrations. *Los Angeles Times*, September 22, 1990.

10. Madani quoted in "Islam Divided," *The Economist* (September 22, 1990), p. 47.

11. Abdurrahman Alamoudi in *The Washington Report on Middle East Affairs* (October 1990), p. 69.

12. Poll from the Pakistani *Herald*, September 1990, p. 30.

13. Philip Robins, "Iraq: Revolutionary Threats and Regime Responses," *The Iranian Revolution: Its Global Impact* (Miami: University of Florida Presses, 1990), esp. pp. 90ff.

14. Alan Cowell, "Iraq Raises Its Volume, and Arab Hopes," *New York Times*, April 4, 1990.

15. *Message International* (April 1990), p. 35.

16. Wafa Amr, "Jordan Welcomes New Government, Political Freedoms," *Middle East Times*, July 9–15, 1990, p. 4.

17. For a discussion of events during this period see Susan Waltz, "Islamist Appeal in Tunisia," *Middle East Journal* 40 (Autumn 1986); Marion Boulbi, "The Islamic Challenge: Tunisia Since Independence," *Third World Quarterly* 10, no. 2 (April 1988); and Dirk Vanderwalle, "From the New State to the New Era," *Middle East Journal* 42 (Autumn 1988).

18. "The Mass Trial of Islamists Before Military Courts in Tunisia" (New York: Lawyers Committee for Human Rights, 1992), Introduction.

19. For analyses of Islamic politics in contemporary Algeria see Robert

Mortimer, "Islam and Multiparty Politics in Algeria," *Middle East Journal* 45, no. 4 (Autumn 1991), pp. 241–256; and John P. Entelis and Lisa Arone, "Algeria in Turmoil: Islam, Democracy and the State," *Middle East Policy* 1, no. 2 (1992), pp. 140–156.

20. *New York Times*, July 26, 1991.

21. "Human Rights in Algeria Since the Halt of the Electoral Process," *Middle East Watch* 4, no. 2 (February 1992), p. 5–6.

22. *New York Times*, August 20, 1992, p. A5.

23. Entelis and Arone, "Algeria," p. 34.

24. *New York Times*, May 20, 1992.

25. *New York Times*, March 30, 1992.

26. For an analysis of this issue see John L. Esposito and James P. Piscatori, "Democratization and Islam," *Middle East Journal* 45 (Summer 1991), pp. 78–91.

27. *Middle East Times*, June 19–25, 1990.

28. For an example that the critique of U.S. policy extends beyond the Middle East to Malaysia see "Exposing U.S. Motives," *Aliran* 10, no. 11 (1990), p. 40.

29. "Text of Remarks by the Vice President: Commencement Address, Graduation and Commissioning Ceremony for the Class of 1990," pp. 5–6; "Remarks Delivered to AIPAC by the Vice President of the United States," *American-Arab Affairs* 33 (Summer 1990), p. 168.

30. Daniel Pipes, "Fundamentalist Muslims," *Foreign Affairs* 69, no. 3 (Summer 1986), p. 958.

31. *The Economist*, May 18, 1991, pp. 47–48.

32. *New York Times*, July 26, 1991.

33. U.S. Congress. House. Hermann F. Eilts, "Prepared Statement Before the House Subcommittee on Europe and the Middle East," in *Islamic Fundamentalism and Islamic Radicalism* (Washington, D.C.: U.S. Government Printing Office, 1985), p. 41.

Suggested Reading

Ayubi, Nazih, *Political Islam: Religion and Politics in the Arab World*, London: Routledge, 1991.

Esposito, John L., Islam: *The Straight Path* 2d ed., New York: Oxford University Press, 1991.

Esposito, John L., ed., *The Iranian Revolution: Its Global Impact*, Miami: Florida International University Press, 1990.

Hunter, Shireen T., ed., *The Politics of Islamic Revivalism: Diversity and Unity*, Bloomington: Indiana University Press, 1988.

Hudson, Michael, "After the Gulf War: Prospects for Democratization in the Arab World," *Middle East Journal* 45, no. 3, pp. 407-426.

National Democratic Institute for International Affairs, *Democracies in Regions of Crisis*, Washington, D.C., National Democratic Institute for International Affairs, 1990.

Rustow, Dankwart A., "Democracy: A Global Revolution," *Foreign Affairs* 69, no. 4, pp. 75–91.

Sonn, Tamara, *Between Quran and Crown*, Boulder, Colo.: Westview Press, 1990.

Voll, John Obert, *Islam, Continuity and Change in the Modern World* 2d ed., Syracuse, N.Y.: Syracuse University Press, 1994.

9

Strategies for an Era of Uncertainty: The U.S. Policy Agenda

Phebe Marr

The global environment of the 1990s has been dramatically changed by the collapse of the Soviet Union and the emergence of a number of independent states tied together, if at all, only loosely. As they attempt to salvage their economies and shape new political futures, these states, and most specifically Russia, which inherits the lion's share of USSR military power, will have neither the capacity nor the interest to challenge the United States for a preeminent position in the Middle East. This development has already begun to reshape the Middle Eastern geostrategic environment in a form more favorable to U.S. interests.

At the same time, the collapse of the Soviet Union has created a more complex international climate. The new states of the former Soviet Union can be expected to compete with each other for influence in or favor with Western Europe, the Middle Eastern states, and in some cases, the United States. Western Europe and new regional blocs in the Middle East and North Africa are developing their own agendas independent of or at variance with those of the United States.[1] Within the Middle East the interests of the United States may appear less relevant to the problems of some regions, for example, North Africa and the Sudan. Other regions and countries, notably the Persian Gulf, Turkey, and Egypt, may still see themselves as being dependent on U.S. strength.

The views expressed in this article are those of the author and do not reflect the official policy or position of the National Defense University, the Department of Defense, or the U.S. Government.

Paradoxically, the advantages gained from a U.S.-led victory in the cold war must be weighed against an offsetting factor on this side of the Atlantic. As the only remaining superpower, the United States may be unable to fully capitalize on its advantageous position because of domestic economic and social difficulties and a restive public unwilling to support an active policy in the Middle East—one demanding time, energy, and a substantial transfer of economic resources. Painful budget deficits, unfavorable trade balances, a deteriorating infrastructure, and widening social problems confront the United States with domestic challenges that vie with foreign affairs. In the Middle East, as elsewhere, the United States is increasingly compelled to reexamine its interests and goals, to evaluate them against available resources—financial and human—and to develop freshly honed strategies that reflect carefully considered priorities.[2]

Given these domestic constraints, the United States must be pragmatic in shaping its future objectives. The absence of a global adversary capable of undermining vital U.S. interests makes it possible for the United States to be selective in its future involvements. The United States almost certainly will not serve as the region's sole policeman, maintaining stability throughout the area.[3] Washington will be compelled to make clear to friends and allies that the United States cannot serve as a ubiquitous referee or solve all of the Middle East's many intractable problems and that it will focus heavily on protecting the most important U.S. national interests. This might well involve disengagement from the problems of some geographic subregions. Although the United States may employ military forces on behalf of international humanitarian efforts, as it did in Somalia, such activities are likely to stop well short of a unilateral military commitment to maintaining order in such regions. Middle Easterners will be encouraged to shoulder more responsibility for resolution of their own difficulties—to learn the price of failure and the satisfaction of success—rather than remain dependent on the world's remaining superpower.

Given the complex and multifaceted dimensions of Middle East conflicts, as well as the important yet diverse U.S. interests that converge in the region, no single strategy is likely to be universally effective. Instead of a grand design, the United States will have to devise policies that address specific problems and issues. Although no overarching blueprint can be fashioned for the decade immediately ahead, this chapter is designed to identify the main challenges and opportunities that confront the United States in the Middle East, to outline U.S. goals and priorities, and to propose strategies for meeting the challenges that face the country.

Challenges and Opportunities of the 1990s

The End of the Cold War

Of all the developments identified by the authors in this volume, none is more significant than the demise of the Soviet empire. The collapse of the Warsaw Pact and the implosion of the Soviet state have shifted the international balance in favor of the West and its values, institutions, and political-economic systems. Over the next several years, the United States can reasonably look forward to some cooperation from Russia and from most of the other former Soviet republics on matters of mutual interest in the Middle East. This new atmosphere has already yielded benefits, for example, in support for the U.S.-initiated Arab-Israeli peace process and in tacit acquiescence in the U.S.-led Desert Storm operation in the Persian Gulf. As they confront severe economic difficulties, the emergent republics of the former Soviet Union will be compelled to balance potential conflicts of interest in the Middle East (and elsewhere) against needed assistance from the West. This does not mean that Russia and the other republics will surrender critical interests in the Middle East, but that they may have to set aside some interests for urgent economic and technological requirements that can only be met from Western donors. As Melvin Goodman reminds us, however, the United States will have to be careful not to overplay its hand. Many conservative Russians, resentful of the loss of empire, could generate a backlash against cooperation. The high-water mark of conciliation may already have been reached.

Counterbalancing these newly acquired advantages are three areas in which the collapse of the Soviet empire could impact adversely on U.S. interests in the Middle East. First and most immediately, the collapse could produce a new fault line of political turbulence along the northern rim of Southwest Asia. The independent states of the Transcaucasus and Central Asia will need strong leadership and economic assistance from the West and Japan if they are to avoid economic stagnation. The Muslim republics in these areas are likely to be the focus of intense competition for influence from Turkey, Iran, Pakistan, and even from Saudi Arabia, all with differing agendas. Rising ethnic and nationalist sentiments spurring separatism already threaten to spill across existing international borders, fueling ethnic and religious factionalism in Turkey, Iran, Afghanistan, and Pakistan. Ethnic strife within Central Asian republics, combined with the presence of Russian forces—in some cases involved in "peacekeeping" missions—has given rise to charges of resurgent Russian imperialism by the newly independent states.

Second, failed economic policies may result in the proliferation both of weapons of mass destruction and of advanced conventional weapons in the Middle East. Some newly independent republics in need of hard currencies already feel compelled to compete for a market share in arms sales, while unemployed scientists, engineers, and technicians threaten to sell their services to Middle Eastern governments interested in acquiring assistance in their efforts to build domestic weapons systems. Centralized control over arms sales may have been lost, at least temporarily. Military equipment is sometimes sold by plant managers on a hard-currency basis without Moscow's knowledge or approval.

Third, regardless of the regime finally established in Moscow, any future Russian leadership cannot be indifferent to the forces emerging in Iran. Continuing ties—economic, political, and military—are likely to remain a high priority concern. No government in Moscow is likely to countenance Iran again falling into a special client relationship with the United States, although that seems highly unlikely during this decade. At the same time, Moscow will fear the spread of militant Islam to the republics on its southern border.

Arms Proliferation and the Balance of Power

The termination of the cold war and the disintegration of the USSR has removed a major threat to U.S. regional interests, but a new challenge has emerged—proliferation of weapons of mass destruction. As William Lewis points out, despite the best efforts of the United States, proliferation will probably increase in the course of the decade. This trend is spurred by continuing regional insecurities, and, ironically, by the very success of the high-tech weapons demonstrated by the United States in the Persian Gulf War. Sales of sophisticated conventional weapons and long-range delivery systems are also likely to increase. Indeed, the two categories of weapons will blur in the course of the decade, making distinctions for purposes of arms control increasingly difficult. Although efforts to constrain the flow of such weaponry to the Middle East can and should be made, the traffic can at best be slowed rather than stopped.

Continued proliferation of CBN weapons will impact on U.S. interests in several ways. They will make future armed conflicts far more lethal, increasing the potential that adversaries will bypass military theaters and strike population centers. The human cost of such wars—even short wars—will multiply dramatically, for the victor as well as for the vanquished. And they will contribute to the destabilization of the strategic balance. As high-tech weapons become more widely diffused, the potential for intimidation will grow. Concomitantly, the costs to the United States of any involvement in regional conflicts will be incalculable. Without diligent U.S. diplomatic efforts to build deterrence attitudes and confidence-building mechanisms, conflicts and crises in the Middle East may increasingly take on a hair-trigger quality.

Regional Conflicts

Another category of challenges confronting the United States in the Middle East concerns the endemic conflicts between and among regional states. Some of these are unlikely to unhinge the emerging regional security arrangements, but in two areas U.S. interests could be eroded if conflicts cannot be contained or resolved; the first is the Arab-Israeli imbroglio, the second, the Persian Gulf. Neither represents a new challenge, but the parameters of each have changed.

The Arab-Israeli Conflict. William Quandt in his chapter concludes that although the Arab-Israeli conflict persists, prospects for resolution have improved. The initiation of peace negotiations among the frontline states and the Palestinians in the aftermath of the 1991 Gulf War, the election of a Labor government in Israel more favorably inclined to compromise, and U.S. involvement in the peace process all point to an improved environment for settlement. Moreover, eruption of open hostilities among the Arabs and Israel is less likely, though still possible. The recent Gulf War has removed Israel's most dangerous Arab threat—Iraq. Egypt appears firmly committed to its peace treaty with Israel. Syria has lost its former superpower patron and is unlikely to initiate a conflict with a country technologically and militarily superior to itself.

Though the dangers of a general conflagration have abated, as Quandt reminds us, the absence of war is no cause for complaisance. On the one hand, if some measured progress is not registered on the Arab-Israeli problem in the next several years, a wide range of U.S. interests would be adversely affected. For example, the United States would find it increasingly difficult to insulate its relations with Israel from its dealings with the rest of the Arab world, especially the Persian Gulf countries. In the wake of a failure at the negotiating table, actions taken by Israel, Syria, or the Palestinians could cause regional security relationships to erode or collapse. Egypt, threatened with economic problems and a significant Islamic movement domestically, would be hesitant to maintain a cooperative relationship with Israel and close ties with the United States. Extremist forces, especially those embedded within Islamic movements, would widen public support throughout the region, shifting the climate of opinion in an anti-Western direction.

On the other hand, if the conflict moves toward resolution, threats to U.S. interests will be reduced and the climate for economic reform and political liberalization will both be considerably improved. A resolution of the Arab-Israeli conflict is also a critical element in curbing weapons proliferation. For these reasons alone, the United States will have to maintain high-level involvement in this perennial Middle East problem.

Persian Gulf Conflicts. Conflicts in the Persian Gulf present the United States with a challenge of a different order. As Marr indicates, the Gulf situation is more complex than that in the Eastern Mediterranean because simultaneous, crosscutting conflicts are involved. These include the historic, geographic, and cultural competition between the Arab and Persian sides of the Gulf, border disputes emanating from boundaries drawn by colonial powers, ideological rivalries, and competition over the distribution of market shares and other benefits accruing from their petroleum resources. An outbreak of armed conflict or a significant shift in the regional balance of military or economic power could affect Western access to oil at stable and reasonable prices, long a key U.S. interest. Marr concludes that renewed war in the Gulf is unlikely in the next few years, mainly because two of the main contenders—Iran and Iraq—are economically depleted and war weary. GCC states have also seen their treasuries reduced by the cost of two wars and need a respite to replenish them. However, the underlying causes of the conflicts persist and could erupt into violence, upsetting the existing balance again sometime in the course of the decade.

Iraq has the greatest potential as a regional destabilizer. Badly damaged by two wars, it will need time to rebuild before it can once again contemplate another military adventure, but it faces an uncertain domestic political future. If Saddam Husayn remains, Iraq is not likely to receive the financial and technological support it needs to recuperate. A change of government in Baghdad might improve Iraq's long-term prospects, but it could also precipitate a period of political instability. Worse, collapse of authority at the center has the potential for national dismemberment and attendant disorder. Such an eventuality would leave Iran dominant in the Gulf.

Iran, potentially the strongest of the Gulf rivals in terms of population, has been traumatized by its 1980s revolution and its eight-year war with Iraq. Tehran must direct its energies toward economic recovery. To meet this imperative, it needs technology and help from the Western industrial countries, a factor that should induce pragmatic behavior. But Iran continues to harbor ambitions for Gulf hegemony and seeks to expand its influence in Central Asia and elsewhere. It is already rearming with Russian, Chinese, and North Korean help, and by the end of the decade may be in a position to challenge the existing military balance. Until the future direction of the two northern Gulf countries becomes clarified, it will be difficult to resolve long-standing conflicts between them. As a result, the United States may have to devote more of its attention to managing Gulf conflicts and containing aggressive behavior than to solving underlying problems, although this should not preclude attempts to reduce tensions where possible.

The GCC lacks the population and military capacity to protect itself and must be assured of non-Gulf help. Saudi Arabia and the other Arab Gulf states will need continued military protection from the United States and the West to counter their far stronger neighbors. In addition, all of these states must balance domestic pressures for modernization with demands from Islamic forces for less Western influence.

The challenge for the United States—as an outside power—will be to devise security arrangements sufficient to protect Saudi Arabia and the GCC and to maintain the balance without becoming intrusive and engendering domestic instability. Meeting this challenge will become imperative for the United States because its interdependence with Gulf economies is expected to grow in the course of the decade.[4]

Regional Instabilities

An additional major challenge to the United States will be regional instabilities of varying kinds. These are likely to have a differential effect on U.S. interests, however, depending on the geographic region in which they occur and on their impact on surrounding areas. The United States and other outside powers can probably do little to influence these changes, particularly those that take place within the nexus of domestic politics. However, this does not mean that the United States should neglect instability or its root causes. It can help shape an international environment that encourages peaceful settlement of disputes, and if this fails, it may be able to play a constructive role in damage limitation through the effective application of diplomatic instruments. In other cases, the United States may join with the international community in initiating efforts to redress some root grievances that cause instability, but it will have to adopt a discriminating stance, being careful to strike a balance between counterproductive interference and harmful neglect.

This volume's authors have identified three broad trends likely to cause turbulence during the coming decade. First, as noted in the chapter by Abdul Aziz Said, ethnic and sectarian rivalries are likely to be a major source of instability in the Middle East (as elsewhere). Such cleavages may weaken some state structures, threatening fragmentation of existing countries and generating regional instabilities. Turkey, Iran, and Iraq are vulnerable to Kurdish aspirations for autonomy; Shiite messianism will continue to infect Lebanon, Iraq, and the Arab Gulf states. The example of the newly independent Muslim republics of the Caucasus and Central Asia may act as a catalyst for separatist tendencies in the region and these may spill over into Iran, Turkey, and Pakistan. The United States will be compelled to monitor developments closely in the latter two countries because of strategic and economic interests.

The second trend, economic scarcity and maldistribution of resources within and among the Middle Eastern states, will also fuel regional tensions and contribute to instability. As the 1990–1991 Gulf crisis illustrated, the wealth of the Gulf states is greatly resented by populations in the poorer countries of the Mediterranean rim—Egypt, Jordan, Syria, Israel, and Turkey. These countries also confront a demographic explosion that will double their populations by the year 2010. At the same time, they must shoulder burdens of debt, inflation, and poorly organized economic structures.

In addition, as Thomas Naff points out in this volume, water scarcity is likely to become acute in some countries (notably Jordan and Israel) in the course of the decade or to become a bone of contention among neighbors in others (for instance, in Turkey, Syria, and Iraq). These disadvantaged Mediterranean countries are important to the United States because they control strategic waterways (in Egypt and Turkey) and, with the exception of Syria, help to provide a balance of power favorable to U.S. interests in the region. In some cases, they extend military cooperation to the United States. Destabilization of these countries or replacement of friendly regimes with anti-Western leaders would make attainment of U.S. objectives in the region more difficult.

The final trend identified by the authors of this book is the turbulence likely to be caused by populist ideologies that exploit social and economic grievances that could reinforce antipathy toward Western influence as well as to regimes supportive of a Western presence. Chief among these mobilizing forces are various Islamic revival movements. Although some are confrontational, as John L. Esposito observes, the United States must be wary of treating the Islamic revival as a homogeneous phenomenon. It is not. Islamic movements have responded to differing conditions in their own countries. Some of the more militant ones concentrate on reducing or eliminating Western influence in their countries and have espoused violence as a legitimate form of political opposition. Such movements constitute a challenge to U.S. influence and to the longevity of friendly regimes in key countries.

Also emerging in the area are movements urging more open, representative, and accountable governments. Their goals, although congruent with those of the United States, may pose a challenge to U.S. security interests. The movement from authoritarianism to more open political systems in the region may well be accompanied by domestic turbulence and may bring to power forces that are antipathetic to U.S. influence in the region.

These more amorphous forces will constitute the real challenge for the United States in the 1990s. Regional conflicts and instabilities, often intractable in nature, may not lend themselves to military solutions. Rather they require the application of a discriminating, diplomacy, including an ability to act with complex strategies and to employ an array of nonmilitary instruments. Above all, in the face of a declining U.S. economy, U.S. commitments must be brought into line with available resources. The United States must identify its interests in the region with parsimony and establish the order of their importance with attention to domestic concerns and attitudes.

U.S. Interests and Priorities: A Policy Agenda for the 1990s

Given the global and regional trends outlined above, what interests are essential to the United States? What is enduring and achievable? If the United States cannot pursue these concerns indiscriminately, where should its priorities lie? It is suggested here that containment of Soviet influence in the Middle East, long the primary U.S. obsession, can be safely put to rest. The rapidly changing post–cold war environment now calls for a new agenda.

Although some traditional U.S. interests in the Middle East remain, their importance may be downgraded in some instances. Meanwhile, new concerns are coming to the fore. The trends outlined in this volume suggest that the United States will have to concentrate on the following issues, listed in order of their importance: (1) preserving access to oil at stable, and reasonable, prices; (2) curbing proliferation of weapons of mass destruction; (3) protecting the state of Israel within recognized international borders; (4) limiting the damage from instability; and (5) promoting political and economic reform.

In an age of increasing interaction and complexity, one in which competing interests will continually have to be balanced, no overarching grand strategy is able to secure all of these interests. A more pragmatic alternative is to establish a range of policy options available to the United States to deal with each issue and to weigh both the risks and the benefits inherent in each option. The remainder of this chapter will explore the implications of this agenda for U.S. security interests and some of the policy options that should be considered.

Access to Oil

With the eclipse of the Soviet threat to U.S. regional interests, priority on the U.S. agenda should be accorded to oil, notably to the protection of its free flow through the Persian Gulf. The vital importance of Persian Gulf oil to the U.S. economy and to the stability of the global economy has long been an article of faith.

Increased international economic competition and a U.S. economy in need of revitalization will lend particular weight to this source of energy.[5] So, too, will the regional trends outlined in this volume. As William C. Ramsay makes clear in his study of energy trends, the United States and its allies in Europe and Japan will be locked into an economic embrace of interdependence with the Persian Gulf for the remainder of the decade. The Persian Gulf is the only area with the excess capacity to absorb increased world demand for energy, and it is likely to remain so throughout the 1990s. As a result, the industrial democracies are likely to become more, rather than less, dependent on supplies of Gulf oil. Moreover, increased world oil production is likely to be concentrated in the hands of five producers—Saudi Arabia, Iraq, Iran, Kuwait, and the UAE. At the same time, Gulf producers are investing heavily in downstream facilities in the United States and Europe, tying their economies more closely to those of the West. In the United States, the flow of investment capital, generated by oil resources, will be needed to reduce the national deficit and to stimulate a slow-growth economy, and the reverse flow of goods—primarily military equipment and technology—will further tie the United States to the Gulf, particularly to Saudi Arabia. Although these developments will tend to inhibit proclivities on the part of the Gulf oil producers to disrupt oil supplies or markets, the West cannot count on economic rationales to prevail. The greatest danger to stable oil prices is political volatility. Domestic political instability in the Gulf states and the potential for renewed conflict among them is the real threat to oil access and price stability. For this reason the United States is compelled to remain focused on the Persian Gulf. Given the global shift from military concerns to economics as the main ingredient of international power, access to Persian Gulf oil at stable—and reasonable—prices may be the only *vital* interest the United States will have in the Middle East in the future.

Policy Options

Given the importance of Persian Gulf oil to the global economy and to the United States, what policy options are available to assure its free flow, to reduce the potential for disruptions of supply, and to protect against undue price volatility? Available strategies fall into two categories: economic and political. The United States must address the challenge of increased economic interdependence while maintaining a reasonable political balance in the Gulf region.

Economic Policy. The U.S. strategies for Middle East oil need to function simultaneously at several levels. The following measures are suggested: First, the United States must adopt an effective program of energy conservation at home and diversification of supply dependence abroad. Numerous conservation measures have been suggested; the most effective would probably be a gasoline tax. Although conservation measures will help reduce consumption, and prudence dictates that such measures be taken, they cannot substantially alter the long term trend of growing Western dependence on Persian Gulf supplies. In recognition of that fact, the United States should encourage oil exploration elsewhere, with a view toward diversifying supply dependence. In this area, investment in oil and gas production in the former USSR might yield the most promising long-term results.

Second, the United States should foster constructive interdependence of producers and consumers. This strategy would make a virtue of necessity. Rather than raising tariff barriers or introducing protectionist measures, the United States should seek to enhance mutual benefits for consumers and producers. The wealth that flows to the Gulf producers will in turn create export and investment opportunities in the United States and will return flows of badly needed capital to the United States. In exchange, U.S. technology, consumer goods, and military assistance for the Gulf will help expand U.S. employment opportunities. These ties should additionally help develop incentives for price stability and put constraints on temptations to use oil as a political weapon.

Third, the United States should encourage regional investment of oil wealth. Even mutually beneficial economic interdependence between the United States and the Gulf countries must be balanced against a countervailing consideration—regional resentment of the

maldistribution of wealth and privilege in the area. Distortive interdependence will bring regional charges that Gulf countries are mere
satrapies of the United States and that the U.S. security umbrella is
extended to assure cheap oil for the West at the expense of the Arab
world.

Fourth, the United States needs to develop hedging strategies to
limit damage from disruptions of oil flows, if and when they occur.
Several hedging mechanisms, already in place, need to be strengthened. These include the Strategic Petroleum Reserve (SPR), which can
be enlarged, and rapid response mechanisms available to Europe,
which can be extended.[6] The United States can also intensify economic
contingency planning with Gulf states, including expansion of oil production and export facilities in the region to meet unexpected disruptions. Saudi Arabia's ability to rapidly increase production and export
of oil in the recent Gulf crisis kept oil prices relatively stable—after a
brief initial rise—and was a major factor in the coalition success.

Such economic measures will not eliminate the political factors,
which are the most likely catalysts for oil disruption. These must be
addressed in the context of Persian Gulf political dynamics and the
potential for violence, instability, and war.

The Political Context: Political-Military Options

The Gulf War reversed Iraq's aggression and restored a modicum of
equilibrium to the region. But it failed to resolve the underlying causes
of conflict among the major players. These could provoke renewed
tensions and armed hostility. First, the borders at the head of the Gulf
between Iraq and Iran and between Iraq and Kuwait are still at issue
and are a source of bitter contention. Second, substantial numbers of
exiles and other displaced persons survive under reduced circumstances
in several Gulf countries, with the potential to be used by their hosts
as pawns against their neighbors. Finally, oil patrimony will likewise be a bone of contention. Iraq has not withdrawn its demand for
portions of the Rumaila oil field which lies in Kuwaiti territory (nor
accepted the newly drawn borders imposed by the UN commission in
the wake of the war). In addition, oil production and pricing issues
promise to be divisive.

These long-standing issues suggest that conflicts in the Gulf are not
yet ripe for resolution. A regional security system involving all Gulf
countries is preferable to an "armed peace" maintained by U.S. power,
but this is likely to come about only slowly. The United States must
concentrate on reducing tensions, establishing effective crisis

containment mechanisms to limit conflicts, and on using its Gulf military presence to maintain and stabilize the balance and keep the peace. To do so, the United States needs to integrate three, overlapping components of Gulf policy.

The first should be devoted to protection of the GCC. Over the past decade U.S. policy has been evolving into the framework that resulted in the successful Desert Storm operation. With the notable exception of a need to clarify deterrence doctrine, the policy has been successful in preventing any one power from dominating the Gulf in such a way as to interfere with the flow of oil to the West. While hostile regimes with hegemonic ambitions remain in Iran and Iraq, the United States may have to play a more active role in maintaining the balance of power in the Gulf than it did in the decade of the 1980s. The following aspects of the existing policy should be maintained:

1. The U.S. military presence in the Gulf should continue to have as its mission the protection of GCC states from external aggression. Part of its role should be preservation of GCC flexibility in foreign policy to allow these Arab states to shift their political and diplomatic weight, as needed, to preserve order and stability in the Gulf.
2. The United States should seek a level of military presence compatible with what is acceptable to GCC states. It should emphasize the use of military early warning systems as well as better intelligence on the intentions of other regional actors. Its forward force posture should contain sufficient air and naval assets to provide an effective deterrent to potential aggressors— and should have enough lift to get to the region quickly with ground forces when necessary.
3. The United States should avoid entanglement in GCC boundary disputes. The U.S. presence should not be construed as support for regime preservation or even for border maintenance.
4. The United States must exercise flexible diplomacy and exhibit sensitivity in its dealings with GCC states to avoid the perception, current in the Arab world, that its military presence is intended solely to protect "Western" oil and preserve local regimes.
5. The one area that requires clarification is deterrence. The United States must be prepared to give a clear signal that it has the will and determination to protect its interests and those of its friends. Otherwise, a repetition of the failure to deter Saddam Husayn could occur.

The second component of this policy option is encouragement of Iranian pragmatism. In the post-Khomeini period, Iran has moved in a more pragmatic direction, but it is not clear whether this is a permanent change or one driven by expediency. By 1992, Iran appeared to be taking a more aggressive posture and giving support to militant groups in the Middle East. The United States should be prepared to set limits to Iran's attempts to establish regional hegemony or to relapse into encouragement of extremist forces in the Gulf, while encouraging the pragmatism that has begun to emerge inside Iran. Several steps would be helpful.

1. The United States should seek to restrain Iranian rearmament efforts, confining them to legitimate defensive needs, in return for assistance, directly or indirectly, through Europe and Japan, in developing Iran's civilian economy. Any such trade-off, however, should have as its basis strict monitoring of Iran's development of weapons of mass destruction.
2. To improve the Gulf security environment, the United States should attempt to ease tensions between the GCC states and Iran without impairing GCC independence or security.
3. The United States should also encourage Iranian inclusion in a Gulf security framework in return for nonaggressive behavior. There is little likelihood of Iran's acceptance in the GCC in the immediate future, given GCC traditional suspicions of Iranian intentions, but informal consultations and a continuing dialogue could create a more relaxed security atmosphere.
4. The United States, in collaboration with its European partners and Japan, should insist on stringent standards of behavior with respect to terrorism and attempts by Iran to destabilize other regimes. These should be met before the United States restores normal diplomatic and commercial contacts with Iran. In this regard, U.S.-Iranian relations might benefit by some clear Red Lines for Iranian behavior as indications of what needs to be done if relations are to be improved.

The third element of U.S. policy centers on Iraq. Iraq will provide the United States with its most immediate Gulf challenge. An improved security framework in the Gulf is contingent on a change of government in Baghdad, but the United States has few effective instruments to produce the removal of the existing repressive regime. Moreover, a collapse of government in Baghdad could bring a high risk of national disintegration, a virus that could spread in the region. Although the United States can encourage a change of regime in

Baghdad and would support a viable replacement should one emerge, such a change can only be brought about by political-military elements within Iraqi society.[7] In the absence of such a change, however, U.S. goals should be to induce modification in Iraqi behavior and to contain Iraq's regional ambitions. The following long-term goals are suggested:

1. Maintaining the territorial integrity of the Iraqi state, without precluding peaceful border accommodations with Iraq's neighbors and a reasonable degree of local self-government for Iraq's Kurdish population. The United States should not seek the collapse of central authority in Baghdad, although it should be prepared to contain the political damage that might ensue should this occur. Without a unified Iraqi state, Iran would achieve Gulf hegemony by default. Under such circumstances, Turkey would feel compelled, for security reasons, to extend its influence into northern Iraq. The United States should, however, make a distinction between disintegration of the state and the kind of instability that would inevitably ensue in the wake of a change of regime, which could ultimately bring a more stable domestic outcome.

2. A change of regime should be encouraged, but should not be made the sole focus of policy. In the absence of such a change, the United States must be prepared to deter Iraq from aggressive military action to limit its ability to repress its citizens and continue to limit its military capacity and its ability to play a spoiler's role in the Gulf.

3. Modification of government behavior, internationally and domestically, preferably through application of UN resolutions, should be a goal. Intrusive UN inspections should continue until the UN resolutions on elimination of CBN weapons and long range missiles are fulfilled and satisfactory monitoring and verification procedures against future revival of such weapons programs are in place. An embargo on arms transfers and sales of military parts for advanced weapons technology should be maintained.

4. The United States should be prepared, in the event of a suitable change of regime, to seek to organize the international community to support Iraq's reconstruction through gradual removal of economic sanctions, reduction or elimination of reparations, normalization of diplomatic relations, and a reintegration of Iraq into the international community, in return for a change of behavior.

Arms Proliferation

The second item on the policy agenda should be the intensification of efforts to curb weapons proliferation in the Middle East. Such proliferation could threaten U.S. interests in several ways. As states increase their inventories, they will have the capacity to intimidate neighbors, including those friendly to the United States. In doing so, they could shift the regional military balance in an unfavorable direction. If Iran or Iraq should acquire nuclear weapons and the attendant missile systems, the balance of power in the region would dramatically change.

Policy Options

Differing perceptions of security imperatives between the United States and Middle Eastern countries will be a contentious issue as the United States seeks to curb flows of weapons to the area. To be effective it will have to follow a multifaceted strategy, one that takes into account supply and demand factors, as well as one that addresses local security concerns. U.S. initiatives should proceed along two tracks: strategies to control supply and diplomacy directed at curbing demand.

Supply-Side Efforts. These have received the most attention from policymakers. Despite pessimism about restraint regimes and other arms control initiatives, particularly those relating to surface-to-surface missiles, and to chemical, biological, and nuclear weapons, the United States and its allies can achieve significant gains by strengthening international restraint and control regimes. In this regard the following steps should be taken: The United States should seek to tighten inspections and encourage punitive measures for infractions of international agreements. Agreements on control regimes, especially the MTCR, should be expanded within the Middle East. More important, challenge inspections should be tightened and made more intrusive. As the Iraqi case illustrates, such inspections may be the only mechanism to insure compliance with international treaties. In addition, the international community must put more teeth into punishments directed against violations for serious infractions, including economic sanctions and embargoes on arms, spare parts, and technological transfers. Punitive measures must be accompanied by more positive steps to encourage Middle East countries to participate in and abide by the rules of international regimes. Their cooperation in establishing a framework of constraints should be sought.

The United States could also add pressure to international arms control efforts by publication of the names of international suppliers of prohibited technology together with carefully considered trade restrictions on offenders.

The United States should encourage development of a cadre of Middle Eastern arms control experts. Such a contingent lodged in Middle Eastern bureaucracies could constitute a new constituency in favor of arms control with some practical knowledge of how to make arms control work.

Curbing Demand. More effort needs to be put on the demand side of the equation. Supply-side strategies are likely to have marginal impact unless they are accompanied by a substantial change in the Middle Eastern security environment. For such a change to occur, the demand side of the equation must address the causes that drive weapons acquisition, including threat perceptions, the doctrines that govern their use, and measures to manage conflicts before they lead to armed hostility. Three kinds of initiatives might bear fruit over time.

First, more should be done to move political elites in the Middle East toward deterrent doctrines rather than war-fighting doctrines. Attitudes in the region now emphasize use of weapons, rather than acquisition of weapons for defense. Governments should be encouraged to develop mechanisms and procedures to enhance deterrence, possibly using the U.S.-USSR experience as a guide.

Second, Middle Eastern governments should be encouraged to develop early-warning and crisis-management techniques such as Red Line agreements and exchanges of information on planned military maneuvers and large-scale exercises. Such arrangements can help to prevent misunderstandings and preemptive actions caused by misperceptions. Such exchanges would also establish a network of contacts that could become an institutionalized framework for crisis management.[8]

Above all, the United States should work to achieve more stable military power balances within the region. It should recognize that one overall balance is unachievable, given the multiple conflicts in the region and the constantly shifting alliances. Three such balances are important: the balance between Israel and its potential adversaries; that between Iran and its Arab Gulf neighbors; and that among the Arab states. If there is no restraint on external arms supplies, these balances will be more difficult to maintain. Such balances should allow local governments to pursue their national interests without fear of intimidation and should leave states that are willing and able to cooperate with the United States free to do so.

Protection of Israel

The survival of Israel will remain near the top of the U.S. policy agenda, although it is unlikely that Israel's adversaries would require the United States to become engaged militarily on Israel's behalf. This commitment is based less on strategic necessity than on four decades of political and cultural ties. Every U.S. president since 1948 has affirmed commitment for Israeli security. That commitment is likely to be sustained throughout the coming decade.

However, the tone and texture of the commitment may be changing. Israel is confronting deep economic problems and difficult choices, particularly as its security concerns continue. Israel's future relationship with the United States is undergoing some modification. Henceforth, there is likely to be more emphasis on economic ties than on security issues. Israel is burdened by a number of problems—increasing military expenditures, water scarcity, unemployment, and a bureaucracy that stifles economic growth. Even without the inflow of substantial immigration from the former Soviet Union, Israel would have to concentrate on these difficulties. With such immigration problems, Israel will face difficult choices concerning its territorial issues, increasing its military arsenal, and its economy. Success in U.S. efforts to resolve the Arab-Israeli dispute would greatly enhance Israeli security and make U.S. protection of Israel less of a burden.

An Arab-Israeli peace, as William Quandt has indicated, is essential as regards other U.S. interests in the region. It is closely tied to efforts to curb arms proliferation and to enhance the climate for economic reform and political liberalization. Indeed, if some measured progress is not made on the Arab-Israeli problem, the United States will find it increasingly difficult to insulate its relations with Israel from the rest of the Arab world, especially in the Gulf, on which the West's oil supply is heavily dependent.

Policy Options

For these reasons, pursuit of the Arab-Israeli peace process should be at the forefront of U.S. efforts in the region. Following the 1991 Gulf War, President Bush began to move U.S. policy from conflict management to conflict resolution. The success of the effort may depend more on U.S. domestic factors than on the situation in the Middle East and on whether the U.S. administration will have the time, energy, and resources required for active involvement in this problem over a considerable period of time.

The outlines of a final solution, long recognized by successive U.S.

administrations, should include some formulation of the following: Security for Israel, its recognition by all Arab states, and its gradual acceptance within the region as a legitimate entity. Self-Determination for Palestinians on the territory of the West Bank and Gaza, and agreed on borders between Israel and its Arab neighbors, including Jordan, Syria, and Lebanon. Stabilization of the Arms Race through arms control and the introduction of effective confidence-building measures.

The peace process underway at the present time seems clearly designed to accomplish these aims. What is necessary is perseverance by the United States and a continuing perception in the region that it intends to remain engaged, despite domestic pressures and expected lapses and pitfalls in the negotiations.

Limiting the Damage from Instability

As the contributing authors make clear, instability will dominate some of the Middle Eastern landscape for the remainder of the decade. Regime changes and the emergence of a new generation will produce new leaders with differing values and perspectives. Ethnic and sectarian tensions will put stress on fragile states; economic problems, water shortages, and population growth will also strain the finances of many; and ideological movements will facilitate antipathy to Western values and goals. The issue is not *whether* instability will occur, but *where* it will occur, with what effect, and how the United States will respond to it.

The United States should not perceive all instability as threatening. Some change may be positive, or at least neutral in its effects on U.S. interests. Desirable economic and political reform cannot be accomplished without some instability, especially in the short term. The U.S. dilemma will be to contain the damage from short-term instability that may result from changes of regimes or from populist expressions of discontent, while finding ways to encourage more constructive economic systems and political institutions.

The United States cannot undertake to guarantee stability throughout the entire region. With reduced resources, it should not seek to perform the policeman's role. There is a danger that the people of the region will perceive the U.S. role in Desert Storm as a precedent for the use of force whenever trouble emerges. Any such attempt is likely to fail and to be costly in terms of time, energy, and, possibly, lives. Moreover, dissatisfied groups in the Middle East are likely to view such activities as an attempt to preserve an unjust status quo and may turn their wrath on the United States and its regional allies.

Policy Options

As regards the matter of how to deal with instability, there are few general policy options that can be enunciated for the region as a whole. The United States needs to develop criteria for selective involvement as well as to develop methods to deal with the root causes of instability. In the post–cold war era, a U.S. policy debate is likely to ensue between those advocating an activist approach designed to help reshape the world "order" and those looking to a reduced U.S. role based on case-by-case pragmatism. As Lawrence Freeman has observed, "Attempts to make stability the central strategic value of the new age are doomed to continual disappointment. . . . Any relevant framework must reflect the creative opportunities as well as the dangers inherent in perpetual instability."[9] The answer lies in a discriminating approach, one that identifies enduring interests and goals and develops strategies to ensure their protection and attainment.

In the establishment of priorities, the stability of several countries should remain high on the U.S. list. Without doubt these include Israel, Turkey, Egypt, Saudi Arabia and the GCC. Their importance can be attributed to several factors. Some control resources critical to the U.S. economy (Saudi Arabia and the GCC); others sit astride strategic waterways essential for commerce (Turkey, Egypt, the GCC). Virtually all provide access to military facilities essential for the U.S. military presence in the region (Turkey, Israel, Egypt, and the GCC states). Perhaps most important, they are governed by a pragmatic leadership that helps set the tone of discourse and cooperation with the West in the region. In general, political elites in these states tend to be internationalist in outlook and accommodationist in style. They are willing to build a framework for interdependence, protection of mutual interests, and a willingness to engage in constructive compromise.[10] In a fractious and potentially turbulent Middle East, these are precisely the attitudes the United States should be encouraging. This is not to suggest that the United States should always support existing regimes in these countries. To the extent possible, however, it should be using its influence with the leadership of these countries to make their countries attractive models of development in the region—political, economic, and social.

In addition to these countries, two others are important for U.S. interests—Iran and Iraq. In both, relatively hostile regimes now exist. In both, change may be favorable for the United States, but at the same time, the risks of instability, especially in Iraq, would be high. The United States will have to deal with instabilities in a matrix that takes these risks and likelihoods into account.

What of the rest of the region, where U .S. interests are less engaged but where instability of varying degrees of intensity may occur? Can the United States afford to disengage, and to what degree? How might the United States help identify and defuse tensions likely to lead to disruptive instability without intervention that may make it worse? The United States has several options available in these areas.

In some, European allies and others in the international community are better situated to take the lead. Instability in North Africa, for example, is of direct concern to France, Italy, and Spain. These states, with a nexus of political, economic, and cultural ties, are more directly engaged. The United States can play a supporting role. The same may apply to such countries as Iran and Iraq, within which commercial ties with Europe and Japan are likely to develop more extensively than those with the United States. These countries can also help encourage changes favorable to the West.

The United States can also work through the UN and other international organizations to deal with instability and its potential results. Desert Storm and its aftermath have redirected the efforts of the UN and have provided a number of precedents for new kinds of collective action. For example, the UN and its agencies may be better prepared today to serve as "early warning" institutions capable of identifying situations likely to give rise to armed conflict. Within the UN system, the international community can develop capabilities to prevent conflicts or to bring them to an early conclusion. The United States can cooperate within the UN on humanitarian aid, refugee assistance, and peacekeeping functions, all of which were undertaken in the aftermath of the Gulf crisis, and it can provide precedents for application elsewhere.

Promoting Political and Economic Reform

In addition to specific national interests, the United States also has broad ideological goals that Washington desires to further. It bears repeating here that the United States has an interest in promoting economic development within the framework of a market economy and political reform in more democratic directions. These goals are congruent with the values and ideals of U.S. society and will continue to inform and shape U.S. foreign policy, even though they may not always be carried out in practice. It is in the U.S. interest to encourage the countries with which it has close ties to move in this direction. To the extent that countries and regimes in the region espouse or approximate these goals, relations are likely to be smoother and U.S. interests better protected. Moreover, experience has shown that these goals are more likely to produce stability *over the long term* although it may require some short-term instability to move in that direction.

In the economic sphere, the United States will face real constraints in the transfer of resources to the region. Moreover, regional funding to ameliorate problems will also be scarce, and Europe's resources are likely to gravitate to Eastern Europe and the republics of the former Soviet Union. Nevertheless, the United States can encourage the region to take steps in several directions that would improve their economic situation. These include:

Encouraging regional economic integration, a trend that was disrupted during the Gulf War and one that will take time to reverse. Some inter-Arab flows of capital investment and labor need to be restored, even at reduced levels.

Supporting regional mechanisms, such as development banks, *designed to reduce maldistribution of wealth.* Emphasis should be less on redistribution and more on investment in productivity and the restructuring of inefficient economies.

Encouraging better integration of Middle Eastern states into the emerging global economy. This will be easiest for Israel and the Gulf states where the process is well advanced, but it is important for such countries as Turkey and Egypt as well. Participation in the developing global market economy holds the best prospects for the transfer of technology, the development of institutions and structures of a modern economy, and the raising of living standards. It will also help develop economic and professional constituencies within the Middle East with a better understanding of the West and a stake in mutually beneficial ties.

Encouraging regional solutions to water problems. In the Jordan Valley, where the situation is acute, the United States could act as a mediator, facilitator, and clearinghouse for data. It should also encourage Turkey to move on basinwide agreements concerning the Tigris and Euphrates rivers with its downstream neighbors, Syria and Iraq.

In the political sphere, the United States has a general interest in promoting political reform and improving human rights in the region. Where feasible, the United States should promote orderly development toward the following:

- governments with improved human rights records
- the creation and strengthening of civic organizations that can buffer society against repressive regimes
- more tolerance for freedom of expression

- more accountable governments
- greater participation of the population in governance

Encouraging these trends, however, will require a continually calibrated balance between undue interference in the politics of Middle Eastern states—which can generate counterproductive backlash and encourage rising anti-Americanism—and incentives to move in a direction deemed more compatible with goals and values that are widely shared in the Western world. The United States—and some of its more vociferous partisans of democratic reform—should proceed with caution in "imposing" on a region with different historical, cultural, and political values its own concept of "democracy" or its unique institutions. What the United States can, reasonably, do is to lend encouragement to such tendencies when they appear and censure groups adopting objectionable practices of repression.[11]

Conclusion

In summary, the collapse of the Soviet Union and its military potential means that challenges and threats to U.S. interests in the Middle East will be regional, rather than global, in the coming decade. These may include interstate conflicts—between Israel and the Arabs, between Iran and the Arab Gulf states or between various Arab states. But these are not likely to materialize, at least in the near term, because of economic constraints and resource limitations. The United States also faces a serious challenge to its interests from the proliferation of weapons of mass destruction, a trend that could adversely affect the regional balance of power, intimidate U.S. friends, or make U.S. military interventions more costly if it is not blunted. The major challenge throughout the decade is likely to arise in the form of local instabilities caused by a variety of factors—maldistribution of resources (including water), ethnic and sectarian tensions, demographic pressures, and populist ideologies. The latter do not lend themselves to military solutions, but demand subtle and sensitive diplomacy as well as an array of political and economic initiatives.

These trends point to a new policy agenda with a reordered set of priorities. Some U.S. interests remain—access to oil and protection of Israel. Others, such as curbing arms proliferation, containing the damage from instability, and promoting economic and political reform, will assume new importance. As always, some of these interests are likely to prove difficult to reconcile. The most obvious and long-standing concern has been the difficulty of continuing support for Israel while preserving and developing relations with the Arab world. This is why perseverance on the peace process is a high priority for policymakers.

A second area of competing requirements lies in the potential conflict between security needs and the generalized goals of economic and political reform. Yet without some movement toward regimes that better satisfy the aspirations of their citizens the long-term potential for instability will continue to exist. A third area of potential competition exists between the need to limit and, if possible, reduce arms proliferation and, at the same time, preserve a balance of power likely to deter aggression. Supply-side efforts to reduce proliferation must be balanced with regional security concerns on a case-by-case basis.

Given U.S. domestic concerns and the need for fiscal retrenchment, the United States will not have the resources—economic or financial— to play the role of regional policeman. Nor is such a role desirable, given local sensitivities. Rather, the United States will have to concentrate on those problems, and those countries, that are essential to its interests, while supporting efforts by others to promote conflict resolution in areas of lesser importance to its national cohesion and well-being.

Notes

1. Tim Niblock, "Regional Cooperation and Security in the Middle East: The Role of the European Community." Unpublished paper, Middle East Studies Association Conference, Washington, D.C., November 1991.

2. Don Oberdorfer, "Opinion Builds for Smaller U.S. Role Abroad," *Washington Post*, October 27, 1991, p. A20. For an excellent discussion of this issue, see "America and the World, 1990–91," *Foreign Affairs* 71, no. 1.

3. A poll taken by *Time* magazine in 1991 found that 75 percent of those interviewed were opposed to playing world policeman. David Gergen, "America's Missed Opportunities," *Foreign Affairs* 71, no. 1, p. 16.

4. These strategic imperatives were well laid out before the crisis, in William Olson, ed., *U.S. Strategic Interests in the Gulf Region* (Carlisle Barracks, Pa.: U.S. Army War College, 1986).

5. According to Henry Schuler, "The Middle East and North Africa have the capacity to dominate world oil trade for as long as we can see into the future." G. Henry Schuler, "The Aftermath: New Forces Unleashed in Middle Eastern Oil Policy." Unpublished paper, Center for Strategic and International Studies (CSIS), May 1991, p. 4. Based on some estimates, a severe disruption of oil—a 50 percent cut over a year—could cause a loss of U.S. GNP as large as 5–8 percent, worse than a major recession; Zalmy Khalilzad and Paul Davis, *Protecting Persian Gulf Oil After the Cold War* (Santa Monica, Calif.: Rand Corporation, May 1990), p. v.

6. Ibid., pp. 23–26.

7. The degree of U.S. activism desirable in inducing a change of government in Iraq is a subject of serious disagreement among policy analysts. For a reflection of this see *After the Storm: Challenges for America's Middle East Policy* (Washington, D.C.: Washington Institute for Near East Policy, 1991), p. 45.

8. U.S. Institute for Peace, *Middle East Arms Control After the Gulf War* (Washington, D.C.: Washington Institute for Peace, November 1991).

9. Lawrence G. Freedman, "Order and Disorder in the New World," *Foreign Affairs* 71, no. 1, p. 43.

10. Ann Lesch, "Notes . . . On the Palestine Question in the Context of the New International Regional Middle East Order." Unpublished paper, American Political Science Association Convention, Washington, D.C., August 21, 1991.

11. The balance and the degree of U.S. activism in promoting democracy within sovereign states has been a subject of controversy among scholars and policy analysts. For diverse views see Robert Rothstein, "Democracy and International Conflict," *The Washington Quarterly* 14, no. 2, 1991; John Waterbury, ed., "Toward New Orders in the Middle East: The Role of U.S. Policy." Report of a workshop, Center for International Studies, Princeton University, May 18–19, 1991; Dankwart A. Rustow, "Democracy: A Global Revolution," *Foreign Affairs* 9, no. 4, 1991, pp. 75–91. One political scientist fears that U.S. leaders will face vital interests in the Middle East but confront a region populated with people who perceive the United States as a hostile imperial power, responsible for the persistence of regimes they see as illegitimate; Richard Herrman, "The Middle East and the New World Order: Rethinking U.S. Political Strategy After the Gulf War," *International Security* 16 (Fall 1991), pp. 42–75.

Suggested Reading

Arnett, Eric H., ed., *New Perspectives for a Changing World Order*, Washington, D.C.: American Association for the Advancement of Science, 1991.

Chace, James, *The Consequences of the Peace: The New Internationalism and American Foreign Policy*, New York: Oxford University Press, 1992.

Fuller, Graham E., *The Democracy Trap: The Perils of the Post–Cold War World*, New York: Dutton, 1991.

Hendrickson, David, "American Foreign Policy," *Foreign Affairs* 71, no. 2 (Spring 1992), pp. 48–63.

Institute for International and Strategic Studies, *New Dimensions in International Security*, parts 1 and 2 (Adelphi Papers, nos. 265, 266), London: Brassy's, Winter 1991/1992.

Nye, Joseph S., Jr., "What New World Order?" *Foreign Affairs* 71, no. 2 (Spring 1992), pp. 83–96.

Tucker, Robert W., and Hendrickson, David C., *The Imperial Temptation: The New World Order and America's Purpose*, New York: Council on Foreign Relations, 1992.

About the Book

Dramatic changes in the global security environment have necessitated a fundamental reassessment of U.S. interests and policy worldwide. This book focuses on the underlying forces at work in the Middle East, the challenges the United States will face in the region in the coming decade, and how they will influence U.S. interests and future strategy.

The contributors go beyond traditional perspectives in analyzing such critical issues as state-to-state conflicts in the Arab-Israeli and Persian Gulf arenas; growing Western dependence on Middle East oil; an increasingly lethal arms race that may upset the regional balance; competition for scarce resources, such as water, in non-oil states; and ethnic, sectarian, and ideological forces, such as the Islamic revival and pressures for democracy, that will affect regional stability and U.S. interests. Throughout, the authors take a fresh look at strategic priorities, the policy options available, and the dilemmas presented by conflicting U.S. interests. The many layers of analysis are woven together intricately but realistically.

About the Editors and Contributors

John L. Esposito is the Director of the Center for International Studies and Professor of Religious Studies, College of the Holy Cross. He is a leading authority on the Islamic resurgence. His most recent work is *Islam and Politics* (1987). He recently has visited Egypt, Tunisia, and Iran researching this subject.

Melvin Goodman is a career Soviet analyst and Professor of International Studies at the National War College. He has served in the State Department and the Central Intelligence Agency and has written widely on changing Soviet policy toward the Third World under Gorbachev. His works include *Soviet Military and Economic Aid to the Third World* (1989), *Third World Clients and Third World Dilemmas for USSR* (1988), and *The Soviet Union and the Third World Military Dimension* (1987).

William Lewis is the Director of Security Policy Studies and a Professor of Political Science at George Washington University. He has written widely on European and Middle Eastern security affairs, particularly on arms transfers and weapons proliferation in the Third World. He is a specialist on North Africa, with emphasis on Libya, and has served in the State Department in various posts dealing with security and defense policy.

Phebe Marr is a Senior Fellow at the Institute for National Strategic Studies, National Defense University and has spent thirty years as a scholar and analyst of the Middle East and Southwest Asia. She has taught at the University of Tennessee and California State University, Stanislau, chaired the Near East North Africa program at the Foreign Service Institute, and worked as a research analyst for the Arabian American Oil Company in Saudi Arabia. She has published widely on the Persian Gulf and is the author of *The Modern History of Iraq* (1985).

Thomas Naff is an Associate Professor of Oriental Studies at the University of Pennsylvania and is a specialist in the politics and diplomacy of the Middle East. He has developed Middle East training and research programs and has authored studies on water resources and demographic changes in the Middle East, including *Water in the Middle East: Conflict or Cooperation?* (1984).

William Quandt is a Senior Fellow at Brookings Institution and is a leading authority on the Arab-Israeli problem and on U.S. policy toward the Middle

East. A key member of the National Security Council staff during the Camp David Accords, he has written numerous works on the Arab-Israeli conflict, including *Camp David: Peacemaking and Politics* (1986) and (in conjunction with others) *Toward Arab-Israeli Peace* (1988).

William C. Ramsay is the Deputy Assistant Secretary of State for Energy, Resources, and Food Policy and has been involved in formulating and implementing U.S. energy policy for over fifteen years. He has served in Saudi Arabia and in Brussels where he was responsible for the U.S.-EC dialogue on energy. He holds degrees in chemistry, zoology, international marketing, and international trade.

Abdul Aziz Said is a Professor of International Relations and Director of Peace and Conflict Resolution Studies, American University. He is an authority on the international and regional politics of the Middle East. His current research has been on ethnicity and conflict in the Middle East. His recent trips to the area have included interviews with a number of leaders, most notably Yasir Arafat.

Introduction